ESOTERIC
MYSTERIES
OF THE
UNDERWORLD

"A deliriously speculative and erudite examination of caves. Echoing the modes of writers as divergent as Bachelard and Eliade, Jean-Pierre Bayard's examination benefits enormously from a deep draft from the font of esoteric wisdom. With these tools he creates a narrative that presents the myth of the cave as a story of human initiation, knowledge, and self-discovery."

JESSE BRANSFORD, CLINICAL ASSOCIATE PROFESSOR
OF VISUAL ARTS, NYU STEINHARDT

ESOTERIC MYSTERIES

OF THE

UNDERWORLD

The Power & Meaning of Subterranean Sacred Spaces

JEAN-PIERRE BAYARD

Translated by Jon E. Graham

Inner Traditions
Rochester, Vermont

Inner Traditions
One Park Street
Rochester, Vermont 05767
www.InnerTraditions.com

Text stock is SFI certified

Originally published in French in 1961 under the title *La Monde Souterrain* by
    Éditions Flammarion
2nd edition published in French in 1973 by Éditions PAYOT
3rd expanded edition published in French in 1994 under the title *La symbolique du
    monde souterrain et de la caverne* by Éditions de la Maisnie
4th edition published in French in 2009 by Éditions Véga
First U.S. edition published in 2020 by Inner Traditions

Cataloging-in-Publication Data for this title is available from the Library of Congress

ISBN 978-1-64411-062-1 (print)
ISBN 978-1-64411-063-8 (ebook)

Printed and bound in the United States by Lake Book Manufacturing, Inc.
The text stock is SFI certified. The Sustainable Forestry Initiative® program
promotes sustainable forest management.

10   9   8   7   6   5   4   3   2   1

Text design and layout by Virginia Scott Bowman
This book was typeset in Garamond Premier Pro with Argent used as the display
typeface

Contents

PART TWO
◆◆◆◆

The Cavern

♦ ♦ ♦

To my grandsons, Matthieu and Christophe,

so they can learn to love the beauty of caves

Preface

LE MONDE SOUTERRAIN (The Underground World) was published by Flammarion Editions in 1961. When the series "Symbols" that was directed by Marie-Madeleine Davy was canceled, a revised edition of this book was picked up by Payot Éditions for their series "At the Boundaries of Science" under the title *La Symbolique du monde souterrain*.

Guy Trédaniel Éditions, which brought out my book *La Symbolique du feu*, published in similar circumstances, expressed an interest in adding this often-quoted book to their list. We looked at republishing this book—either with a new design and perhaps a new title and with some revisions or keeping the 1973 edition as is in order to respect the analyses that had been made—but adding a more recent study to expand the book's subject.

In November of 1986 my friend Michel Random had asked me to write an intentionally short text for his book called "The Cavern." But—as happens in any number of publishing houses that do not follow through on their plans and abandon what they have asked people to write for them—the collection he edited was canceled. I was not overly concerned about the fate of this text, but in the context of the republication of *Le Monde Souterrain*, publisher Guy Trédaniel and I thought we could update the whole book by adding this unpublished text to the end of the original book. The present volume was born from the combining of these two texts.

JEAN-PIERRE BAYARD
LE PUY BARBET, JANUARY 1993

PART ONE

•••

The Symbolism of the Underworld and the Cave

1

Preamble

THE INFINITE AND UNTOUCHED WEALTH of the world underground haunts the human imagination. This mysterious domain does not reveal itself to those who dwell above those deep, dark caverns, whose strange, dull noises inspire dread and superstition. But if we go even a short way down into these *inferna immanis,* we are soon struck dumb with wonder: vast halls sparkling with crystals open up before our eyes. Before us lies a luxurious and fabulous landscape. It would come as no surprise if we were to encounter fairies here, the guardians of all this wealth.

Despite so much bewitching beauty, the reader will not find descriptions of caves and the legends connected with them in this book. I will devote a short chapter to the inviolable citadel that retains traces of artistic activity, but these Sistine Chapels of prehistory with their wall paintings only concern us in light of the idea of magic and the cult of enchantment. There remains quite a good deal to say about a poorly known civilization whose long intellectual heredity provides us this way with an acute, conscious, and evolved observation. Nor will I speak of the troglodytes* or the flora and fauna of the underground realms. I am going to pass over in silence the extraction of metals, all the various mining techniques, the search for combustible fluids and gases, excavating the earth, and the related technology, as these fall into a domain

---

*[French term for modern cave dwellers. —*Trans.*]

of knowledge that has no place in this book. We will likewise merely touch on all the works created by the hand of man, such as sewers, water conveyances, underground construction, and highway tunnels. My chief desire, to the contrary, is to study all the manifestations of the underground fire, and to interrogate these mouths of hell in which giants have been interred, and to examine sacred caves and labyrinths. I hope with this to show that aspect of initiation offered to us by all the mythology and legendary accounts of the world below.

With this book, dedicated to symbolism, we are in the presence of the Egg of the World. An androgynous substance is engendered in the entrails of the earth. Every human being is born from clay, and to clay he shall return. The cave therefore is no longer perceived as a fay and enchanting place but rather the dark womb in which the genesis of the world takes shape. According to Ossendowski, this supreme center went underground some six thousand years ago, at the onset of the Dark Age. We are still living in an era in which all is becoming darker and more confusing; however, this Tower of Babel era will eventually end. In order to find this central point, made of brightness and radiant strength, the human being strives to communicate with Mother Earth.

This allows us to come into contact with the theme of the descent of the spirit into matter. One must possess great courage to approach this underground palace of the double axe. Cerberus, the monstrous hound with fifty heads, also has a voice of iron whose dreadful sound waves will bring the most intrepid explorer to a complete standstill. Cerberus becomes the dog Garm in Germanic mythology. Theseus has to slay the Minotaur, but the labyrinth offers its own dangers, as it is all too easy to get lost in it. To find the secret chamber it is necessary to have outside assistance, divine aid that already knows and can put us on the path of understanding and spiritual realization.

It is necessary to suffer, to undergo physical torments, to show proof of your valor in order to merit the bliss that comes with the fullness of being. The hero must descend into hell, the lower but sacred place and abode of shades. In the center of the earth he will find the subterranean fire. If he can cross through it without being burned, he proves that he is worthy of returning to the surface of the world and to the light. The Eleusinian initiation offers us this mystery that is also found in Japanese mythology with Izanagi, who is inconsolable over the loss of his wife. We also see the goddess Ishtar descending into the infernal realms, while the ancient Greeks offer us a chthonic Artemis who guides humans through the terrors of the underworld. Hell is therefore not only the place of eternal suffering. Montessus de Ballore has shown that it is not located in the center of the world, although "the internal fire of our planet, like that of Hell, never goes out." Cicero tells us that near Lake Avernus, in the vicinity of Pozzuoli in Campania, the souls of the dead are evoked, thanks to the many cavities that pierce the hills with their sacred groves. According to Strabo, the cave of Acherusia in Hierapolis, sacred to Cybele, was nothing other than the gate to the underworld. This passageway should be sought out, as it not only allows the individual to reach the "middle hall" and enjoy its regenerative powers, but also puts him or her in contact with the souls of the dead—whose knowledge can be quite useful. The human being is fully realized in the primordial lair. The dead body is buried in order to not delay the cycle of earthly lives, to activate his or her reincarnation, and to allow the soul of the deceased to avoid long periods of torment. There is a very specific ritual for establishing contact between the dead body and the Earth Mother. The crypt—which is the source of the word *grotto*— is associated with the underground chapel intended to serve as a tomb for the saints and martyrs of the early Church.

The spirits of the underworld do not remain inactive: divine smiths create miraculous weapons in their underground smithies, and alchemists and Hermeticists search there for the Philosophers' Stone; but the quest for the Great Work can only be envisioned as a spiritual discovery. The Neolithic cave became the site of prehistoric initiation and the cult of Eleusis. The Earth, the Great Mother Goddess, is paid her most enduring worship here, which can still be seen in the adoration of the Black Madonna, the figure of the divine feminine. But the natural site was followed by the temple that placed the human being back in his original conditions: taking after the mazes and the dense, dark forests, the chamber—in which the initiate sleeps, guarded by the green scarab—was carved out of the solid rock. I will only mention the corridor of the pyramid that we know through copious documentation and will devote more analysis to the curious Tomb of the Christian Woman.* With all its underground rooms and chambers for reflection we can feel the presence of Moses, Pythagoras, Triptolemus, and Orpheus, who, after being immersed in the darkness, were reborn in the sparkling light of illumination, as Plato tells us in an allegory in the seventh book of *The Republic* as well as in *Phaedrus*.

But over the course of the chapters that make up this book, we will find stable values that still belong to this earth. Water plays a major role in human life. After the waters of our birth, green algae and baptismal water purify the spirit. This water appears mysteriously in the crypt where the Black Madonna is enthroned. The tree takes root in the great secrecy of the world below; it establishes communication between the earth and sky and makes possible the exchange of waves that remain poorly defined. We also find in the underground realms the stone whose magnetic and virginal life remains a witness to the past. These stones of the sun and moon, these dolmens and menhirs, all make concrete a balancing point, the initial crystallization of the universe; the sparkling gem takes part in this sacred life. But in the midst of these stones, the Hermetic foreshadowing of the Black Madonnas, we find subterranean serpentine passageways. These "strait gates" allow the serpent to enter. Those tunnels that start in the banks of the Nile and extend toward the Libyan Desert are called "passages of the serpent." Here is where the mysteries of the "cycles of necessity" unfold. Through a similar underground passage we reach Luz, the city that assumed a celestial blue color. It so happens that Luz is located on the spot where Jacob had his dream, and *beth-el*—which became *baetyl*—means "house of God."

This is the basic outline of my research. But beneath the analysis of a broad symbol I wish to show that all civilizations and all philosophies

---

*[Royal Mausoleum of Mauretania in Algeria. —*Trans.*]

contain the same basic teachings and beliefs that are all subject to local modifications. This notion of a universal foundation led me to question the numerous movements that respond to a higher idealism. Every social body contains ritual ceremonies, and some of these rites are more or less accessible: the ordination of priests, the taking of the veil by a sister, the coronation of a king, and some of the ceremonies we find in universities, folk celebrations, and cyclical ceremonies. Books that have reached a large audience reveal some aspects of the trade and craft guilds (Compagnonnage and Freemasonry), alchemical circles, some of the knightly orders, and Hermetic groups with a more or less Christian bias. All these many studies show us that symbolism remains an eternal means of correspondence.

In order to show all these analogous secrets it is necessary to refer to some texts to show evidence of the symbol's integrity. I know unusual terms will complicate the reading, but I am obliged to provide the material needed by other authors to go beyond the framework of this study. But I am primarily seeking to make tangible the communication between the visible and the invisible and attempting to partially draw back this veil in which the real assumes the appearance that is seen every day, but in which the true represents the revelation of the pure Forms and Essences. Truth is what should be.

Esotericism should develop the spiritual knowledge of human beings. Just as some studies predispose an individual to think or act a certain way, and just as mathematics forms a rigorous form of reasoning, symbolism improves the human being. It is necessary to make people understand that in life everything is linked, everything is connected, that all is one. We shall then realize that we are merely one link in an endless chain, that we are all united. And because of this we should become better people with greater understanding. Some people will think that my dream is utopian, but others will be able to contemplate the fable and extract the truth it carries.

In his preface to *Cosmogonie des Rose-Croix* (Rosicrucian cosmogony) (Leymarie, 1947), Max Heindel writes:

In all schools of occult philosophy, the student is advised, when a new teaching has been given, to not allow himself to be swayed by preferences or prejudices, but to keep his mind in a state of calm and dignified expectation.

Before penetrating the spirit of the mysteries it is necessary to find one's own way to the intelligence of the arcana. The guru or spiritual teacher can only put you on the right path; the teacher is the initiator, he who sows, but it is still necessary for the ground to be favorable. No one can go directly to illumination and fraternal goodwill. Knowledge can only be acquired slowly, but its benefits are in proportion to how long the effort has been sustained. As Saint-Yves d'Alveydre said, "There is no occult science, only sciences that have been occulted."

This study on the subterranean world revolves around this form of thought. Those whose minds think scientifically will find it implausible because many of the points in my argument cannot be physically checked; our era loves everything that appears logical and demonstrable. In reality, this places severe limitations on the mental thought of human beings, as it excludes dream, intuition, and imagination. Are we correct to deny these abilities that we admire so greatly in some artists? Our science only rests on postulates; it can therefore only represent a philosophical position of our mind. Over time our scientific understanding may come to appear quite relative and provisional. For my part, I have tried to get myself out of the habit of intellectual reasoning so I can go back to a more synthetic way of thinking. I would like to stress the fact that I am not denying the exact sciences that are, moreover, the base of my education, but I want to lift myself to a higher plane. Some of my hypotheses may appear gratuitous, but in reality I am using traditional cosmology as my reference. The eternal laws of nature remain poorly understood. Éliphas Lévi said that the knowledge of the law of fluidic tides and universal currents would amount to possession of the secret to all human power.

We should not forget that Socrates was unjustly condemned because he was "a learned man, curious about the things of heaven, having studied all that is underground and attributing superiority to the lower orders of the Word." Let us not dare claim that our civilization—a term that dates from the eighteenth century—is the preeminent "civilization." Auguste Comte also spelled out his reservations about evolution, which can be nothing other than a curve with an asymptote. Because each of us calls progress that which conforms to our own disposition, and each of us may be right. Those whose tendencies remain in harmony with their era think that life is making progress, but do those others who speak of this rhythm of progress that is too often confused with the evolution of science but that does not concern itself with understanding the spiritual value of aromas, sounds, and colors?

It is my wish that these several keys will make it possible to go beyond our reality for a moment. By freeing ourselves of our prejudices we can manage to rejoin the fullness of Unity, and we will be able to make the descent into matter so as to return transfigured.

2

Earth, Mineral Blood

BEFORE BEGINNING THIS STUDY of the underground world it would be helpful to consider briefly the mysterious signs of the Earth. In the series of the four elements, Earth is placed between Fire and Water (Fire, Earth, Air, Water), and it alone possesses a resistant quality (see fig. 2.1 on page 10). Mavéric wondered about the order of these elements,[1] and Pierre Génillard sought this sequence in astrology.[2] According to one natural series we have Air, Fire, Water, and Earth, or by opposing each of the forces in accordance with the law of balance: Fire, Air, Water, and Earth. If we consider the qualities, we come up with Air, Water, Earth, and Fire, but if we think of the seasons, we find Air, Fire, Earth, and Water. It is therefore fairly risky to try to classify these elements one to another.

I should add that in Taoist teachings and in the theory of the seals of the hand,[3] the little finger represents the element Earth.

Through geological study of the depths of the earth, the telluric forces—volcanic or electromagnetic—can be envisioned as the effect of cosmic radiations. These subterranean forces also assume the names of deities such as Rhea, Cybele, and Demeter; and according to Hesiod's *Theogony,* the sky is none other than Uranus and the earth, Gaea. This wife of Uranus is still known as Gaia or Gé, but she is Tellus for the Romans, Semele for the Thracians, and Tailtiu in Ireland—where she is the foster mother of Lugh—while in Peru she assumes the name of Pachamama or Mamapacha.

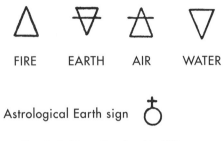

Fig. 2.1. Fire, Earth, Air, Water

For the ancients, these mysterious forces influence the actions of their lives, and all these phenomena reveal the presence of a god. Phrygia, by the very nature of the ground, encourages this aspect of worship. Cretan deities were underground, and the cult of Poseidon was connected to a seismic notion.[4] Montessus de Ballore was merely summing up the generally accepted opinion that the conflicts of underground gods were responsible for earthquakes. The earth is comparable to a human body.

The knowledge of the ancients was often much more extensive than we think, and in fact, it clearly seems that these telluric forces could be comparable to etheric forces and mirror the complexity of our blood vessels. The sun—the heart—governs the cosmos considered to be a living being. It should be pointed out in this regard that, while the priests of ancient Egypt knew of the circulation of the blood, their embalming science remains a complete mystery to us. They were able to completely empty the skull by extracting the brain and the cerebellum through the nostrils. They rinsed the cranium and soaked it in brine without touching the individual's exterior, which demonstrates a profound understanding of anatomy. The physician Erasistratus of Iulis on Ceos was performing experiments on the heart in 300 BCE and stated that the blood carried the pneuma; in other words, spirit. Later scholars mocked these theories while giving no thought to the spiritual element, and they believed that blood transported air. In the same era, 200 CE, Ptolemy placed the earth at the center of the universe, while Galen stated that the heart was not the source of the heartbeat. Is it the animated blood that causes the heart to beat or is it the heart that gives movement to the bloodstream? Similarly, because of its central position the sun becomes the heart of the world.

> *For high raised above th'aetherial plains,*
> *And in the world's bright middle orb thou reign'st,*
> *Whilst all things by thy sov'reign power are filled*
> *With mind-exciting, providential care.*
> (PROCLUS, "HYMN TO THE SUN,"
> TRANS. THOMAS TAYLOR)

For Macrobius (*Commentary on the Dream of Scipio,* 1:20), the sun is the "intelligence of the world."

A connection therefore exists between the heart, the sun, and wisdom or intelligence. The heart is the vital center, but more significantly "the principal center of the total being."[5] For Pliny the Elder (*Natural History,* 11:69), the intellect resides in the heart. René Guénon cites the Chandogya Upanishad to say that the *atma*—the universal spirit—is set in the heart.[6] "The Earth has a body, a soul, and a spirit," says Pernety,[7] and Tantrism states that Shakti is the universal force. According to Eliade, an Indian prophet of the Umatilla tribe refused to work the earth because it would have been a sin to "wound or cut or tear or claw our common mother."[8] By this reasoning stones are seen as the bones of the mother, the soil her flesh, and plants her hair. According to Marie-Madeleine Davy, Saint Hildegard established an analogy between the macrocosm and the microcosm.[9] In the human body viewed as an image of the cosmos, the head corresponds to fire, the chest to air, the feet to water, and "the belly is the image of the soft and fruitful earth," for we are subject to the elementary nature of Aries, Gemini, Pisces, and Virgo. Isidore of Seville established the same relationship in his *De Natura rerum* (chap. 9) as did Honorius Augustodunensis, who explicitly describes the kinship between man and the elements.[10] Flesh is drawn from the earth, blood from water, breath from air, and heat from fire. The Iroquois and similar societies believed that their ancestors once lived under the earth in the telluric depths. In this way the earth depicts the mineral blood of the universal mind and is the soul of all things.

This helps us better see the close kinship that connects the earth to woman. The woman, for Plato, imitated the earth: the chasm at Delphi represents the female generative organ, which was called *delphi*. Mircea Eliade has done a study of the etymology of names that compare the cavern to woman.[11] In the earth, where minerals grow, the mine becomes the womb, the earth the belly of the mother from whom all is born and to whom all returns. This dark material, black by definition, becomes green through vegetation. The Black Madonna symbolizes regeneration: "When the contemplative man looks at the earth he understands why it is both always a virgin and always a mother. It is virginal because it is constantly in expectation of the divine seed; mother because she gives birth successively to many harvests."[12] For Paracelsus, the Great Spirit fertilizes the earth; the elements are given the names of sylphs, salamanders, gnomes, and undines depending on whether they move in the air, fire, earth, or water. For George Sand, as well as Buffon, the center of our globe is an immense glass crucible, and "the crystal is a mysterious mirror that reflects this way the cosmic drama of the world's genesis."[13] Bernard Palissy thinks that the earth is never idle: whatever is naturally consumed within it is once again renewed and reshaped. If it is not of one kind it will remake it into something else. In parallel, the interior and the matrix of the earth are also working to produce."[14]

This is how all of life is crafted in this subterranean world. And while a magical force causes the seed to germinate, the human being will go down into this primordial egg, this philosophical egg, in order to be regenerated at the site of his first birth.[15] It is the rediscovery of the first connection, the one that preceded the Fall. The elect will find the spiritual light through the digestion of a telluric force. This dark radiance will be visible with the descent into hell where, after sublimation, the individual will acquire the status of initiate. He finds happiness here because we should recall the words that

Buddha spoke to his faithful follower Ananda at the end of his life: Don't let yourself be deceived, Ananda. Life is a long suffering. The child has good reason to cry upon being born. This is the first truth.

The initiatory hut, the cave, the temple, and sacred enclosure where the adolescent is transformed represent the maternal womb. The candidate puts himself in a place preceding his biological birth in order to have a second birth.[16]

The earth as womb is also found in the alchemical notion of the process in which the three colors of the work go from black—the color of the earth and the god Osiris—to red by way of white. However, this white is probably only the representation of "the absence of color," this transparent color of the Great Ray of emanation, the sole one that is true. White is the color of initiates, and the pope clothes himself symbolically in white. The French flag is said to have been designed by the Mason Louis David based on the principles of these three alchemical colors: the deep blue or black corresponds to the bourgeoisie, the white to the people or peasants, and the red to royalty.[17] In his *Dictionary,* Dom Pernety makes a comparison between the earth and the alchemical work:

This chaos is developed by volatization; the abyss of water disappears from sight, little by little as the earth is formed and the humidity is sublimed at the top of the vase. This is why the Hermetic Chymists thought to compare their work, or that which occurs during the operations, to the development of the Universe at the time of creation.[18]

This concealed universal life has been represented by the crux ansata, the hieratic Egyptian sign. But the swastika—a symbol we find in all civilizations and that also adorns the dolmen as well as the Tomb of the Christian Woman—has often been envisioned as a symbol of the earth. Its four branches are oriented toward the four cardinal points, and Charles Diot has established that the hooks are drawn by the vertical radiations from the sources.[19]

The first man was formed from red clay—or *adamah*. *Adam*, which also means "red," is in this way connected to the Atlantean tradition, and the role of the potter has been "the symbol of the production of manifested beings." Stanislas de Guaita noted (*Le Serpent de la Genèse*, 88) that in fact we merely deduce that the Lord formed man by kneading a little clay between his fingers because the name *Adam* was formed from *adōm* (red or reddened) and *adamah* (earth or clay). But when Adam was conceived he represented a state of perfection; he was a culmination. It was only later that he fell because of his sin. The color of the earth can therefore symbolize power on the human plane. The cavern painted in red by Leonardo da Vinci retains the same symbolism. René Guénon often conjectured on this value of the earth and the sky, in which the universal man serves as an intermediary.[20] The universe, according to numerous traditions, is made up by seven earths that are arranged and inhabited in a hierarchy. The "higher earth" would be our own; the six others would represent lower degrees. This world involves notions of time and physical space and sensory perceptions that are denied by other traditions that do away with time in particular. Leo Schaya finds in this notion the "Sabbatic Cycle" of seven times seven years and at the end of which, in the fiftieth millennium—the Great Jubilee—the world will be reincorporated into the Divine Principle.[21] It is fairly obvious that we can compare this construction of the universe to the value of the seven *sefirot*. The forty-nine *sefirotic* degrees emerge from Binah, and to Binah they return. Binah is therefore simultaneously the one and the fiftieth degree.

This jubilee number is that of Moses, of the fifty interpretations of the law. Before we attain this stage—a paradisial state—we will have to pass through many tribulations, but between these temporary restorations we may enjoy periods of rest characterized by the cycle of the Fiat lux, the perfect balance between spirit and matter. This notion of the universe with the seven earths still pushes us to hunt out the great center of rest in which we will touch on infinite consciousness. To end up at the cosmic Sabbat we only possess three values: the earth, the sky, and our presence. The Chinese tradition also includes three creative principles. The sky is depicted as a vertical line and the earth a horizontal one. The human being is found where these two lines intersect, at the spot where spirit and matter meet. The human being is therefore located at the very center of the cross. Heaven and earth and man form the three poles of the Great Triad. The geometrical depiction of this figuration forms the cross and esoterically retains the same power. The same notion can be found in the *Sepher Yetzirah*: "There are three fathers, fire, water, and spirit. The fire is above, the water below, and the spirit joins them together." Activity lowers toward contemplation, and it is through this polarity that the powers are balanced. "The body," says the *Zohar*, "is the garment of Nephesh; Nephesh is the garment of Ruach, and finally Ruach is the garment of Neshamah." These are the three elements of the human being: body, soul, and spirit.

This Great Triad is related directly to the subject at hand. The triple enclosure thereby symbolizes the heavenly Jerusalem, the primordial city. In geometric figures the square represents the earth. Three squares inserted within one another with a single focal point can depict the three worlds: the earthly world, the world of the firmaments, and the heavenly or divine world in which God resides with these pure spirits. The Celtic cross is also inscribed in a combination of three circles, each of which is the triple of the other, in a relationship with the numbers 9, 27, and 81 (see fig. 2.2, on page 16). These three circles of universal life are defined as follows in the Bardic Triads:

> The circle of Keugant, the empty circle in which no being can survive except for God himself. Neither the living nor the dead can reach this point and only God may enter it.
>
> The circle of Abred, the circle of inevitability and unavoidable destiny, in which each new state, each new life is born from death (conditioned by the one before). And this circle is one that human beings travel through.

The circle of Gwenwed, circle of bliss, the "White World," in which every state is derived and born from life. "And this circle is one that humanity will cross through one day."

Paul Bouchet has reconstructed the Celtic cross in this way and given proportions to these three circles—which in reality break down in turn into other triads.[22]

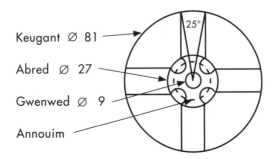

Keugant Ø 81
Abred Ø 27
Gwenwed Ø 9
Annouim

25°

*Fig. 2.2. The Celtic cross.
Keugant 81; Abred 27; Gwenwed 9; Annouim*

This triple enclosure, which has given rise to some interesting analyses,[23] can be found in Hindu literature. The mandala, which in Sanskrit means "circle," represents the divine world. From the square, one is directed to the focal point, which is to say, from the outside toward the inside. Thought progresses from the perimeter toward the center, which is reduced to a dot identified with the divine. At this heart is found the residence of the god beneath the cosmic mountain, Mount Potalaka or Mount Meru. There are several representations of this progression toward paradise in the Guimet Museum. In Hebrew mysticism, the Shekinah is the core in which the God of Life is enthroned. And I cannot help but mention the Tomb of the Christian Woman and the dome that sits atop a square foundation. This may help us better understand what Isaiah had in mind when he said: "Thus saith the Lord, The heaven is my throne, and the earth is my footstool" (66:1). But this footstool is the fundamental stone that Isaiah defined in chapter 28, verse 16.

This triple enclosure can be found in the graffiti drawn by the Templars. Charbonneau-Lassay has analyzed these symbols: figure 2.3a is from the castle of Chinon; figure 2.3b is in the Abbey of Seuilly (Indre-et-Loire); elsewhere the octagonal design was a chief preoccupation of this order. The cross may traverse the three squares, as we can see in the former round keep of Loudon (fig. 2.3c). But it is inside a stone of the ancient Merovingian or Carolingian church—at Ardin (Deux-Sèvres)—that God's abode, the central point, appears best (fig. 2.3d).

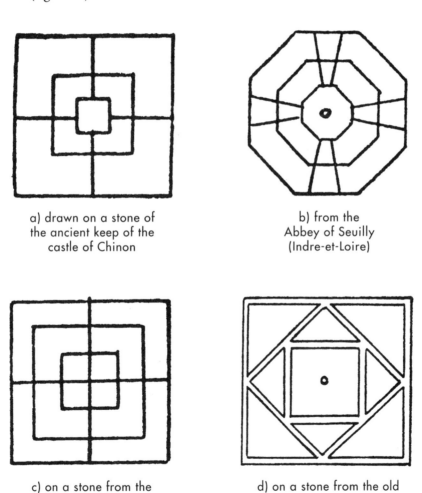

a) drawn on a stone of
the ancient keep of the
castle of Chinon

b) from the
Abbey of Seuilly
(Indre-et-Loire)

c) on a stone from the
keep of Loudon

d) on a stone from the old
church of Ardin (Deux-Sèvres)

Fig. 2.3. The triple enclosure in graffiti drawn by the Templars

The earth is a passive material, the *prakriti,* the support material of manifestation. The earth, as yin, displays a negative aspect. Conversely, the sky represents the positive male principle, or yang. This thereby gives us the two poles of manifestation. They are two opposing yet complementary phases. Does this mean that we have here both ends of duality? No, because we must give more study to that extraordinary yin-yang symbol in the I Ching, which are inseparable because everything is connected in nature. Men and women are opposites, but they aspire to union. It is through this androgynous principle that earth and sky become two additional principles that make it possible to detect the light in the darkness. The old yin and yang are stable states: the young yin and yang are states of maturation and transformation. We should never forget that the more summons the less; the wheel must turn perpetually; the "permanent imbalance" consists of alternating compensations. This brings Tarot cards to mind.

The action of the sky (represented by the number 3) on the earth (represented by the number 2) gives us 5 and 6, ratios of manifestation.[24] With this earthly number, we find the mysterious pentagram, symbol of the regenerated human being. There is a 72-degree gap between each point, but this blazing star must revolve because it is a symbol of omnipotence and because the third letter of the Hebrew alphabet* is located at its center, equated with the letter *G*. This power of the Logos makes the definitive reintegration possible. Solomon's seal symbolizes the union of heaven and earth, and this star with six branches is on the earth plane the union of spirit and matter. This outline of the universal man sheds light on the thought of Saint Thomas Aquinas as well as that of Albertus Magnus, and because in life everything intersects, we can still muse on the sixty-four hexagrams of Wen Wang that appear in the I Ching. We are touching upon the handwriting of the Logos.

We must study yet further this union that is the origin of time. Once upon a time, Izanagi and Izanami were not separated. Euripides knew that heaven and earth were only one. According to one widespread

---

*[Gimel. —*Ed.*]

myth, the Chinese Tuang-ku* separated heaven from earth. We can now understand why we can connect the nervous system of the neophyte to that of the earth and the cosmos, and to all those magneto-telluric currents that spread in accordance with laws we no longer know. We must place ourselves before the rupture of the primordial unity took place, in that cosmic unity that is the basis of harmony and beauty. Even science has rediscovered a few thoughts from antiquity on indivisible matter, but they are at best only a few stammerings. In this unity, we shall succeed in finding our reincarnations because, according to the doctrine of Pythagoras, every man preexists himself, but he is still necessarily subject to the influence of telluric currents.

---

*[Or Pangu. —*Ed.*]

3

The Telluric Currents

THE ORIGIN OF THE EARTH, its construction, and its age are all highly controversial questions. For Laplace, Maillet, Alfred Maury, and Figuier, the earth is an igneous planet: a globe of fire. According to the plutonian theory, the earth was once covered in water or ice. Some authors think that our planet is hollow, while others believe that the four elements are incorporated within it; the core would be subject to intense heat. But some other scientists feel that this core can only be frozen and that in this core an extraordinary energy is deployed. This slumbering force can be compared to one that exists in the human body: the *kundalini* or fire serpent. Gravity, density, and solidity have reached their maximum limits in this place,[1] making this center "the extreme point of manifestation in the state of conscious existence: it is a veritable stopping point." The heat of thermal waters would not be due to some natural form of heating akin to an enormous furnace, but rather their temperature would come from contact with the radioactivity of granite, like a catalytic phenomenon.

The temperature increase is 1° centigrade every 31 meters,[2] and pressure also increases as we descend. This allows us to calculate that the pressure at the center of the earth should be 3.5 million kilograms per square centimeter, which would make Jules Verne's vision in his *Journey to the Center of the Earth* impossible. But who tells us that our calculations will respond "logically" to what might happen?

Perhaps other laws will govern conditions here, laws of which we are still ignorant.

According to Jacques Baurès, the fine terrestrial crust—or *sial*—is formed from silica and aluminum.[3] A next layer that is 3,000 kilometers is called *sima*—silica and magnesium. The density increases the closer we get to the center and goes from 3 to 6. The fluid core, which is 2,000 kilometers thick, would have an average density of 10 and at the center would "contain a solid grain that is around 17 in density." Some other authors are of the opinion that the crust is from 120 to 180 kilometers thick, while yet others believe that it could have a thickness of 1,300 to 1,600 kilometers.[4] By accepting the presence of an enormous central core with a 3,000-kilometer radius, Louis-Claude Vincent calculates that the density of this core would have to be 33.5 in order to obtain the average density of 5.52.[5]

The earth's age also remains unclear. Some scientists argue it is 15,000 years, while others say it is 148 million years, and yet there are others who claim it must be 300 million years old. I am citing these figures to clearly demonstrate that everyone believes they are holding the scientific truth, but in reality we are completely ignorant on this matter. Perhaps we may be able to sense this fluidic soul of the earth—the "guardian of the threshold—in this unconscious spirit of birth and death, the blind agent of the eternal becoming."[6]

According to Hayford, in 1919, the dimensions of planet Earth were

6,356,912 meters for the polar radius
6,378,388 meters for the equatorial radius.

In 1956 the geographical department of the United States Army stated that the meridian was actually half a mile shorter than previously thought. In 1957, the Soviet astronomer Jonglovitch wrote that the diameter of the planet was 500 meters smaller than the accepted figures. M. Guettard, without providing any reference, stated that in accordance with traditional Druidic figures, the two radii of earth would measure

6,356,777 meters for the polar radius

6,378,197 meters for the equatorial radius.

But there is good reason to define the yardstick, as we know that our meter only measures 0.999771 in relation to the cosmic meter. The English yard, as well as other ancient measures, are similar to the cosmic meter and thus have a more logical relationship with it: 70 yards represents 74 cosmic meters. The Russian arshin (0.718m) is similar to the common Egyptian cubit.[7]

According to Plato, our system is derived from the dodecahedron, "that combination used by God to design the Universe." The Bible says that "God measured the boundaries of the abyss," and that he placed "a marker in the East, and one in the West, and one in the South, and one in the North, and one at the Zenith, and one at the Nadir." He thereby demarcated space. For M. Guettard the junction of the opposing markers determines a cruciform system that orients us toward the cosmic revelation based on the projection of the cross with equal branches over the sphere. This closed universe appears to be a curve, and Guettard has summed up in a table the characteristics of the two universes it is possible for us to know:

Euclidian Universe
1. Is flat and boundless.
2. Is based on the straight line.
3. Through one point only one parallel can be drawn to a given straight line.
4. The sum of the angles of a triangle is two right angles.
5. Has a human character, useful for the professions.

Pythagorean Universe
1. Is curved and limited.
2. Rejects the straight line.
3. Through one point an infinite number of parallels can be drawn to a given straight line.

4. The sum of the angles of a triangle is different from two right angles.
5. Has a divine nature that is cosmic and architectural.

Here we arrive at the very abstract thought of Einstein, for whom the world is closed, just as Saint John indicated it was.

For Paul Bouchet, the earth—Gaia—is constructed like an atom around a central core (or neutron).[8] Planets (or electrons) follow elliptical revolutions around this core or follow a spiral line. The earth is therefore a living being whose magnetic activity is displayed by telluric currents "about which practically only the sea currents are known and categorized." These wave series circulate in the same direction following sinuous lines and branch off much like the human nervous system. "If we truly consider these currents to be nothing other than the external manifestations of the planet's intense life, we will have to conclude that existing beyond the barysphere, inside the planet, some 30,000 meters deep, there is a gaseous mass whose high pressure is equal to the gravity of a full body, inside of which this atomic world is in motion." Instead of a central core, there would be two magnetic poles around which three planetoids revolve in an elliptical movement that takes place in 471 years.[9]

In reality the three planetoids—Steropes, Brontes, and Arges—do not revolve around their "sun" on an equatorial plane but on planes that are very oblique in relation to each other. We find a similar notion in Arago, who also gave consideration to a "black sun." Finally the observations by Michelson demonstrate that the sun rises and descends periodically beneath our feet, dragging with it all the cities and mountains (a difference in height of about a foot).

The emigration of men and animals would be affected by the flow of these currents, which might explain "that drive to move westward." According to Paul Bouchet, megalithic monuments mark out the paths of these waves. Cathedrals are built over the "nodes" of currents at the sites of former dolmens, and the uneven heights of the church towers correspond to the intensity of these fluids. The Chinese knew of forces they called "dragon veins," and African magicians used similar ones to communicate psychically with each other.

Human behavior remains subject to laws that are still poorly known, and because everything is a survival, the builders and Saint Bernard—who some maintain was a Culdean Druid—built their monasteries on the sites of Druid sanctuaries, which had themselves been established close to sacred springs.

We know very little about the earth on which we live. I am going to try to describe several ancient rites that will allow us to fill the gaps left by science, starting by diving directly into the plant kingdom.

4

The Root

THE TREE ENDOWED WITH MARVELOUS PROPERTIES lives like a human; it teaches the human being and remains a receptacle of religiosity. In the center of a holy site it becomes the primordial tree, the mythical tree bearing twelve wonderful fruits that govern life and knowledge. But in the book at hand, I am going to try to establish its correspondence with the subterranean world from which it draws its nourishment, since the worship of the tree is associated with that of the Great Mother Goddess represented by the cavern.[1]

Odette Viennot has meticulously studied the cult of the tree in India.[2] But whether they are found in Vedic, Brahman, Buddhist, or Celtic literature, we learn that these trees possess the liquor of immortality and that fire circulates within them. Endowed with marvelous properties, they allow man to communicate with the sidereal world. By extension, the place where the tree grows is sanctified either by enclosing the said area or by erecting a mound on it. In Celtic mythology, the sacred oak stands at the summit of a knoll, and in a similar manner, Brahman texts speak of the aśvattha, the mango, the jambo, and the udumbara. Golgotha was identified in this way with the center of the world. It is the site of creation and the death of Adam and is also the site of the Crucifixion and the redemptive death of Jesus.

The tree can be seen as a vertical axis: by crossing through the earth this axis of manifestation harmonizes its elements, establishes a liaison between life on earth and cosmic life, and allows the human being to climb on its branches or on its notches to make his way to the divine realm. This path leads to perfection, making it so that the tree plays a role on the "universal way." It permits the restoration of an individual's sense of eternity. This tree of life that stood at the center of the earthly Paradise leads man to the reintegration of his Edenic or primordial state. This also explains the dream of King Nebuchadnezzar in Daniel (4:7); in it the king saw a growing tree whose top touched the sky. Christ was also compared to a tree: "The tree is a ladder, for it is cast between heaven and earth; the cross is again a ladder, tree, mountain."[3] The cosmic tree therefore becomes the tree of the world, a ladder of light that leads toward spirituality.

The Tree of Life cannot be uprooted. Life's storms have no power over it. Here we have the emblem of the man who is just and firm in his virtue: "the Christ, who is the virtue of God, the wisdom of God, and is also the Tree of Life upon which we should be grafted." Nowadays angels drive away with flaming swords those who seek to approach the Tree of Life, for we no longer have the right to have consciousness of the Absolute since man was deceived by Satan. With this inversion of the cosmic order, everything that was hidden is revealed, but what was obvious is concealed: the inside becomes the outside, what was outside becomes imprisoned within what was inside. This is how the spiritual light becomes enclosed within the corporeal. It is then that the roots of the tree, turned upside down, reach toward the sky, and the branches reach into the earth. This is an image we can find in the Upanishads, in Dante (*Paradiso,* 18.28–30), and in the *Zohar.* The Major Arcanum card 12 of the Tarot (the hanged man) reflects this same notion. The tree or the burning pole—the fire ceremony of Saint John—materializes the separation of heaven and earth. The "dew of light" carries out the resurrection of the dead much as rain materializes the descent of spiritual influences. The sefirotic tree is identical in this way to the tree of life, wherein the right column becomes that of mercy and the left column that of severity. This symbolism also appeared in the medieval image of the tree of the living and the dead.

This tree is made sacred because it establishes the liaison between Heaven and Earth. Its proximity makes intercession with higher powers possible and allows the faithful to enjoy the benefits of their prayers.[4] The royal hall is set up around this venerated tree as the home of a god. This pillar, located in the center of the palace, connects the lower palace—first degree—to the higher palace where reigns the mystery of mysteries and where all the cosmic degrees culminate to be reabsorbed into One. Man must climb up this pillar to the seventh heaven. Mircea Eliade emphasized the role of the cosmic tree used in shamanic initiation: "By attaining the cosmic summit one becomes the contemporary of the world's beginning," for the initiate has succeeded in abolishing time. This survival can be detected in the *laribuga* ceremony in which the novice climbs a tree.[5]

According to Odette Viennot the purpose of this pole used in a solemn festival is the consolidation of royal power.[6] In rites related to royalty, the central tree or cosmic pole that is securely anchored in the ground becomes a symbol of the prince who must be the support of his people. The Vedic *chaitya,* after having been the tree itself, becomes the sanctuary built around the tree, thus an edifice that is opened to the sky. For the sake of convenience a roof was desired to cover the entire construction, which soon made the presence of the tree inside the temple impossible. This made it so that the edifice lost its sacred character little by little. In the legend of Siegmund, the son the old king Volsung used a handsome ash tree to create the roof of a round hall. Odin passed by and struck the ash with his sword. Only the great-hearted hero Siegmund could pull this sword back out again. Later his son Siegfried slew the enormous dragon Fafnir—an animal of the earth—because he had reforged the sections of this enchanted sword. This work was done in the lair of Mime. Not only the *Nibelungen,* but Scandinavian mythology also very frequently cites the ash Yggdrasil that possesses three roots. "One stretches toward the Aesir (the gods), the second toward the *hrimthursars* (frost giants) and to the place where once stood the abyss Ginnung, and the third reaches Niflheim (the misty realm, Hell), near the well Hvergelmer (the bubbling boiling cauldron) where it is gnawed upon by the serpent Nidhogg. The well of Mimir is located beyond the root that extends into the Hrimthursars."[7] The tree feeds on the heavenly water in which its roots are immersed, but it breathes an ethereal air through its foliage. It draws its life sustenance from the underground waters, from the primordial water,[8] but a cavern leads from beneath the almond tree to the hidden city of Luz.[9] This explains the Buddhist iconography in which the tree is symbolized by the lotus flower that blossoms next to the river and follows the course of the sun.

This tree that rises from the center of the earth is therefore located close to a spring or close to a river. A bird nests in its branches and defends them, but it causes seeds to fall into the river where they germinate for the benefit of all humanity. This bird is sometimes a griffon and sometimes an eagle; it is always a divine being with wings or else a solar bird.[10] This cosmic tree is the Scandinavian Yggdrasil and the Aśvattha in the Athavaveda. We should note here that the Aśvattha gives birth to the sacrificial fire. The two *arani* gods are formed from this tree and make it possible to light the pyre that is made up of seven types of wood. Its brother tree is the *śālmali* that grows in the hell that is home to the demons known as the Asura; its thorns stand erect. In Chaldea, the Gaokerna stands in the middle of the lake in the garden of Ahura Mazda.[11] Paul Le Cour[12] has noted that the pine was sacred to the cult of the god Attis. This tree of knowledge also appears as the oak of the Druids, and in Christian symbology the resurrected Christ is represented by the acacia, the tree that Freemasons associate with the resurrection of Hiram, the great architect of the temple of Jerusalem. This tree that flowers over the grave of the master builder likely originates in his navel, just like the tree of Jesse emerges from the navel or mouth of the prophet Isaiah (11:1, 3).

Jules Boucher[13] states, according to Tiele, that "over an ark carried by four priests, from which an acacia emerges, is the phrase 'Osiris soars forth.'"[14] It so happens that in the Bible, the Ark built by Moses, the Tablet, and the altar for the holocausts were made from the wood of the acacia (Exodus 37–38).[15] The acacia is therefore sacred, and this immortal tree, the setim, has branches that form roots. Jules Boucher (*La Symbolique maçonnique*, 269) has noted that the acacia with white flowers we see in Europe is actually the *Robinia*, a pseudo-acacia, and that the true acacia, a Middle Eastern bush, is cultivated here under the name of mimosa. Jules Boucher regards the mimosa as the Golden Bough—Frazer had a branch of mistletoe in mind—and its golden yellow flowers are a symbol of magnificence and power. But we can also recognize the image of the sun here.

The tree, endowed with a soul, is a being that advances toward deliverance. The *Mahavamsa* says that being born in the shape of a tree deity is an extremely fortunate state that can only arise as the culmination of earlier lives of piety.[16] But it also directly fertilizes Maya or helps during her delivery. "The descent of the Bodhisattva into the heart of Maya takes place at the Sacred Place, beneath the *śāla* tree next to the cave of gems. And it will be atop a sacred mound, by means of the *śāla* and the mother, in addition to water in the shape of elephants, of Indra, or of serpents, that the arrival of the future Buddha into the world will take place."[17] In many other Vedic texts the queen is impregnated by the tree, the dwelling of God: the vine, one of its limbs can embrace and wrap around. The magical aspect of the vine often appears in this guise in Indian iconography. We also find charms and amulets that have been made out of wood, and the tree subsequently becomes the sacred pillar. Stripped of its bark and branches and uprooted, this pole—to which an entire rite has already been attached—retains the properties of the tree. It can be the sacrificial post, the *yūpa* or Axis Mundi, the "totem" or *poteau-mitan* of Voodoo; but it initially belonged to the stone pillar in which we find the column or menhir, the axis around which the world revolves. In Indian cosmology, this axis takes the name of *skambha*, and the central summit of Mount Sinai in Hebrew cosmology made it possible for Moses to communicate with the Eternal One. A snake is wrapped around this sacred pillar because liturgical prayer ascends toward God by coiling around the shaft: it is the movement that twists in the ether, and it may be helpful to note that all ascendant movement appears to be helical. The wooden pillar can be crowned by the Cretan double-bladed axe or the horns, both of which characterize a sacred monument. The pillars become homages to the tree: columns are found at the temple of Tyre, and these pillars of Melqart resemble those of Attis erected in front of the Cave of Dionysius. Some would call these phallic pillars, but Marques-Rivière thinks that they represent instead the vital human force that travels through the spinal column.[18] If the essential function of the pillar is support, that would make the tree a pillar, since Heaven rests upon it. To hold up this vast expanse, four supporting points are needed, each located at one of the four cardinal points. These boundary markers denote the ends of the lands according to the Bible. In the same spirit, Clave notes that the two pillars are the two principles of creation and destruction, life and death, and light and darkness. The balance of the universe is supported by the play between them. However, the two pillars of time and space can only have value in a material form, as the quest for the supreme center is what makes it specifically possible to be free of the notion of time.

According to Herodotus, the two pillars were attributed to Hercules: the pillar of fine gold represented the psychic energy emanating from the throne of Zeus; the one of emerald that of the Aphrodite of ancient Egypt—the temporal and spiritual powers. I can also mention the pillars of Jachin and Boaz defined in the book of Chronicles.[19] King Solomon allegedly summoned Huram-Abi—Hiram—to oversee the construction, and because of this filiation Papus compared the two columns to two interlacing triangles: a white one rising and a black one descending, thus forming the seal of Solomon, the emblem of alchemical research.[20]

But if the tree root serves as an intermediary between the plant and the mineral, and if the tree develops under the solar warmth, the forest introduces a somewhat different kind of symbolism. Of course this group of trees retains the properties of each species, but the vertical radiations that travel through the trunk and main roots are much more active. The radiations emitted by the trees create a veritable exchange between the earth and clouds. A builder once noted that the fir emits a very large number of radiations with a huge wavelength, varying with the type of soil. The ends of the needles are oriented toward the sky and permit greater contact. Modern lightning rods are designed similarly and discharge the cloud statically, balancing its electrical potential with that of the earth. In addition, the American scientists Ernst Antevs and Professor Andrew Douglas have studied the alternation in consecutive tree layers (dendrochronology). They found evidence for a constant correlation between the speed with which the layers of wood were formed and the solar cycle. The seasonal imbalances were connected to sunspots. This cycle is currently eleven years. The Scythians and the Gauls gathered in vast forests in which dense growth of trees girded clearings—inside of which grew no grass. This wooded, inviolable, and sacred place can be compared to a cavern. The sacred grove, with its triple enclosure, isolated and gave protection to the individual presiding over the religious ceremony. Harmful, occult powers were incapable of breaching it. The forest ritually sets the magic worker apart from the profane world; this enclosure gives birth to the circle and to the magic square, but it also materializes in a circle of flames with Sigurd. This tangled plant growth conforms to the appearance of the theme of the forbidden chamber, a theme treated in Perrault's fairy tale "Sleeping Beauty."[21] It is necessary for Prince Charming to perform many feats of valor in order to earn—through his perseverance and moral elevation—the right to cross through this natural defense. In a Danish variation of the fairy tale "Cinderella," the text tells us that the young girl must travel through two forests. In his *Seven Romanian Fairy Tales,* Bachelin also describes this threefold appearance of a forest that should be made of silver, gold, and diamonds. In similar fashion, before descending into Hell, Aeneas had to cross through a forest. We see that same scenario in Dante's *Divine Comedy.* In Chrétien de Troyes's *Knight of the Lion* Yvain had numerous adventures in the forest of Brocéliande; and Tom Thumb also went through many of his trials there. This would imply that the abandonment of children in the forest should not be considered a savage act. In this sacred retreat and sanctuary, the child shapes himself: Tom Thumb, John of the Bear, Mischievous John, and even Little Red Riding Hood evolve in a place of initiation. I do not share Hyacinthe Husson's opinion that the forest symbolizes night or that of Leo Bachelin, who sees it as winter. If this were so how are we to understand the Deccan version of Sleeping Beauty in which a little girl named Surya Bai is sleeping under the effect of a sting from a rakshasa. She is left to sleep in a small house that has been placed atop a huge tree. Wouldn't this tree be the cosmic tree, the initiatory tree at whose foot the Buddha was initiated?

The Zulu of Africa are initiated in the forest,[22] and the entire corpus of Mircea Eliade has contributed considerably to our knowledge of this subject. Similar customs exist in the Congo and the Gulf of Guinea where these ritual ordeals were considered as exorcism procedures.

Many springs can be found in the sacred grove. Pausanias cites the sanctuary of Demeter Mysia, near Pellene in Achaea. Combats accompanied by ritual insults between men and women took place here. In Ethiopia, and primarily among the Falasha, tree worship was celebrated in a cave near the waters of a spring where a black heifer was sacrificed.[23] With the caves and sanctuaries of the Black Madonna, we also find many more examples of wooded sites surrounding a spring.

However, roots that are not those of trees can also play a similar role. In reality, the tree, which is endowed with a distinctive kind of life, permits the liaison between Heaven and Earth, but it would be helpful to study the roots of some other plants here, which would take us beyond the scope of the present book. I have in mind the mandrake, a herbaceous perennial that originated in southern Europe.[24] This thick, plump, pivoting and often bifurcated root that is a blackish color on the surface often gives the impression of being the bottom half of a human body. Its fairly large green to bluish-green leaves spread out over the surface of the ground. This plant is said to "be

formed from the earth from which the first human being was molded,"
a red adamic dirt that is the transition between man and plant,[25] and
it is possible that "the first men were a family of gigantic sensitive
mandrakes who were given life by the sun and who freed themselves
from the ground."[26] Tercinet reminds us that the mandrake provides
temporary wealth.[27] Joan of Arc wore one near her heart when being
questioned at her trial on March 1, 1431. However, according to
Johann Weyer (*Witches, Devils, and Doctors of the Renaissance*) it is
engendered beneath a gallows from the urine of a hanged man. The
extraction of this embryonic being proves to be difficult because its
gestation is incomplete, and it can only be torn from its mother's
womb with a great deal of trouble. "This type of human being, something like an animated rough draft from which the noble senses have
not yet been freed, and a kind of chrysalis" therefore clings to the
earth. But it seems to give back its original integrity to its happy
owner, and it can also be sold for its weight in gold. In order to gain
possession of one it is necessary to employ a complicated ritual involv-
ing a black dog. This animal is then attached to the plant so that it
can be uprooted without any curse falling on the human being.

While mistletoe, according to Frazer, also possesses the property
of finding treasures hidden underground, I want to point your attention toward another preeminently fertile grain. This is the wheat
offered to Osiris, the god of vegetation and god of fertility. The ear
of wheat often appears in Eastern iconography.[28] In a Welsh legend
from the *Mabinogion,* Ceridwen is pursuing Gwion. After a series
of transformations Gwion turns himself into an ear of wheat, which
Ceridwen, who has taken the form of a hen, swallows. She then finds
that she has thereby been impregnated.[29] Roots can give fertility to
women as well. The mandrake figures among the legends and tales
that describe "miraculous births." It was worn as a fetish on a necklace during the Middle Ages.[30] But the ear of wheat also symbolizes
the burying of matter, which breaks down to create life. From this
simple grain the large ear is born; life follows apparent death and
perpetuates itself.

All seeds can be cited symbolically, but one curious case in particular should draw our attention, that of the fava bean. In his *On the Cave of the Nymphs* (19) Porphyry writes that "the bees do not sit on the beans, which were considered by the ancients as a symbol of generation proceeding in a regular series without being intercepted; because this leguminous vegetable is almost the only one, amongst other fruits whose stalk is perforated throughout without any intervening knots."* In this text we find the principle of generation inasmuch as by "bee" we should understand souls headed toward generation. Pausanias did not dare indicate the reason for the taboo on beans, which were forbidden to the initiates at Eleusis and those following the Orphic mysteries. For Gaffarel, "one side of the bean carries the form and figures of the shameful parts of a man and on the other, that of a woman."[31] This legume that is planted in the ground therefore carries the seeds of men.[32] We can rightfully ask ourselves why the Egyptians worshipped this legume like a god, as it was forbidden to sow it, eat it, and even to look at it—they hid it beneath a veil in their temple—while Pythagoras forbid its use by his students because it prevented divinatory dreams in the same way mandrake did. It has been said that the Sage of Samos, who believed in reincarnation, was afraid that this seed—which turns over in the ground as it grows—will collect through transmigration the soul of an ancestor. Other authors have mentioned that the flower contains infernal letters in the two black patches painted in the wings that envelop the hull of the marsh bean. But what is the point of finding the bean in the king cake that families share on January 6, Epiphany? The bean grants its lucky owner several moments of joy. Is this the sign of the baby Jesus that appeared to the Three Magi?[33] The bean sealed within the galette on whose crust crisscrossing lines have been drawn—snares or nets—shows that one destined to become king receives a sign from heaven.

It was not my intention in a book on the underground world to get into the complexity of the symbolism of the basic tree or of seeds. What

---

*[Translated by Thomas Taylor]

I wanted to show was the universality of the tree as the seat of super-natural powers and the source of blessings. The tree of life allows the human being to attain the cycle of Illumination. This living wisdom puts us on the right path and gives us balance. Through its radiations, through its quality as world axis, the tree leads to higher states. This desire to reach the sky and reestablish connection with the forces of the cosmos is what causes the erection of pillars, posts, columns, and ladders, and in order to materialize this ruptured union the cosmic tree is burned.[34] The tree in the Saint John's bonfire remains first and fore-most the celestial footstool. The signs of the tree are associated with those of water and stone—and thereby with those of the altar, as fer-tility symbols—thus putting all the forces of the cosmos into contact. This tree-pillar is a ladder, a tower of Babel, which permits the passage and access to the ultimate realization, thanks to which we can move from the state of ignorance to that of knowing—from the subterranean world to the cosmic world. However, to be reborn, one must be purified as much by Fire as by Water.

5

Underground Water

THE PRESENCE OF THE SPRING in the underground sanctuary allows the neophyte to purify himself and to be transformed; on the Druid hill, the oak grew near a fast-moving stream; the Black Madonna of the Roman crypt keeps watch over the well. The worship of stones is itself associated with the worship of springs and water. All traditions deify this secret subterranean spring, which, because of that, possesses a sacred nature. This water of life gushes from the rock when invoked by Moses (Exodus 17:6) or by Hercules. In Hades, the river Lethe flows on the left while the spring of Mnemosyne is located on the right. Its cool water makes it possible to retain memory and consciousness. The fountain of youth inspires us to imagine that water possesses healing or miraculous qualities. The fresh water of the well inside the crypt of the Saintes-Maries-de-la-Mer is considered to be miraculous water because all the water around it is salt water.

These subterranean waters emanate from the primordial Water that subsequently became the elixir of the Hermeticists.

Although this chapter refers only to the symbolism of underground water, there is a text by René Guénon in which we can find the definition of the baptismal water that regenerates and recreates the individual.

Water was looked upon by many traditions as the original medium of beings, by reason of its symbolism, according to which it stands for Mula Prakriti; in a higher sense, and by transposition, water is Universal Possibility itself; whoever is born of water becomes a "son of the Virgin" and therefore an adopted brother of Christ and co-heir of the Kingdom of God.[1]

The spirit is the Hebrew Ruach (associated here with water as a complementary principle according to what was said at the beginning of Genesis). It so happens that *ruach* also means "air," and this indeed brings to mind the purification of the spirit by the elements.[2]

Water is symbolized by two wavy lines. This fluid, flowing element is often endowed with the power of fertility. People bathed in springs and fountains in order to have children. In today's world, women take cures at thermal spas when they are unable to bear children; for example, at Luxeuil. When studying the legends concerning virgin mothers, Saintyves noted this power. It appears that water is not innately fertile but that it transports the element of life. "Pleasurably excited by the warmth of the season, they—the gods—often spilled their sperm in the springs and fountain, which corrupted the waters."[3] This provided an easy explanation for a miraculous birth as a virgin bathing in this water could easily be impregnated. These notions are quite hardy and survive even into the present day; someone told me one day in complete seriousness that a virgin had been made pregnant by her father by bathing after him. It is primarily in Hindu literature where we find mention of water transporting seeds and impregnating young girls when they are bathing. In reality, conception responds to much more complex biological laws, but the waters are declared to be fruitful, and sterile women are advised to bathe in them. The primordial waters were themselves fertilized by Ruach Elohim, His Spirit—the gods. This cosmogony is based on the *Manava,* a metaphysical treatise attributed to Manu: "On one side are the Waters and on the other, Him. The primordial water was lying there since boundless time, in the darkness and silence of the tomb."[4] We should not be surprised by this prolific aspect because it is necessary to connect the dual waters to the generating breath and understand that water is the complement of fire. The active and passive principles combine for manifestation.

Under the star sign of the Moon and the Sun—the principle of the two pillars—water is considered in the standard symbolism to be a female power, and earth is viewed as male, even though it is Mother Earth that gives birth to children and provides life. This underground water emerges from the ground—from the lower regions where the human has been initiated—to ascend toward the liberating light. Water, purified by fire, thereby becomes the image of the spiritual work.

Life is only possible because of the element of "water" thanks to the phenomenon of ionization, electronization, and osmotic pressure.[5] Life is formed in the water this way, and this energetic mechanism is recognized by biologists (Laville, Fred Vlès). This element that has a huge part in our diet also plays an equally important role in human health and behavior. Louis-Claude Vincent has observed that very pure spring water maintains health and allows cells to flourish, which can be seen in a fresh complexion and the absence of wrinkles. To combat the desiccation of old age, it is necessary to drink extremely pure spring water that removes salts; mineralized waters are not satisfactory, but siliceous water (such as that of Volvic) gives excellent results. According to the theories of Laville and Coanda the first form of green algae developed in this water. Spiritually regenerating water also possesses medicinal properties. Thermal baths are located alongside beneficial springs that are the emanations of a god or goddess. The Gauls were quite familiar with these springs that remained hugely popular during the Roman occupation. Many Roman remnants remain near our spas: Neris, Evian, Amélie, Saint-Galmier, Dax, and Bourbon-Lancy. While the bathwaters wash away all the body's physical dirt, pure water removes the stain from the soul. In every religion, diving into the water corresponds to an act of purifying the soul. In this way the human being improves himself spiritually. The lotus blossoms on the surface of the water and is thereby continuously restored. Water—*akka* in Sanskrit—is always available on the Mandara temple altar.[6] The Ganges, which originates in the Himalayas, remains the preeminent sacred river because "it is a soaring ladder to the gates of heaven from earth."[7] The Brahman living as a hermit will allow his hair to grow unchecked as well as his beard and nails, but he will bathe three times a day.[8] Pilgrims purified themselves in the waters of the Castalian Spring near the Oracle of Delphi. The convert before he is given permission to undergo the tests of initiation must first be purified in water—the symbol of regeneration and new life.[9] Baptismal water plays a large role in Christianity. Saint John the Baptist worked in the same way as the Pharisees and the Essenes,* thereby making the Jordan the River of Judgment. Christian baptism was practiced by immersion and only given to those who had passed the age of reason. Saint Augustine was not baptized until he was thirty-two.[10] The Anabaptists held on to this tradition because in order for the sacrament to have any validity when given to the new member he or she must understand it perfectly and accept it. The future knight also took a bath on the eve of being dubbed. This custom gave birth to the knightly Order of the Bath, which was established by either Richard II or his successor, Henry IV. In the same way, the statues of gods and goddesses, carried in great pomp, were bathed in the sea, rivers, or springs. Even today the statue of one of the Saint-Maries-de-la-Mer, the black saint Sarah, is placed in the Mediterranen after being carried there by Gypsies and her guardians. This custom can be seen in India, where this bathing ceremony, Lanoë-Villène tells us, was still in vogue but a short time ago. Couldn't this be another sign of a connection between the Bohemians and their Hindu sect? In this way spring water—visible in the church of the Saintes-Maries by its miraculous well—plays an important role in baptism, part of enjoying a second birth. The Magne Tower in Nîmes overlooks a sacred spring.

The siting of the baptistery responds to strictly determined characteristics. While Persigoult believes that the chamber of reflection is placed at the intersection of radiant cosmic forces whose rays intersect, megalithic monuments are supposed to have been erected at the crossing of underground springs.[11] According to this view, the dolmen was

---

*According to the historian Josephus, the Essenes were Pythagorean Jews.

set up at the intersection of two veins, and cupule or sculpted stones were placed at the center of the cross formed by two streams of water intersecting at right angles. Paul Bouchet expands the matter by no longer focusing on springs of water but on telluric currents.[12] It is undeniable, in any case, that monasteries were built in this same way on Druid sites that had been set up near sacred springs.

Miraculous waters form part of a very distinctive devotion. Following the Clitumnus springs in Umbria, those of the Olympian sanctuaries and those sacred to Poseidon, we have the miraculous waters of Lourdes. While much remains to be said about Luz and its Holy Savior church, located in a valley with a wealth of occurrences as well as one that was a Johannite and Templar valley, we should note that our local saints replaced the subaltern gods of the Greek and Roman religions. These regional devotions are in reality nothing but the survivals of a pagan cult.

It is running waters that are worshipped, not stagnant waters. I think that this implies the existence of a spirit in the water that takes part this way in the rhythm of life. Running water represents the animal in some way, the benevolent beast whose spirit is found everywhere and nowhere. Water runs. It has been compared to a snake that also emerges from the depths of the earth and is connected with the depiction of the spiral, the flowering of the human being. Lakes are inhabited by sacred animals that give material expression to the genius or spirit of water— there are lacustrine serpents, bulls, horses, and horned animals that are akin to certain gods.[13] All these legends converge primarily in Germany and the Baltic countries.

Water remains an element that is difficult to cross. To traverse a waterway it is necessary to be able to build a bridge, always a complex undertaking. Ribbons, cotton threads, and vines make this crossing possible. Both in Goethe's *Green Snake* and in iconography the world over, we find countless examples of this ditch filled with running water. The boat makes it possible to go from one bank to the other, but it requires a ferryman. The boat itself has its own supremely complex symbolism, such as that of the cup that should contain the quaff of immortality.

Miniature boats are found in many tombs because they make it possible to cut through the many states of being. Jesus is often the ferryman.

We should finally note that in the Scriptures water is often the symbol of great misfortunes in addition to that caused by the water of the Flood. Jacob compares Reuben to uncontrollable water because of his crime with Bilhah, and the waters of Egypt transformed into blood. But generally water encourages harmony. It has a positive influence on the state of one's health, but primarily it inspires illumination. This pure water, emerging from the nourishing earth, appears like a baptismal bath that regenerates us physically and morally, and restores our original cleanliness, perhaps because it snakes through the rocks where the godhead resides.

6

The Rock

WE NOW FIND OURSELVES in the presence of the stone, that mysterious rock that is often regarded as the home or body of a god. From this was born the cult of the raw stone whose evolution seems paralyzed; then the stone carver presides over an act of magic. As far back as we can go we find adoration of the stone as a synthesis of matter envisioned as support for the spirit and an emblem of the world of manifestation. The standing stone gives the impression of something surging up—a force that was raised and suddenly petrified. Human beings remain attentive to this display of active power and very mysterious sustained effort. Literature has made use of this emotional shock.[1] Victor Hugo describes this enchantment that Michelet deftly described, saying: "And the stone itself, standing on the path, offers you the riddle of the sphinx."[2]

If the material can be identified with a geometrical shape, the stone—the image of the earth itself—symbolically becomes a square. We are all familiar with those depictions of the dual membership—earthly and divine—in which the square is combined with the circle in order to show that everything is part of the Whole. The cart and the palace of the Chinese sovereign, the dais, the cupola, all take part in this symbolism.

The stone in itself possesses the potential of the telluric forces and triggers a complete ritual of sacred art. As an illustration of man's ability to perfect himself, he has been compared to a raw stone that has been carved. To truly grasp what this task of carving implies, it is necessary to realize that this manual task is coupled with an act of mind and spiritual power. The invocation and enchantment resemble an alchemical exercise; this vocational rite surpasses itself, and its mastery leads to inner discipline, thus a realization of consciousness. "The stone carvers have inscribed the echo of the Lost Word within the secular silence of the stone that the predestined alone will hear,"[3] writes Victor-Émile Michelet.

However, I am not going to discuss the carving of the stone or the symbolism of the tools that are used to do it. Yet it is necessary to know how to carve the cornerstone of the Great Work, the stone to which Jesus compared himself and that figures in the *Zohar*. I am therefore going to set aside all this power of enchantment, prayers, spells, and all that magical and religious power that made it possible to work a divine material more skillfully. All I wish to retain here is the totemic aspect of this material, this emanation of subterranean power. I would like to mention some of my conversations with my friend Albert Pichon while we mused as the Petit Morin* snaked by our feet, for this stone may have achieved a state of perfection from which we other humans are still quite far, with our animal life made up of instincts, desires, and anger.

"Because of its immutable nature, the stone symbolizes wisdom."[4] This divine nature should catch our attention. But I am not saying anything about those marble statues that come to life and whose absolute cold paralyzes the reckless individual who was not scared of provoking them. Prosper Mérimée borrowed from fables of antiquity to write his short stories *La Vénus d'Ille* and *Il Vicolo di Madama Lucrezia,* and meanwhile Don Juan was debating with the statue of the Commander.[5]

The stone, the house of God, clearly appears in the story of Jacob's dream.[6]

> And Jacob went out from Beersheba, and went toward Haran.
> And he lighted upon a certain place, and tarried there all night,

---

*[A tributary of the Marne River. —*Trans.*]

because the sun was set; and he took of the stones of that place, and put them for his pillows, and lay down in that place to sleep. (Genesis 28:10–11)

In a dream Jacob saw the ladder on which the angels climbed and descended, a symbol that we can also see in the Tarot:

And Jacob awaked out of his sleep, and he said, "Surely the Lord is in this place; and I knew it not." And he was afraid and said, "How dreadful is this place! This is none other but the house of God, and this is the gate of heaven." And Jacob rose up early in the morning, and took the stone that he had put for his pillows, and set it up for a pillar, and poured oil upon the top of it. And he called the name of that place Beth-el [House of God]: but the name of that city was Luz at the first. (Genesis 28:16–19)

And Jacob went on to say: "And this stone, which I have set for a pillar, shall be God's house" (Genesis 28:22).

The divine stone came down from the sky to become the abode of the Deity. As an axis, it serves as an intermediary between heaven and earth. In the image of God who manifests in the monolith, the human being is born from a stone, and we have here a traditional relationship that we find in a great many of the Bible's prophecies. Mithras was born from a stone, and this rock that brought him into the world was later worshipped in the form of a cosmic stele. This phenomenon of crystallization culminated in the cult that takes the stone as its chief support medium. The Japanese also revered rocks, which could sometimes become a *shintal,* meaning an object that the invisible deity could merge into in order to reestablish contact with his or her believers. This is why the shrine of Himegoso, the dwelling of the princess Akaru, consists of three huge stones surrounded by trees. Carl Jung has drawn a brilliant parallel between Christ and the stone: with the death of Jesus, matter was sanctified by its dissolution into the cosmic night. Apollo was worshipped in Delphi in the form of a stele.

According to Ovid and Pindar, Deucalion and Pyrrha cast stones behind them, which is how human beings—or the various stages of life—came into existence. The less fortunate Jason sowed pebbles that became foes that he was forced to fight. This maturation of the rock inside the earth as a life motif figured in Central and South America among the Maya and the Inca, but Eliade also found this legend among the Greeks and Semites, as well as in Asia Minor.[7] Ripley meanwhile deduced in his philosophical research that every human being possesses the Stone.*

Saint Bernard established a connection between the human body and the temple constructed by masons. For M. M. Davy, the raw stone becomes the symbol of freedom; once carved by the hand of man it becomes a symbol of servitude.[8] While the rock that falls from the sky is raw, when it resurfaces beneath the sky from the ground it is transformed and carved. In its natural state, the rock contains an intense spiritual potential, but on contact with our ground it can lose its Knowledge. It must then regenerate in order to find the path of illumination once again. The raw, androgynous stone loses its sacred nature when cut, because the two principles—male and female—are separated. These two basic principles can be reunited with the placement of the conical stone on the cubic stone.

All of Celtic civilization, drawing from traditional sources, saw unquarried rock as sacred because it was an energetic astral substance that served as a mediator between heavenly and earthly forces. In the tradition of the patriarchs the incarnated Word is worshipped under the symbol of the standing stone, a representation of the world's axis because petrification remains the foundation of the universe. Paul Sedir writes:

A little-known theory that the Templars took from Celtic initiation and which seventeenth-century Rosicrucians borrowed from them:

The Word is the raw stone that falls from the heights of time onto the depths of space, through the ecliptic, by separating the

---

*[Sir George Ripley (ca. 1415–1490), English alchemist. —Ed.]

cosmic Potential from what has not come to pass. This is the first day, the Fiat lux, Beth-Il.

It halts its descent, and stands still before climbing back up: this is Beth-El.

It ascends again, travels through the so often erroneous efforts of man: this is the flat stone, the House of Lies: Beth-Aven.

Finally it reintegrates its starting point and becomes the worked and open cube, the stone that opens, the stone with one hundred and forty-four faces, the cubic stone, the stone of life: Beth-Lehem.

This is how the stone, by virtue of its quality, allows the construction of gigantic cyclopean monuments in which we find menhirs, dolmens, cromlechs, megaliths, and *carneillous*. I naturally exclude monuments such as the Tower of Babel, in which we find bricks made from clay. This is no longer a noble material as it involves manufacture. These extremely simple constructions follow the evolution of taste: they became increasingly ornate and embellished with sculptures.[9] The quadrangular rubble stone forms the oriented altar whose four sides face the four cardinal points. In Christianity the altar has an east-west orientation, following the sun. This altar stone and dwelling place of the divine also represents Christ and the four cardinal virtues incorporated into each of the four faces. All these ritual principles seem to go entirely overlooked today. Jesus, the cornerstone, brings to mind the final cubic burrstone with a point at the top of the pyramid, the supreme spiritual power. In their great wisdom the ancient Egyptians did not make this pole concrete and leveled off the top of their temple.

Moses had twelve stones erected at the foot of Mount Sinai (Exodus 24:4), symbol of the Last Supper and the origin of the cromlech of Bethel that became baetyl. When Joshua located the passage over the Jordan he used the same procedure,[10] and the Scriptures stress the fact that these are raw stones undefiled by the chisel.[11] The Celts established their monuments of stone the same way, as it is impious to carve the house of God. The erection of these coarse standing stones gave the impression of an extremely elementary civilization that was thoughtless and equipped with only the poorest of means. This legend does not stand up to critical observation. When Pausanias[12] tells us that a raw stone* was erected in Hyetta in Boeotia as an image of Hercules, we do not laugh.

On observing the widespread presence of menhirs across the world, many authors have mused on the possibility of a pre-Celtic civilization. According to the maps drawn up by Fernand Niel, the distribution occurs primarily in the coastal regions, although we are familiar with the alignments in the Gard, Lozère, Saône-et-Loire, Oise, and Seine-et-Oise in France. But while France has a wealth of such alignments, we can also find them in England, India, and Tibet. There are two hundred and twenty dolmens in the Deccan plateau of India and there are those on the desert plateau of La-Chung in Tibet, some twenty-one thousand feet above sea level. Korean dolmens are found on the eastern side of the peninsula, and there are others that still exist in Palestine (Jordan—between Assam and Mount Nebo—Galilee, Samaria, toward Lake Tiberiades), Algeria, and in Africa (in the Maghreb, and in the regions of Sous, Marrakech, and Taza).

Why did human beings go to the trouble of erecting monoliths that are at least sixty feet high and often more than three tons in weight like the large menhir of Locmariaquer in Brittany? In countries as far apart from each other as France and Korea there are similar techniques, inasmuch as sixty-ton blocks have been raised to a height of ten feet (Ha-Heum dolmen in Korea). It was through manpower, some say, but the extremely limited area would only allow for a small number of workers.[13] Fernand Niel clearly exposes the difficulties that are encountered: this kind of work requires the establishment of a solid track and the crafting of procedures for raising stones like this—procedures that remain unknown to us. While menhirs are sculpted, all these stones possess a family resemblance, which gives one the impression that they were to honor a universal deity, "a great goddess, whose worship would have been around 2000 BCE." Couldn't these megalithic goddesses be

---

*It is necessary to cite the stones of Thespis and of Pharae near the statue of Hermes.

the virgin mothers? We should note that Shiva's emblem, the lingam, is also represented by a standing stone. It so happens that sterile women come to pray to this third god of the Hindu trinity. There is therefore a relationship between the stone that gives fertility and the standing stone in both the Celtic and Hindu religions.[14] In this way all religions stem from a common tree, which was the Beginning.

Why erect such monuments? The cave could be the origin of the sepulchral dolmen, in which the entombed corpse sleeps curled around itself. There are some dolmens with holes, their cavities having been worked artificially in one of the supports. Additionally, in order to reach the chamber, it is necessary to stoop down and sometimes crawl. The gash across the stone is also executed in the upper slab—as in the dolmen of the Mas d'Azil in the Ariège department of France, these are preeminent rites of initiation.[15]

The menhir is also involved in sun worship. A large number of these stone alignments are determined by the solstice sunrise—either of summer or winter—or of intermediary sunrises (November 8, February 4, May 6, and August 8). More specifically, the cromlech of Stonehenge north of Salisbury poses some fascinating questions. This construction is supposed to have been built around 1850 BCE, and the menhirs that form the lane leading to it are oriented precisely on the rising sun of the summer solstice. One solitary menhir gives an orientation; if one of its sides is roughly square, the long axis locates a particular point. The Champeaux menhir in Ille-et-Vilaine is perfectly oriented, and its four sides face the four cardinal points. When several menhirs are grouped together, the lines connecting them indicate a solar direction. But many menhirs have been destroyed and others moved.[16] This makes our observations less precise. We are no longer certain of understanding the symbol that remains for us because Druidism is only transmitted by word of mouth and avoids the written word. This transmission is proof of the high spiritual authority of our ancestors.

For Bernard Palissy, who was more of a scientist than a ceramicist, stones and crystals are formed through the congealing effect of water; in other words, through the power of the attraction of salts. Master

Bernard, with his positive and practical mind, still asserted that he had seen a petrified man, and he was of the opinion that man, beast, and wood could all be reduced to stone.[17]

This brings us to Jacob Boehme's thinking on the matter: "a stone, however, is nothing but water. This allows us to imagine what kind of great anger would cause water to congeal so severely."[18] Many authors believe that a stone is alive like any other being of creation. According to E. W. Eschmann, its evolutionary law cannot be perceived by us humans.[19] The stone in the womb of the earth receives an increase of stonelike substances that are carried by water and then deposited on the stones that have already been formed. For Palissy, the stone does not grow but increases in size thanks to deposits. He calls this process "the congelation of stones." There is also the case of devotees who want children and seek help from stones that may look like lingams but could also look like breasts, eggs, or rounded humps. These stones shaped like generative organs can restore fertility because they work through magic.

This hidden stone of the Sages, this carbon atom in the pure state, the soul of the crystal, also gives birth to the sparkling gems whose limpid water sets and regenerates the form. The quest for the Philosophers' Stone must be pursued inside of us; our body becomes a laboratory in which the soul reforges itself to become as pure as the diamond that burns without leaving any trace.[20] We must read with our full attention the narrative by Alexandre Toussaint-Limojon, knight of Saint Didier, a text contained within *Le Triomphe hermétique* that is titled "L'Ancienne guerre des chevaliers," with a highly significant subtitle: "Or maintenance of the stone of the philosophers with gold and mercury."[21] The stone is the root of humanity, the navel of the earth,* the central power, and the triumph of all. René Guénon, in *The Symbolism of the Cross,* compares it, as a phallic emblem, to the Sacred Mountain. This is why the standing stone can be a close match to the lingam, the mystical phallus that is the symbol of Shiva and which unites the King with the

---

*The crystallization occurs in the human being in the area around the navel, from the plexus with ten petals, the *manipura* chakra. This comparison deserves further analysis.

Queen. In the mysteries of the High Wisdom it becomes the incident ray: Christ. This connection was broken by the original Fall; initiation is an attempt to recover the paradise that was lost. This Rosicrucian teaching, by introducing Elias Artista or reflected ray, establishes the relationship between the stone and the mineral realm based on celestial mercury.

The Philosophers' Stone prepares itself slowly. By combining it with gold and silver and by cooking it in a glass flask for one year, a person can obtain that precious stone that makes it possible to transmute other substances into mystic gold. It should be noted that the cooking starts from black, before going through a stage of dazzling whiteness before ending at ruby red. This Philosophers' Stone often appears vile and black, but beneath its miserable exterior it contains everything. "The matter is known by all, but all are ignorant of it." The Cosmopolite emphasized this mistake of the common folk who reject the stone "like muck." He entered into evidence the opposition that exists between mineral vitality and metallic inertia, Limajon writes: "Our stone is born from the destruction of two bodies: one is mineral, the other metallic. They both grow in the same earth."

Claude d'Ygé provided some very helpful documents on the stone,[22] and during my research I compared the mystery of Hermetic work with the winning of the Golden Fleece. This philosophical quest leads to the reincarnation of the individual into the three kingdoms, then to the regenerated human being. Jean-Albert Bélin hints at the same search:

> The Philosophers' Stone is a mineral substance, the most perfect kind that can exist, having within a very perfect mixture of elements.[23]

Other philosophers have stated explicitly that three elements are essential; the Philosophers' Stone gives access to initiatory experience like the elixir of advancement.

The material stone holds celestial fire within it. The black stone fallen from the sky gives an esoteric power; it rises up like a pillar of mystical degrees, and it plays the role of one stage as it makes it possible to gain access to the invisible. It is the designation of the pole, and the Holy Spirit reveals itself within it. The black stone of Mecca and the one that Gérard de Nerval discusses with respect to the Druses (*Journey to the Orient*) comply with this notion.

Revering the stone led to an idolatry that early Catholicism sought to fight; Christian rulings forbade this fetishism because the worship strayed from worship to become aberrational magic. Wearing an amulet was made against the law. Fernand Niel gives us some historical facts in his book *Dolmens et Menhirs*. Emperor Theodore II banned this worship in 435 and inserted it into the Theodosian Code of 438: "Canon 23 of the Council of Arles of 425 makes guilty of sacrilege the bishop that tolerates the worship of stones in his territory." The Council of Tours, in 567, "advised the clergy to expel from the Church anyone seen doing in front of certain stones things that have nothing in common with said Church." Canon 20 of the Council of Nantes was even more explicit in 658: "may the stones, which people, deceived by the ruses of demons, worship in ruined places and forests, making vows to them or wearing them, be buried deeply and cast into a place where their worshippers cannot find them." In 681 and 682, the Councils of Toledo fulminated against the *Méneratoires lapidum*. In Rouen, in 698, the council denounced those who swore vows to stones or who offered them candles. Saint Eligius protested in his sermons against those who lit candles or swore vows near stones or stone circles. Even without his *Admonitio Generalis* of March 23, 789, which was renewed in article 41 of the *Capitulaire des Missi dominici* published around the year 800, Charlemagne ordered the destruction of stones worshipped by the populace. Fernand Niel concludes from this: "But judging by the number of megalithic monuments still standing, the public authorities and clergy remained singularly impotent before the opposition or the inertia of the peoples."

Nevertheless, these religious edicts did inspire quite a lot of destruction. The names of a number of French towns keep alive the idea of a similar worship even though the object of this worship has vanished, such as Pierrefitte, Pierre-Levée, and so forth. In 1959 newspapers ran a story on how a stone on which the kings of England had sat during their coronation had been stolen from Westminster Abbey, and the stone returned just as mysteriously as it had disappeared.[24] Did an alchemist need this stone? Let's examine this reddish sandstone that was used during royal coronations; it could be the famous Bethel of Jacob. This stone, which was a support for the Ark of the Covenant, is said to have been spirited away by Jeremiah who, fleeing the destruction of Jerusalem, took refuge in Ireland. Planted on the sacred hill of Tara, this Stone of Destiny, or Lia Fail, was necessarily used in coronations. It so happens that the monastery of Iona, in the midst of the Culdees who protected this stone, was founded on the ruins of a Druid school. This church had also maintained relations with the churches of Constantinople and Alexandria. Is there any need to underscore the strange analogy with this early church between the transfer of this stone and that of the Grail?[25] Twelve Culdean monks left this monastery with Saint Colomba in 573 to reform the Gallic clergy. This famous Irish monk, a spiritual son of the monastery at Bangor established by Comgall, founded the monastery of Luxeuil. It became necessary to reconnect the Roman Church with the Celtic Church. Its rule had momentarily eclipsed that of Saint Benedict, but after Saint Colomba's death in 615 the bishops met in council in Autun (in 670) and imposed the rule of Saint Benedict over the Irish monks scattered throughout Gaul. The kinship between these two groups is much easier to understand.

This Lia Fail, transplanted and held at Westminster Abbey, brings to mind the "white stone" that was used to distinguish the winner of the public games. An unknown name was carried on the "suffrage stone"—likely that of a candidate with public duties in a popular fair. This unknown name could be that of the Savior,[26] for this stone—white like innocence—could be nothing but a symbol of salvation. This "symbol of knowledge" brings to mind the strange pebble that Sheik Escherazy asked from Gérard de Nerval.[27] This black stone is akin to the Baphomet of the Templars to those who are veterans of the Masonic or

Compagnonnage systems. But in reality, Gérard de Nerval, who almost certainly knew the rites of initiatory German secret societies,[28] veiled his thought by using poetic turns of phrase. A black rock seems to hold singular importance at the temple of Mecca. Muhammad revered this worked and polished cornerstone, emblem of a civilization that knew how to use the compass and the square. The Compagnonnage of France retains this symbolism that we find in Isaiah (28:16–17):

> Behold, I lay in Zion for a foundation a stone, a tried stone, a precious corner stone, a sure foundation: he that believeth shall not make haste. Judgment also will I lay to the line, and righteousness to the plummet.

The black stone symbolizes the earth. Apollonius of Rhodes said that the Amazons made their prayers before a black stone.[29]

But the Lia Fail speaks and loudly raises its voice to designate who should rule as king. In the Celtic legend, the *clachabrath,* this stone of destiny and judgment, falls into the category of stones that prophesize like the oracular rocks: here we find ourselves in the presence of the final vestiges of Atlantean civilization. We may be surprised at all these concretions of substances foreign to those found in the region and that are, in fact, from very remote countries. Rocks found in southern Russia, in Siberia, seem to come from Africa. Creuzer wondered about these incomprehensible transports. Our power appears quite weak next to that deployed for transporting these enormous blocks of stone. According to the fairly abstract tale of Geoffrey of Monmouth, the stone alignments on Salisbury Plain consist of stones that were brought there by giants from the farthest reaches of Africa. The fifteen thousand men of King Ambrosius could not budge them. But Merlin took out his golden harp and played his incantation, the enchantment of the precious stones, and magnetized the monoliths that began a fantastic circle dance centered on the sunrise.[30] A man without making any physical effort whatsoever could therefore arrange these enormous blocks of stone. But we do not grasp the full totemic meaning, as Geoffrey of Monmouth stopped short in the telling of his revelation.

In this study of megalithic monuments, whether as the basis for the worship of stones or the mystery of the cavern, we must note the presence of curious earthen huts, sometimes raised some sixty feet and whose diameters vary between thirty-five and two hundred feet at the base. One of the largest is that of Villars-les-Dombes (Ain). It is more than one hundred sixty feet in diameter, is some fifty feet tall, and has a volume of fifty thousand square feet. These truncated cone-shaped monuments are called *poypes*. There are many of them in Bresse, Dombes, and in the Dauphin plains. The butte of Ambronay (Ain) takes the form of a pyramidal mound. Charles Diot maintains that their borders are marked off by underground springs parallel to the edge of the embankment.[31] Nothing has been found in the rare monuments that have been excavated, and researchers have come up with all sorts of hypotheses for explaining the presence of these odd tumuli.[32] Their oval form brings to mind the Egg of the World, a representation of the center of the earth. This tumulus that is also the image of the sacred mountain is found in China, where in the center of each kingdom a mound was built in the shape of a quadrangular pyramid. The soil of the five regions was used to build it. A pyramid was similarly raised in Ireland in the center of each kingdom. Mount Snowdon in the country of Wales was used to test those who wished to become initiated into the knowledge of the bards. A black stone was located at the top of the mountain. The novice spent the night there while a fire of aromatic cedar burnt itself out. It so happens that Snowdon, which in Welsh is called Y Wyddru, means "funerary tumulus," and this mountain can only be a site for a second birth.[33]

In conclusion, life in ascendency seems to go from the stone—mineral realm—to man. This is characteristic of the movement of involution-evolution. But we know almost nothing about the process of this crystallization, and we know absolutely nothing about this captive spirit. However, the stone of generation takes the form of the cave-womb, and in this form it symbolizes the Cosmos as a productive power. The stone, with its magnetic and virginal life, gives birth to prayers. The most miserable of pebbles is worshipped just as strongly as the most beautiful diamond sparkling on the diadem of a king. But the hard, immobile stone, witness to the past, stabilizes this higher cosmic will because God dwells within it. These stones of the sun and moon, these dolmens and menhirs, these covered alleys, materialize a point of balance and freedom. The fundamental stone composed of fire (spiritual light), water (subtle substance), and air (the ether) is located in the heart because it figures at the center of all things, the primordial crystallization of the universe. The stone contains all the secrets within it, and all the riches, and all the power of miracles, and all the strength of the three kingdoms like the gem from deep in the earth. The stone, fruit of the union of heaven and earth, represents life and the sacred, the Absolute Reality.

7

The Gems
from Underground

THE HUMAN EYE IS FASCINATED by precious stones. In addition to their qualities of rarity and beauty are those of inalterability and hardness. Their sparkle casts an enchantment, and each stone has its own very distinctive character. They are unique works made mysterious by their chemical composition and reflection of light. The inclusion of foreign substances gives them a hitherto different nature. Chrome gives the common beryl the green color of the emerald, but some stones take on iridescent subtleties. Depending on the lighting, the stone can change its color range, such as happens with alexandrite, which, green in daylight, becomes red in artificial light. The diamond rules over all these bewitching scales: its clarity is only matched by its radiance.

Human beings admire those jewels that collect the light, harness it, and cast it back. Pliny spoke of their personality, and we can only wonder at their secret architecture that reveals all the wonders of a hidden world. While precious stones have sometimes been found rolling down the streams of Brazil, Sri Lanka, and Madagascar, while seams of sapphires are out in the open in Myanmar, and while rocks have surrendered emeralds in Colombia, it is still safe to say that access to their underground home remains difficult. Nature guards these fragments of eternity in its deepest depths.

And so humans wonder about this mysterious spark that animates the basic elements: carbon, aluminum, silica, lime, and magnesium. The earth is the crucible, the matrix in which the stones are born, and this mysterious crafting that takes millions of years, with pressure and gradual heating and cooling, has been the source of many long commentaries. Indian mineralogical treatises speak of the emerald in its matrix that is nothing but a rock.

The sun penetrates the mineral world through the cave. In this solar mountain the crystalline dew engenders the precious stone that thereby becomes the culmination of a state. This is why stones are situated in very symbolic sites and most particularly in the earth's nervous system. In a Buddhist text—the *Gandhamadana*—one of the four gold mountains* contains at its center the cave of gems. The *manjusaka* tree that produces all the aquatic and terrestrial flowers is covered with a sparkling dust of precious stones. Its roots plunge into the water of Lake Anavatapta, and beneath its shade a *pratyekabuddha* engages in the exercise of *dhyana* or meditation.[1]

These sparkling gems stand for stars; they may also have come detached from the celestial throne; they reflect the image of the sun. "Precious stones are the elementary stars; they take their color, shape, and metallic color through the formation of stars."[2] The same notion can be found in the work of Alphonse Barba, who sees there the representation of the radiance of stars.[3] The light from the beyond penetrates the stone, and this sacred character comes into play in the shamanic initiations of the Australian Aborigines, the Negritos of Malacca, or native tribes in North America.[4]

The formation of these stones illustrates the basic theme of alchemy. In the *Book of the Mysteries of Heaven and Earth,* written by the monk Isaac, we find the myth of the pearl. A white swan impregnated by the sun dives into the sea. Eight months later the swan gives birth to birds on her left side and precious stones on her right. This bird is called the

---

*These four mountains are situated in the direction of the four cardinal points, and they surround the Himalayas.

karbe-dinel: the "purest of all birds." There are twelve pearls the first time, and sixty the second, but on the third occasion the bird only produces a single pearl.[5] This symbol of the white pearl can be also seen, according to Jean Doresse, in a book of the Falashas, *The Apocalypse of Gregorios,* in which "one admirable page develops the vision of the Pearl, symbol of Heavenly Zion."

However, precious stones do not acquire all their virtues unless they are worked and cut at very specific hours, the purpose of which is to increase their potency.[6] They are no longer only astrological stones, but also pentacles that act in the spirit of the planet that corresponds to them.[7] We see here the ideas of Éliphas Lévi on stones sharing the virtues of stars. The knight Jean de Mandeville also recorded in a very strange book that the mineral attracted the astral, and he wrote this regarding the sunstone:

> The sunstone is black and round with white, but sometimes blue, veins, which give off a soft glow like sunlight. If it is placed in a house in sunlight in a vessel with this water, it will produce great clarity. It is pleasing to noblemen because it protects them and makes them doubt everything; it increases riches and principalities and the power to offend; and it protects the virtues of the body.[8]

I will also cite his description of

> the moonstone, a white stone with veins and patches that can be black, red, or citrine; it protects the body and gives those traveling by sea easy passage; or gives protection from storms and peril; it increases worldly goods; it helps the entry into noble things and honors; it heals lunatics and protects thieves.

Mandeville's opinion can be found in many legends in which a precious stone can light up a room with its moral value. It just so happens that the Philosophers' Stone corresponds in sacred language to the stone that bears the sign of the sun. It is for this reason that the gem has been compared to the Philosophers' Stone, that mysterious substance the quest for which can also be compared to that for the Grail.

The writers of the Renaissance asserted that precious stones offered a challenge to the world of darkness. We attain the spiritual value of the stone, a power of enrichment and representation of the will. The Grail, carved from an emerald, leads to spiritual knowledge and full realization of the individual. The words of Hermes are also carved on an emerald that has been cut into the shape of a tablet. This emerald that seems to be the preeminent sacred stone appears in Solomon's seal as well as in the foundations of Holy Jerusalem:

> And the foundations of the wall of the city were garnished with all manner of precious stones. The first foundation was jasper; the second, sapphire; the third, chalcedony; the fourth, emerald; the fifth, sardonyx; the sixth, sard; the seventh, chrysolite; the eighth, beryl; the ninth, topaz; the tenth, chrysoprase; the eleventh, jacinth; the twelfth, amethyst. (Apocalypse, XXI, II, 18, 21)

Bernard Palissy, in his *Recepte véritable,*[9] defines the qualities of the twelve stones of Saint John, which are the twelve foundations of the city. They are congealed water with their own individual characteristics. The pectoral ornament of the high priest Aaron also consists of twelve precious stones that are arranged in four rows of three gems each.[10] All of these stones may be different from one another, but, like the twelve apostles, each has his own road to God, and the supremacy of one over the others is not to be imagined.

Pliny, however, arranged precious stones into the following order: diamond, pearls, emerald. Victor-Émile Michelet[11] stated, "No material could scratch the diamond, and no emotion seems capable of penetrating it. It lives in a state of pure intellectuality, dead to all sensitivity . . . it is also called solitaire." For many writers, the diamond was a condensation of the forces of the universe. When worn as a talisman it was connected to the cosmic power and established the liaison between the astral and human desire. The poet Charles Cros, when studying the synthesis of precious stones, wrote that the gem is a boundless talisman.[12] For Paul Claudel, the stone did not only offer shimmering colors but also perfumes.[13] In this way the jewel became a pledge, an effective presence.

Natural gems were followed by those created artificially. There has been a steady reproduction of synthetic diamonds since 1893. Moissan, by introducing pure crystallized carbon into molten steel at a temperature of 3,500°C obtained cementite from the crystalline powder. Fifteen years later, the Englishmen Noble and Crookes managed to create miniscule diamond crystals. The General Electric Company is still seeking a solution. Based on the experiments of the French chemist Verneuil, it was possible to obtain synthetic rubies from pure aluminum powder to which had been added chrome oxide; when he replaced this later with cobalt oxide, Verneuil created the synthetic sapphire. France, Germany, and Switzerland also produce aquamarine and spinel on an industrial level. These products are used in clock making and are exported to India. But what we have here are no longer "sexed crystals, subject to the law of love."[14] The sign of quantity can never replace that of quality. These industrial stones give birth to monotony because they have not received the radiance of the "sun of the earth," and they no longer have any correspondence with the astral. According to Pliny, the emerald can recreate life or soothe eyestrain, but the artificial emerald has lost this divine power. The artificial stone no longer attracts any blessing. It no longer stands in opposition to the temptation of the demon. Did you know that the corundum protects against witchcraft and madness? That the garnet makes the person who carries it invulnerable? That the spinel offers a haven from anger and hatred? That the agate guarantees eloquence and wealth? And that the diamond attracts happiness because it reflects purity?

The precious stone symbolizes a portion of eternity. With its astral and magical power it illuminates the most stubborn darkness, and far from our modern laboratories we seek it in the mysterious ground, for this drop of dew emanates from the heart of Mother Earth, into which we must descend.

8

Descent into Hell

THE NOTION OF HELL FIGURES as a fundamental element of Christian tradition. In my book on the symbology of fire I provided numerous evangelical accounts about this subterranean region devoured by "the lake of fire." I mentioned there these terrifying frescoes in which horned demons exult over the damnation of man. There is therefore no need to revisit this role of hell with its eternal fire. What I have in mind here is only the symbolism of its location.

It is curious to see that all forms of religions place hell in the underground world, which represents the lower state of the human being as earth corresponds to the physical human state. The fables of the Hellenic poets come close to those of Eastern Jewish traditions, which themselves appear to come from Egypt or Assyria. There can be no doubt that an equivalence exists between the Greek Hades and the Sheol or Gehenna of the Jews. The merger of the pagan hell and the Christian hell was made thanks to Honorius of Autun, Raban Maur, and Saint Chrysostom.[1] Gaia, personification of the Earth, wife of Heaven, has a snake as a servitor. As for Cybele, her worship introduces the stone in its raw, natural state, then the veneration of the cave, which Strabo saw as "the gate to the underground world where the infernal deities rule."[2] Pluto is the master of the subterranean fire there. In Khmer mythology, the eight large hells sit one beneath the other and become more terrible the deeper one descends. The periods of suffering are also longer the deeper the hell. But each of these big hells has sixteen small hells adjoining it, which brings their number to one hundred and twenty-eight, and in the deepest one—the Avici—the suffering is 128 times greater than in the first one.

But as I noted earlier in my book *La symbolique du feu,* this infernal region hardly matches the one described by Christianity in any way. The damned do atone for their sins, but their suffering is not eternal because they will be reborn to start a new life. The torturers are also damned souls who are doing penitence for their sins, and in order for every soul to be informed as to the kind of torment he must undergo, the list of tortures forms a moral code. This list is depicted on the southern façade—the gallery of bas-reliefs—of Angkor Wat and describes thirty-two hells. Last, the Asuras—or Yeaks—living beneath the ground guard the riches that are buried there. They are fallen demigods, reduced to being permanent prisoners of the underground kingdom beneath Mount Meru. But while these giants are paying for their sins, they still retain magic powers that make them superior to men.

In current Chinese notions that have been formed from the blending of Buddhism and Taoism, the ten hells are ruled by the Ten Yama Kings of the Ten Tribunals, Che-Tien Yen-Wang. Each of these Che-Wang is the master of one of these places, and this takes us to a scenario much like Dante's. The book, the *Yu Li Chao Chan* (Ten courts of purgatory), describes and subdivides each one, and in the novel *Journey in the West* we learn that the emperor Tai-Tsung of the Tang dynasty made the descent into these regions in order to bring back a description.[3] This is how every living being goes through cycles of life broken up by more or less long sojourns in the hells. In Japanese mythology, barely any descriptions exist except that of Izanagi's descent into the Land of Darkness—Yomi-tsu-Kumi. Izanagi was searching for his wife Izanami. Generally speaking, Shintoism had little to say about death and corpses. Sometimes we see seven hells, the dwellings of impurity at the lowest edge of the cosmos. These worlds of elementary formation are in reality the shadows of the seven creative sefirot—the reversed image of the seven ascending models. The seven hells thereby have a connection with the sefirotic hierarchy and play a role in the reintegration concept.[4] The seventh hell reconnects with the upper boundary and "its windows look out upon the Holy Light." Following the seven hells we have the seven earths that end with the earthly Paradise and culminate with the paradise of Heaven.

The hells—where fire resides—are traversed by water. The Acheron remains one of the primary waterways; one of its tributaries, the Cocytus, is a river of tears. The most dreaded waterway, the Styx, encircles the dark realm seven times. The shades that drink the water from the infernal river of forgetting, the Lethe, lose all memory of the past. Charon is the ferryman of Hell. As noted by Mircea Eliade,[5] the bridge—or rope—that permits the heroes to cross the infernal river, and the benevolent figure, the bridge's animal guardian—are all classic motifs from the descent into hell, a myth we can find in all civilizations.[6]

Volcanoes serve as the gates of hell and as the dungeon windows of the infernal realm. These include Vesuvius, Etna, and Hecla. This notion echoes the thought of Saint Gregory the Great (*Moralia* 4.35) and Tertullian (*On Penance,* 12). Montessus de Ballore sums up the idea of situating hell in the fiery core at the middle of the earth by saying that there "the fires never go out like those of hell." Humans fear storm and Saint Elmo's fire as much as earthquakes; this manifestation can only be the work of giants or demons living inside the earth. In the *Aeneid* (book 6), Aeneas crosses through the woods surrounding Lake Avernus and enters a cave where he reaches the threshold of the infernal abode ruled over by mythological monsters. He forces his will on Cerberus, the monstrous three-headed dog, to let him pass, and he can then make his way either to Tartarus—the vast prison surrounded by three walls—or to Elysium—the evergreen kingdom of gentle light. This man thus suffers the attack of underground forces, overcomes them, and chooses his path. Likewise, Theseus fights against monsters so that he may rejoin the kingdom of light, and one Manichean notion indicates that the soul "is led" and that man cannot be free.

Telemachus also ventures into the land of shadows, but like the Sybil, he finds another exit than the entrance he used. Yudhishthira, before Saint Paul, went down into this place of revelation, whereas the second Faust made his way to Persephone's lair after that classic wild Walpurgis Night. In Lord Byron's *Manfred* (1817) Manfred succeeded in reaching the cave ruled by the evil genie Arimanes, just like Ibsen's Peer Gynt.[7] Cassou, in *Souvenirs de la Terre,* has also borrowed this theme of a journey to the infernal circles, which was described as well in the Latin poem *The Zodiac of Life* by Marcellus Palingenius—in his true name Pierre-Ange Manzoli—in the sixteenth century. We are also dragged into these strange worlds by Victor-Émile Michelet, who wrote prose poems of a Gnostic nature such as *The Gates of Bronze* (1919) and *On the Threshold of the Gates of Light.* Tuoni and Tuonetar are the Finnish god and goddess of the underworld. Persigoult muses on the Masonic chamber of reflection that represents the depths of the earth and in which the postulant must stay in order to vanquish his passions and earn the benefits of initiation.[8] But among these places of knowledge we should also cite the Ungunja of the Aruntas, the Olkapara Cave in the central tribal lands of Australia. According to Herodotus, the legendary Egyptian king Rhampsinitus went into the underworld while still a living man, where he played dice with Demeter, who gave him a golden towel when he went back to the surface. The details of this story are quite colorful, and Herodotus's symbolism remains quite appealing. For Guénon,[9] this descent into hell becomes "the recapitulation of the states that preceded the human state." Hell would depict a lower state of being, and initiation achieves a "conscious realization of higher states." Jung has analyzed this symbolism.

Initiatory knowledge implies degrees that must be crossed; often these degrees are represented by concentric walls. The adept must cross through them in succession in order to earn the last degree that leads to the center. There is no way death can be nothingness; it is only a transformation of matter. The grain of wheat doesn't die when buried because it bursts open and a new stem emerges. The human being also gives birth to some part that we have trouble imagining. Every generation must pass through a preliminary corruption. In the book of Psalms (91:13) we read:

And you shall flourish again like the phoenix, which is to say, from death and burial.*

Louis Jacolliot[10] recorded the following discussion with a Brahmin: "Why," he said, pointing to the piles of refuse surrounding them, "why is there so much grandeur in the past and such wretchedness in the present?" The old pandit answered:

It is destiny. The plants rot to make fertilizer for new plants; the father sleeps in the grave after he has raised his son, nations die to make way for new ones, and everything becomes decrepit for the arrival of death, and the land of the lotus reaches its final hour. . . . Happy are those who know that death is but the dawn of a new transformation.

But Jacolliot could scarcely comprehend the metaphysical side of Hindu thought, and this is what he wrote:

How can you regenerate a country where the best talk this way, and despair of the energy and vitality of their race?

I think for my part that at this stage the soul of the sages does not need to be "regenerated," but that to the contrary, it can teach us on the spiritual plane what it cannot on the material plane. Our feverish agitation astounds the placid Asian whose spiritual mind is perhaps more awakened than our own.

The initiatory death involves a fictional death, and this death can only be achieved in the depths of the earth, the nurturing Mother Earth in which we shall be buried upon our terrestrial death. Jung has noted that through his initiatory death, man approaches the reintegration of cosmic night.[11]

"The man of desire"—according to the expression of Louis Claude

---

*[This version of psalm 91 is via Tertullian, *On the Resurrection of the Flesh*, 13. —*Ed.*]

de Saint-Martin—seeks to purify himself and to free himself from material chains in order to better penetrate the mystery of all things. All traditions teach that one must first reach the depth of hell in order to begin the ascent to the worlds of heaven. It is impossible to reach heaven unless one goes through hell, thereby providing proof that one is worthy of moving up to a higher world. The wicked individual will be burnt or remain in hell, whereas the good individual will not be burned in a world he knows not and in which he cannot remain. Valentinus, concerning the *Pistis Sophia,* speaks of a river of fire that some souls can cross without feeling any pain. This river of fire resembles the Egyptian hell, as we can see the river of fire on the tomb of Seti I, accompanied by the indication of broken lines, a representation of water, a water that must figure in Egyptian initiation.

In order to regenerate, the human being wishes to descend into the underworld. There he will find the primordial subject indicated by the word *vitriol* (Visita Interiora Terrae Rectificando Invenies Occultum Lapidem, which means "visit the interior of the earth and through purification you shall find the hidden stone"). With the descent into hell, we seek to discover the nature of the secret fire of the sages, and this is how Dante's admirable story should be analyzed. Claude d'Ygé interprets the words of Rabelais in the same way when Pantagruel visits the underworld in book 5 (chapters 48 and 18).[12] Bachelard proposes a more Freudian interpretation:

> It is the need to penetrate, to go inside of things, inside of beings, it is a seduction of the intuition of intimate warmth. Heat can insinuate itself where the eye cannot go and the hand cannot enter. This communion through the inside, this thermic sympathy, will find, in Novalis, its symbol in the descent into the hollow space of the mountain, in the cave, and in the mine. This is where heat spreads and evens out. Where it blurs like the contour of a dream. As Nodier recognized quite strongly, every description of a descent into hell has the structure of a dream.[13]

This is how the initiatory ceremony came to be achieved in the telluric shadows, and while this crossing of the infernal world is made without suffering, it is because the test for obtaining immortality is positive. Cybele borrows the underground ways of Eleusis, and this walking at random, with its laborious detours and its harrowing courses, gives us the impression of a labyrinth. The din of initiation reflects the horror the human being feels when he is left alone in the underground tunnel where the echo of the slightest noise makes a frightful racket. The blindfold over the eyes symbolizes this underground night, a night that on its own shows the straying of the man who has not yet received the light. The corridors of the pyramids were partially planned for this initiation.

This radiance of the earth chains the neophyte and surrounds him in the magical action.[14] By descending into the depths of the earth a person can communicate more easily with its currents, which thereby become more powerful and thus more effective. If we imagine that these forces can be represented by yin while the yang would represent the energy above the surface, we are venturing toward the interpretation of universal harmony as well as toward the notion of nuclear physics. The spiritual man manages to act directly on the etheric elements by rediscovering the primordial center and the entirety of its energy. The same concept appears in the Tibetan Tantric work, the *Bdemchog Tantra,* in which we see that in order to benefit from the development and externalization of psychic powers—the centers of manifestation being the chakras—it is necessary to descend so that "the beings of the three regions escape from the six realms of 'samsara.'" These descents are the *avatāras,* magical reflections that correspond to the informal states.

Plutarch, in his *Morals* (6th fragment), describes several phases of initiation received in the passageways of the tombs, subterranean corridors that are akin to the tracks of labyrinths. However, not wishing to reveal any secrets, Plutarch restricted himself to generalities. We can learn however that Thespesius is in a lethargic state that lasts three days, that he follows an ascending stair on the spiritual path, and that at the end of this quest that invokes Bacchus and Semele, he sees in the sky a triangle—the emblem of the Trinity. An angel of feminine appearance, marked with stigmata of the faith, appears to him—it is the androgynous being. The one who goes through the test of the tomb will be called "a resurrected one,"[15] and Plutarch has shown the concordance between death and initiation in *On the Face in the Moon* (§§ 27 and 28). These three days—which do not necessarily have a twenty-four-hour duration—are in accord with the worship of Demeter: the first day is called the burial of the seeds in the earth; the second day, their germination beneath the ground; and the third day is the rise of the sprouts and the resurrection in a new world. The convert attains a world of spirituality and faith.

These two complementary phases occur again in that spiritual quest that contains two stages: a descent and the climb back. We shall have an opportunity to revisit this point, but let's simply note for now that the man who has achieved the first stage must return to the surface. When Mephistopheles gives the key to Faust so he may descend to the world of the Mothers, Goethe writes: "Sink into the abyss—I could just as easily say climb toward the heights." And in another story by Goethe, *The Green Snake and the Beautiful Lily,* the underground temple emerges "when the times are fulfilled." This subterranean, initiatory temple also contains three sacred statues—three pillars—which imply the still invisible fourth pillar.

Descent and ascension thereby form two complementary phases; they are the representations of two poles, just like the cards of the Tarot and the Hermetic Great Work. As Diricq wrote, the heavens and hells constitute the two solsticial portals, the two ways of "Janua Coeli" and "Janua Inferni." In the Hindu tradition these two paths are known as the "Way of the Gods" (*devāyāna*) and the "Way of the Ancestors" (*pitriyāna*).[16] This is why the descent into the hells became the preeminent theme of initiation. Following the dramatic event of Calvary, Christ went down into hell. Paul Le Cour[17] connects Christianity to Orphism. This theme appears in Cicero's *Republic,* in the "Dream of Scipio" (4, 6–14). The author of *The Vision of Saint Paul*[18] imagines that the saint went down into hell guided by an angel. There he sees the seven furnaces* vomiting flames and the wheel of fire that turns one thousand times a day and tortures a thousand souls every time it turns.

In his *Divine Comedy,* Dante gives hell the appearance of an immense subterranean funnel consisting of nine circles that get smaller the deeper one descends. The fallen angel Satan is found at the center of the final circle, and the extremities of his body lead to the antipodes of the earth and the funnel. It is here where stands the conical mountain of Purgatory, which consists of seven circular platforms. This Luciferian myth is in agreement with the tragedy of Dionysus, genius loci of the infernal world, and we can see that this fallen angel who maintains the cold and death could reside nowhere but the immutable and frozen center, apart from all ethereal and fluidic material. He situates himself at the central core of matter, at the ultimate center of condensation. This is like revisiting the fall of Adam expelled precipitously from Eden; his freedom can only come from an effort toward the law of attraction. The access to this underworld is beneath the mountain of Zion, as Dante considered Jerusalem to be the center of the world.[19] On the sides of the double circle of fire is the large swamp with its muddy waters. According to alchemical theory, it is obligatory to go through the stage of putrefaction to attain the "fire of nature." The worm develops in the ashes, and after a transformation becomes the fledgling. Nothing dies in nature.

Gérard de Nerval in his renowned *Journey to the Orient*—the *Nights of Ramazan*—mentions the mysteries of the mountain of Kaf where Adoniram descends into the depths of the earth with Tubal-cain. Nerval's cosmic conceptions extend over two chapters, and Jean Richer thinks that Nerval had become aware of Kircher's *Mundus Subterraneus* in which the interior of the globe is the subject of meticulous descriptions.[20]

In this telluric test, apart from Ishtar, the Celtic imagination would

---

*Seven here is the preeminent Roman number, as it combines four (the number of the body) with three (the number of the soul). It is the union of the two natures. The six deployed faces of the cube provide the septenary, as we have three horizontal faces and four in a vertical line. It also brings to mind the crux ansata, the cross of life.

repurpose this symbolism that professes the immortality of the soul, in which all dies to be reborn. This is what explains the boat of Saint Brendan, the light craft made from reeds and cattle hides painted red.[21] This boat appeared with Dante and in Michelangelo's fresco of the *Last Judgment*. While Saint Brendan caught a glimpse of hell, the knight Owen traveled through it.[22] His entry took place on an island in Lake Derg, and we see again the fiery furnace, the wheel* of fire,[23] and the frozen river. The soul of Tungdal[24] also travels through these sites of torture, during a span of three days, in order to report his experience to other men. It is therefore a moral value that is being referred to her, and the purgatory of Saint Patrick shows the transformation of the Druid hell into that of the Christians.

The same philosophy presides over the half-satiric, half-dramatic *La Papesse Jeanne* (twelfth century): the compassionate lady descends into hell to wrest a supplicant free of it. The woman is therefore a path of purification, and medieval thought developed this character more fully. The *Roman de la Rose* (vol. 3, p. 248, v. 1999, ed. Méon) shows that the description of hell was very popular in France, but it is the Manichean hell in reality because the entire thought of the Middle Ages revolved around dualism. The worship of Satan could not assume its true value until after the flowering of the thought of Zoroaster that symbolizes the antagonism between Ahura Mazda and Ahriman. But in reality we should not forget the existence of a third principle—Mithras-Mithra—a balancing principle. Concerning Satan, it should be noted that the illustrators of the Middle Ages depicted him carrying a pitchfork: the trident became the insignia of the king of Hell. It stands for sovereignty and absolute mastery. We can see this emblem with the Greek Poseidon and again with the Roman Neptune. Hades, the king of Hell, received the trident as a symbol of sinners as it resembles the harpoon. This fork of sovereignty is akin to the heraldic fleur-de-lis.

---

*The wheel expresses the instability of all things. On the wheel of fortune at the Cathedral of Amiens, eight small figures appear to be rising while another eight are descending. A man is seated at the top wearing a crown on his head. The same image is evoked by the Tarot's Tenth Arcanum.

So the descent into hell represents an initiatory quest. It requires the knowledge of an initiate to knock at the door of the underground cavern. The stone that blocks the cave of Ali Baba only swings aside when the kabbalistic phrase "Open, Sesame" is spoken. It so happens that the sesame is a very tiny seed, comparable to a grain of wheat. This worldly wealth inspires thoughts of a more spiritual value. But Ali Baba's brother, a greedy man who has not taken the pains to evolve through the degrees of wisdom, does not know this world of reflection and dies uninitiated. He thought he held possession of a "secret," whose uniquely spiritual essence cannot be communicated. The secret therefore remains in a pure state and cannot be violated. Even when it appears to have been divulged, it remains valueless in the hands of a person who has not made the mental effort necessary to assimilate it.

This is why some ceremonies appear luxurious to profane eyes, while the initiate knows there is a teaching to be discovered therein. The ritual gesture permits the transmission of the symbol that acts in accordance with the degree of initiation or knowledge of the person who receives it. The words of Jesus are quite revealing: "Therefore speak I to them in parables: because they seeing, see not; and hearing they hear not, neither do they understand" (Matthew 13:13). In a book with an unfortunately reduced format,[25] I interpreted several legends and briefly said how each one had a mystical explanation and that each story argued in favor of a theory and gave a teaching at the same time it entertained. The perfection of their poetic form allows us to see beforehand the search for initiatic themes capable of elevating the individual.

This is why a minority seeks to protect the forms that are known to them alone. These spiritual theories have been raised to the rank of the sacred. These mysteries can only be interpreted far from the profane. The temple therefore remains underground, and the depth of the darkness only makes more radiant this light that radiates the chosen one, this transparent light that comes from the summit of the building. Salomon Reinach connects to this custom the practice of taking the veil by initiates, and the veiling of brides and the dying.[26] For the soul to win eternal bliss and go beyond its own nature, it must return to the source and descend into hell. It must be able to disregard the self and detach itself from everything, yet still love everything. "For whoever wants to save his life shall lose it, but he who loses his life for me shall gain it." The descent into the hells makes it possible to hunt for and bring back the Stone that can only be found in the depths of the earth. The initiation will only be effective once the Salt and the Stone have been fixed. It is necessary to descend lucidly into the pit by degrees, rediscover its successive stages, because in order to reach paradise a person is obligated to pass through hell, one of the stages of initiation. With this initiatory death, realization takes place in the core of the stone, and the second initiatory death resides in the subtle crystallization.[27] But if the elect can draw from there the ascending strength that will allow them to reach Heaven, it will have been from meditating in the underground temple.

9

The Underground Temple

THE CAVE

The hero goes down into the depths of the earth, led by an unknown force or guide.[1] He is seeking the center in order to restore his psychic, etheric, and physical energy. In this sacred zone he should rediscover his absolute reality. But it can be quite difficult to find this natural sanctuary: it is as diaphanous as the adventure-filled castle of the Fisher King that appears and vanishes before the eyes of the knights on the quest for the Grail.

Also, in the image of the den of divine initiation, man creates—according to his temperament and knowledge—a temple that can replace the site of the first initiation. Before tackling artificial constructions, the individual thinks to move closer to natural elements. The more or less well-fitted-out cave or cavern condenses these telluric forces, but it is a natural place that is very often regarded as a gate to the underworld.

The cavern becomes this way the den of the mysteries; its very shape can evoke the image of the primordial egg that provided the androgynous substance,[2] but it is also a belly—that of the regenerative earth—since it is in this place that the initiate dies symbolically to be reborn purified and freed of his coarse envelope. The cavern therefore represents the universal womb, and Mircea Eliade analyzes this ritualistic character[3] by noting that in Hebrew "pit" or "well" also means women or spouse. Springs are naturally born in the generative organ of the Great Goddess who also contributes to the mineralogical gestation of stone.

So the cave engenders, but most importantly the cave permits the human being to conquer his or her immortality. This is in agreement with the notion of a regenerative hell, inasmuch as death is only a necessary transformation without becoming a form of annihilation. We have come upon the two faces of a transitional state that is one and the same, just as the two faces of Janus belong to the same individual.

The Masonic writers—Oswald Wirth, Persigoult—have found in the symbolism of the cave a parallel with the chamber of reflection, then with the middle chamber where the central light glows. But in a general way, the worship of caves is always more or less connected to the idea of an "inner place" or a "central place." In this regard, the symbol of the cave and that of the heart are fairly close to each other. The cavern or the cave represents the heart cavity considered as the center of the being as well as the interior of the "World Egg" (René Guénon, *Le Roi du Monde*). The cave, a site where condensation of the forces of the world occurs, demonstrates the union of the two major cosmic vessels in which the Magna Mater resides. This cave—or lodge—is only used for the first initiation, but it provides access to the true underworld. Illuminated from within, its vault depicts the sky while outside the darkness reigns; it is the heart of the world. For Porphyry[4] the cave becomes the image and symbol of the world because its abundance of water, dampness, and darkness depict the symbols of "all that is in the world because of matter." With Plato, the cave, the cosmic lair of initiation, assumes its full significance. The beginning of the seventh book of *The Republic* establishes the difference between the two worlds of consciousness. We see the emergence of the disenchanted image of the sensorial world into which the reflections of a transcendent reality penetrate, but in order to avoid violating the law of silence the poet expressed himself in veiled images.

In this cave, men have been chained since the time of childhood.

Deprived of the ability to move, all they see of the outside world is the shadows projected on the back wall of their prison. They think these images are real and represent life, whereas intelligible reality belongs to the person who sojourns in the light outside of the cave. The man that is content with his vision, without looking for the cause, remains a slave chained in this "dark place." His senses are deluded by a reflection. The slave must cause his chains to fall,[5] then struggle against his ignorance if he wishes to reach the door that gives access to the true light. Only several elect will manage to contemplate the higher realities. This process is part of an initiatory elevation with gradations of knowledge. Plato notes that the man who reaches the light is often blinded by it and cannot perceive the true form immediately, and "what he discovers most easily are shadows, then images of men . . . then finally the objects themselves." In agreement with Plato's story we should note the Javanese shadow theater, the Wayang Purwa, in which the spectators sit around a screen. The men place themselves in such a way as to see the flat leather marionettes with movable arms, while the women can only see the shadows these puppets project.

Many episodes of sacred history have taken place belowground. The Annunciation given Mary by the angel Gabriel took place in a cave, which, according to the iconography, was located near a spring.[6] Here we find water again—in the form of springs or wells—and it is pure and superior water, a notion of the highest form of femininity where the Virgin rules. A striking example of this can be seen in the cave of Lourdes. According to Saintyves, the natural caves of the land of Canaan were always equipped with a spring.[7] It is likely that the water fed a baptistery or vessel of absolution. The cave, called that of the Virgin in the mountain of Batroun near Sghar, possesses two stalactites in the form of female breasts from which water is dripping constantly. The underground sanctuary of the Virgin surrounded by a forest displays a new aspect of the eternal feminine, the creative principle to which all forces and energies return.

Goethe and Gérard de Nerval, following Leonardo da Vinci, have illustrated the power of these Mothers.[8] Fourteen miles from Cairo, near Heliopolis, there is a display of the remnants of a place (Matariya) where the holy family sought refuge when fleeing Herod's executioners. A very old sycamore stands within this enclosure, and several yards from it there is a spring. Joseph is said to have taken the water of this spring to quench the thirst of Mary and the child. This episode can be found in Catherine Emmerich's visions of the childhood of Christ.[9]

There are columns inside the cave of the Annunciation that bring to mind the pillars of Attis and Dionysus, or of those that Hiram erected in front of Solomon's temple. And in reality, this cave of the Conception was a pre-Christian sanctuary sacred to Cybele.[10] The same comparison can be made between the caverns housing the Nativity and those of Mithras. Both Jesus and Mithras were born on the winter solstice; both received the consecration of shepherds and animals because they represented the rising sun. We can find the same correspondence between Jesus and Adonis—or Attis. Both were born in a cave and are buried there. Like Zeus,[11] Agni also entered the world in a cave among the cows and shepherds who hailed him.[12] The Mexicans believe that the cave of Chicomotzoc—which means the "Seven Caves," and therefore is a sacred place—was the cradle of their race. The aromatic cave in which Dionysus grew up was often situated in the middle of an immense forest,[13] often on the center of an island—therefore surrounded by water—and had been carved out of purple-colored boulders bordered by trees in which birds perched, perpetually singing. Homer and Porphyry note the existence of venerated trees, often olive trees, which cross near its purposefully oriented entrance. Pausanias, when speaking of the cave of Mount Elaion, sacred to Black Demeter, writes (8.42): "The cave is surrounded by a sacred grove in which there is a very cold spring." This enclosure of greenery is not dark but sunny. The cradle of Bacchus is described in a similar way.

The caves of Cybele in Eleusis deserve mention. These birthplaces bring to mind the seashells that share the symbolism of the goblet. Venus emerges from a conch shell whose volutes form a spiral. The divine spark—or uncreated spiritual seed—is contained in the womb of the waters. It is from this that Brahmānda or the "World Egg" is born.

Bethlehem, according to Saintyves, was surrounded by Christianized caves, some of which were tombs.[14] Sixth-century apocryphal texts mention that Adam stored gold, myrrh, and incense stolen from paradise in a cavern. These were the presents of the Three Magi. A Syrian book, *The Cave of the Treasures,* tells how Adam was created in the center of the earth, and that the splendor of this cave evokes the beauties of the cave of Ali Baba.

All the caves made sacred by the passage of Jesus or Saint John the Baptist are extremely hard to reach, characterized by dangerous climbs and narrow entranceways.[15] The entrances of the initiatory temples, which were always oriented in alignment with the four directions, force the postulant to lower himself, most likely into a respectful posture. It is probably helpful to mention that Egyptian occultism has left traces in the initiatory systems such as that of the Marquis de Chefdebien, the Rite of Memphis, and the Rite of Misraïm.* But this spiritual realization, based on the teachings of the ten sefirot, can also be detected in the occult order of the A.A. (Astrum Argentinum) founded by Aleister Crowley around 1905. We again find these overly low entranceways in the tests of the Compagnonnage and Freemasonry, and the same imperative was responsible for the hole made in one of the walls of the dolmens, most particularly in the Deccan region of India. The dolmen pierced at the top can be integrated into another symbolism, as it allows the light to come from on high, a notion of inner illumination. But this opening cut into the vault is often the only access.† This stone dolmen with the domed roof thus brings to mind the Pythagorian basilica of Rome, in which the light is filtered through the oblique openings placed at the top of the atrium.[16] We find this same style of lighting in Mont Saint Michel. Its visitors go into raptures over a construction procedure that in reality is designed to support spiritual seeking. Lighting with no direct source becomes a metaphor for illumination.

Plato mentions the presence of two openings: one that gives access

---

*These last two rites were merged in 1880.
†Like at Notre-Dame de Pitié of Chaudes-Aigues (Cantal).

to the sky and another that gives access to the underworld. Dante leaves hell, and its upward force gives him passage to the world of On High. This vault corresponds to the cosmic vault and the hole to the solar portal. In this way the light enters through the roof of the world, establishing itself in the form of a pyramid. This illumination of the axial world, situated at the mountain summit, has as its correspondence the crown on the head. This inspires thought of Montsalvage, Montségur, and the blue city of Luz, the complementary symbol of the cavern. This piercing of the vault brings us back to the opening placed in the head, to this third eye of Shiva and the crown chakra; the saint's halo and the priest's tonsure correspond to this metaphysical concern. In Tanganyika initiated men are called "serpent men," like the serpent that only has one hole for entering his subterranean lair. But wouldn't the snake be the symbol of the universal substance that vivifies the human being and escapes at death through the hole of Brahma, that imperceptible hole located at the top of the head? Guénon, in an article entitled "La Porte Étroite,"[17] has shown that the rite of posthumous trepanation allows the soul to free itself more quickly, and, when the camerlengo knocks three times on the top of the deceased pope's head, it is again to evoke the restitution of this universal substance.[18] These low and narrow passages therefore characterize the circuit of the fluidic material, and Egyptian temples illustrate these concepts perfectly.

The "third eye" or "pineal eye" provides all the powers of cosmic and superterrestrial consciousness. After some extremely pertinent notes from Claude Valence,[19] here is a scientific text by Belzung (Anatomy and Physiology):

The reduced epiphysis cerebri, which in the human being is a small oval body placed between the two superior quadrigeminal bodies, in some saurians, for example, in the *Hatteria punctata* of New Zealand, a survival of the Permian lizard, pursues a remarkable development and culminates in an ocular organ known as the pineal or third eye. The pineal eye is located beneath the transparent skin of the middle of the head, in an orifice of the skull.

Thus, in addition to ordinary eyes the *Hatteria punctata* possesses a third eye that certainly corresponds with the other optic nerves. It so happens that this tiny gland we all possess at the top of the skull prevents the fontanel from closing before the age of five, but according to Lotus de Païni (*Les Trois Totémisations*), complete ossification does not occur until between sixteen and eighteen years of age. This author wonders if there might not be a need to discover here the climate of this very distinctive world in which the toddler evolves. Cosmic consciousness would require a vigilant plan, and this pineal gland would inspire manifestations of a prophetic nature. Léon Langlet told me that he has noted the presence in children of a spiral center sketched out by the body hair. Couldn't a possibility be found here for getting access to psychic powers? Just what does what the tonsure priests wear represent? Body hair plays the role of a receptive organ—the holy thinkers who wish to live as hermits have long hair, while the active monk becomes bald. The importance of the crown is demonstrated in all the iconography. The chakras are connected to the plexuses; the rituals intended for the ordination of priests and the coronation of kings corresponds to a magical realization. Conrad (*Goéland*, n. 75) has noted that according to the Roman ritual the priest's tonsure is 3 inches in diameter, the deacon's tonsure is 2.5 inches, and that of the subdeacon is 1.75 inches. A minor cleric's tonsure is 1.5 inches while that of someone receiving their first ordination is 1.25 inches. The pope's tiara should cover almost the entire upper part of the head. The halo therefore becomes larger and larger as the churchman assumes higher positions in the church hierarchy, perhaps to symbolize that the knowledge dwells within him and that he should share it with other individuals. On the other hand, the wearing of a skullcap becomes mandatory. Linen is used to make the pope's head cover. In addition to its white color, this fiber holds magical properties. The hat has the same significance as the crown or the bishop's miter. Dr. Henri Allaix has studied the value of the hat.[20] We should take a brief moment to note that the Indian's scalp tends to remove the seat of the soul and that the wearing of any piece of clothing implies the avoidance or development of a relational rhythm between an organ of the body and astral powers. In the same spirit I could include the pigtail of the ancient Chinese. The masters in the Masonic lodges customarily wear a hat, which could signify that the master has nothing more to receive but has reached the final grade.[21] This hat could have the same meaning for Pernath, the gem cutter of Gustav Meyrink's extremely curious novel, *The Golem*. The magistrate covers his head when it is time to deliver a verdict, for no influence should be allowed to color his judgment. Beneath their veils nuns were tonsured, and both Buddhist priests and Egyptian hierophants officiated with their heads shaved. Conversely, the parishioners were obliged to keep their heads covered, as are men in the synagogue.

In each case, we see the survival of a notion that light comes from above and enters through the top. This illumination of the individual therefore comes from a cosmic consciousness. But the passive force of women requires the covering of this focal point, because it is feminine nature to receive and not give. Female initiation thereby only plays a subaltern role. Shared idealism among men cements powerful bonds: the need to find and identify one another as fellow seekers gives birth to insignia and words of recognition. Ceremonies with an accentuated ritual character mark each stage. These groups include craft, industrial, and agricultural guilds; universities; Hermetic or alchemical circles; the priesthood; knighthood; and even thieves' or beggars' guilds. But women are given no role in these whatsoever. The same circumstances appear in other civilizations. Pueblo Indians gather in kivas, underground chambers that women are not allowed to enter. Women were not admitted into the *kozges* or kashims of the Bering Strait Eskimos except for public dances. However, while women are excluded from brotherhoods, they do figure in the Old Testament, but the Talmud was even harsher toward women than the previous examples: a woman was forbidden to even enter the temple. Other religions prescribe the same intolerance, and a Japanese woman cannot even enter the sanctuary of the goddess Sengen Sama, who is worshiped at the top of Mount Fuji volcano. Moses drew up a hierarchy of female impurities. A woman who gave birth to a girl was more impure than one who had a son, as all a girl brings to the world is a new source of sin. We have to wait until Muhammad for women to be granted a less humiliating role. The woman became an intrinsic part of man in the New Testament. These polarized beings, subject to the law of love and magnetic attraction, have been analyzed by Guatia.[22] He maintains that women follow the evolutionary law of the primordial androgyne dear to the Kabbalah. He adds that she reflects the supreme deity and captures a portion of that solar energy for which temples are built.

The cave can house temples. Those of Nubia consist of four rooms, only the first of which is lit by natural light. Vast in its proportions, this room is called the "pronaos." The other spaces are known as the "naos" and the "sekos." The underground layouts are luxurious. Enormous statues, generally in pairs, guarantee protection of the temple on the outside. The colossi of Karnak and Memnon are actually surviving pillars. Among these *speos** we should point out the immense underground complexes of Samoun—or of the Crocodiles—located in Upper Egypt near Manfalut. A *hemi-speos* is an underground temple that has exterior extensions consisting of stone buildings decorated with colossal statues. One such temple is Girché (Gerf Hussein) on the left bank of the Nile in Lower Nubia. The Holy of Holies in the Egyptian temple is inaccessible to the profane. The narrow entranceway most often leads to two halls with no openings to the outside—the sanctuaries of the barque and the statue.

The Hindus hollowed out temples comparable to those in Egypt for celebrating the worship of Buddha, and they display colossal proportions, wealth, and ornamentation. One of the most remarkable of these is located in Ajanta in the Deccan region. This temple at Elephanta, near Mumbai, is enriched by sculpted walls. In central India, in Ellora (state of Nizan), the region is crisscrossed by underground galleries. The depth of the Visvacarma temple is around 140 feet, and of the two attendants of this temple, one bears a scepter and a lotus flower, and the other holds a square. Above Visvacarma—personification of Brahma as

---

*[Temples carved into the rock.—*Trans.*]

architect—we find the eye of organizing wisdom. The Naljorpas, who follow the Tibetan tradition—greatly influenced by Hindu Yoga—seek the "direct path" by living in caves. They learn to regulate their breathing in order to place their minds in a calm state.[23]

These caves offering access to the lower world make possible a direct connection with the spirit that dwells at the immutable center. According to Strabo, the cave of Acherusia in Avernus, or that of Campania, permits the telling of oracles, an initiatory method that facilitates the regeneration of souls. These notions crop up in many tales: the future Australian magician must make his way to the Olkiapara Cave, and this also brings to mind the underground lairs of the Hindu nagas. Charles Deulin, in his *Mother Goose Stories,* often mentioned this underworld ruled over by a dwarf people, one of whom—the dwarf Allis—carried off Thor's daughter to this realm of darkness to consecrate their marriage. The invisible husband in the fable of "Eros and Psyche" is called the "Lord of the Underworld." Some versions of the "Beauty and the Beast" story take place in caves. Wouldn't the "forbidden room" be a simulacrum of this cave in which a specifically determined act unfurls? This theme is found in "Bluebeard" in which the incriminating blood, with its ceremonial phases, evokes the "sorcerer's apprentice." This is a set of legends, the oldest of which appear in Hindu literature. *The Thousand and One Nights* provides us some savory details: the cave of Ali Baba is filled with fabulous wealth; the thieves are forty in number; the magic word that allows the door to open is the name of the smallest seed, and in addition to the Logos and its injunction, I am thinking of the Pagad, the first card of the Tarot, whose value appears to be zero and yet is the card that opens the deck. Something that might appear insignificant can hold great value. In other tales, the evil genie comes out of a bowl or an earthenware pot in which he had been imprisoned. He is preceded by a thick vapor. The same taboo is implied in "The Story of the Third Calendar" told by Scheherazade, and the initiate can only triumph after receiving the teaching and going through the three stages of purification, knowledge, and power.

We should also note this curious narrative of a wonderful journey through a land located at the center of the earth. I am thinking of the one imagined by Casanova, who wrote: *Icosaméron: Or the Story of Edward and Elizabeth, Who Spent Eighty-One Years in the Land of the Megamicres, Original Inhabitants of Protocosmos in the Interior of Our Globe.* After this fairly evocative title, we should note the journey made by Antoine de la Sale to the mountain of the Sybil. This story appears in his book with the title of *La Salade.*[24] The entrance to a cave can be found at the top of this mountain.[25] It offers access to an underground passageway that is so narrow that a person can only travel through it lying down. This path crosses over an abyss and becomes wider. Artificial dragons are enthroned in a place where doors of metal and crystal are slamming repeatedly. Queen Sybil resides in the central hall. Similar symbolic notions figure in the story by Andrea de Barberino, *Guerino il Meschino,* in which a serpent offers helpful advice to anyone who enters the cave. While considering this series of literary works,[26] we should not overlook Rabelais and his temple of the Dive Bouteille.* Pantagruel was dazzled there by the lamp that was next to the transparent chalice, and we should not forgot the Holy Fountain (presence of a superior water as it is an image of blood), that flows following a logarithmic spiral, the universal movement of life coiling in the ether.

The underground temple built in the cave, in memory of the descent into hell, permits the postulant to make contact with the forces of the earth. It puts him back in his original environment and thereby prompts his regeneration. But after having developed the natural cave, man began thinking of ways to recreate this ambiance. This is what we are going to study in the next few chapters.

---

*[A bottle of wine. —*Trans.*]

10

Initiatory Passageways and the Tomb of the Christian Woman

THE INITIATORY CEREMONIES that take place in the telluric darkness permit the individual to regenerate. They enable him to earn immortal life. In order to depict the crossing of the infernal world the tests take place in caves, or if such are lacking, the forests in their darkest recesses.* But man wished to reconstruct these natural sites and thereby, without forgetting the value and forces of natural currents, he symbolically established initiatory places. In order to make all these occult forces receptive to his desires, these sanctuaries were equipped with the greatest possible number of ritualistic amenities.

This immediately brings the pyramids to mind and their passageways created for perfectly defined purposes. Beneath the step pyramid of Zoser, galleries are laid out on different levels to a depth of 100 feet. This formation that radiates with ratios of divine harmony and geometrical forms has surprising properties that we shall look at briefly. If we were to build a pyramid of wood or cardboard according to the proportions of that of Cheops, and if we oriented one of its faces to magnetic north, an animal substance placed beneath this ensemble would

---

*Mircea Eliade has spoken in all his work about the value of this sacred enclosure (primarily for Africa).

mummify in a dozen days. These pyramids with their very distinctive proportions emit ultrashort waves that would belong to the "negative green" area.

With the pyramid humans tried to use "the influences of telluric waves for vitalizing purposes obtaining success after much trial and error, which we can see by following the evolution of the great funerary architecture of Kemit."[1] Furthermore, M. A. de Bélizal found that, on a diagram of the solar spectrum, the radiation of these waves would correspond to a hypothetical color in the opposite direction of green, which he defined as "negative green."[2] These influences, which are particularly detectable to dowsing, give us grounds to think that the very shape of the pyramid prompts the activity of telluric waves from the same family as those encountered in underground waters and fissures. We are meeting up with the law of numbers and harmony. The esoteric cut—the ratio of the circle to the square—gives the number of man, 2.618, from which the golden number is derived. And it is helpful to note that the pyramid of Couhard (which should be spelled Kouhard), near Autun, has a close connection to the pyramid of Cheops. This Druid monument, which was built long before the coming of the Romans, was studied by H. Guettard, and his conclusions lead to the recognition of one of the doors of knowledge in this construction. H. Guettard explained the regulating theme of these two pyramids:

1. The esoteric cut of the great pyramid of Egypt gives, within the limits of the monument's base, the diameter of the circle whose circumference is equal to the perimeter of the quadrangular space.
2. The esoteric cut of the pyramid of Couhard gives, within the limits of the pyramid's base, the diameter of the circle whose surface is equal to that of the square of the base.[3]

The problems raised by the construction of the pyramid remain an almost entire mystery. Moses's knowledge came from a teaching received on the banks of the Nile, and we can see there the debt of Christianity, direct heir to ancient Egypt. Plutarch made note of the "bright light" and pure air that prevailed in the passageways of these constructions. We are still at the stage of supposition here and have been unable to discover the nature of this light.

It would seem that many modern theories and inventions were discovered, using other means, back in earliest antiquity. Aristotle seems to have been familiar with the telescope; the compass was called "the southern chariot" in early Chinese antiquity; and the idea of a submarine was presented in a German poem, *Salmah und Morold,* which dates from 1190.[4] Hippocrates and Apollonius knew the blood circulatory system, which was rediscovered by Harvey.[5] An amusing question that might possibly make us think is one passed along by Jules Boucher.[6] The oracle of Apollo at Delos predicted that the plague in Athens would end once its altar had been duplicated. Immediately each side of the cube was doubled, thereby increasing the volume of the cube eight times. The plague did not stop, and it was Hippocrates of Chios who was able to reduce the cube by finding two mean proportionals in continued proportion between two given straight lines. This problem required the resolution of a third-degree equation: if the volume of the first cube is 1, the edge of the second is equal to the cube root of 2. It so happens that a chest of polished red granite without a lid exists in the Egyptian king's chamber. The exterior capacity of a parallelepiped shape is exactly twice the interior capacity of the same shape. The two parallelepipeds should have proportions that are identical in every sense, a problem that is difficult to resolve. The physical solution of this problem can be found in the pyramid, however. This is how stone contains the oldest accounts of human thought. The very shape of the pyramid is the reflection of the *tetractys,* the fundamental image and basis of the theory of numbers held in honor by the Pythagoreans (see fig. 10.1).

Because the sum of its elements makes ten, or in other words, one, the decad symbolizes unity.

While the Couhard pyramid could represent the sacred mountain, we should also cite some other Druid monuments. After the Irish tumulus named Newgrange, located on the Boyne between Drogheda and Tara, we have the tumulus with the chamber in a dolmen, Gavrinis,

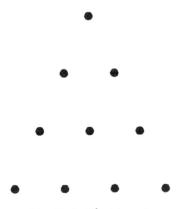

Fig. 10.1. The Tetractys

located on the archipelago of Sept-Iles in Brittany (Morbihan). The covered alley of Gavrinis leads into a square chamber, and in both monuments we can see the presence of the spiral, the Celtic emblem that shows cosmic evolution and involution. The Christ in majesty of Vezelay has two majestic spirals on his robe. This may well be a remembrance of Saint Colomba. Also, at a certain degree of initiation, the path to be followed takes the form of a spiral. Plotinus alludes to this when speaking of the Eleusinian Mysteries.[7]

The spiral-shaped underground corridor is found in the Tomb of the Christian Woman, a curious monument located in Tipaza near Algiers. Little has been written about this temple that can be seen from the entire Mitidja chain—seven thousand feet above sea level—in a barren and sad place.[8]

In Marcel Christofle's book, with its valuable architectural knowledge, we need to go back to the description of this tomb in which nothing was found.[9] An enormous cylinder topped by a tiered dome sits on a square base (63.40 meters × 62.99 meters). The building measures 60.90 meters in diameter and is slightly over 33 meters tall. This cylinder is decorated by sixty columns—separated by four false trapezoidal doors located at the four cardinal points—ornamented with cross-shaped moldings. For this reason visitors view it as a Christian monument. There are flowers on the capitals, "a kind of dog rose with four, five, six, seven, and even eight petals, whose arrangement is consistent: one flower with four petals is followed by one with more petals, then a flower with four petals, and so on." The cone ends in a kind of platform at the top, and Marcel Christofle, abandoning his role as architect, writes that this point "might end in a roof light with small columns" (page 13). The only known entrance opens beneath the fake door on the east. It is quite narrow and has grooves. It is imaginable that a sliding slab of stone blocked the entrance and the inside end of the tunnel was sealed by another slab. The passageway leads to the "cave of the lions." A second passage similar to the first leaves from this room, sealed by a third door/slab. After going up seven stairs, we enter the circular gallery, which is vaulted and about 140 meters long. This semicircular gallery is 2.05 meters wide. The curve abruptly changes direction, and its volume shrinks and resumes normal proportions. After a fourth sliding-stone door there is another arched vault. The fifth and final sliding-stone door gives access to the last vault, whose walls are oriented perfectly. It is 4.04 meters long by 3.06 meters wide and has a height of 3.43 meters. All these chambers are semicircular vaults.[10]

Numerous visitors describe this as a crude monument. Yet all the stones that form "the shirt" of the tomb are connected by plugs carved in dovetail joints. These plugs are made of cast iron, lead, or wood in lead. The floor of the paved vault is made from large stones whose joints are all oriented northeast and east-west. There are so many minute details in the construction of this monument, details we have trouble perceiving precisely as such and that are invisible to the superficial glances of tourists. We are therefore in the presence of a perfectly oriented monument whose low entranceway or "strait gate" is located on the east. Like the pyramid, this truncated monument shows that we are in the presence of human wisdom; the placement of the final tip—the triangular stone—would lead to divine knowledge. The monument has therefore been built for a symbolic purpose. The circular monument rests on a square platform demonstrating the covenant between heaven and earth, a symbol we also see in the palace or the chariot of the Chinese emperor, topped by a dome. In the perspective of this cosmic unity, Marco Polo said that in Persia, in Saveh, the Three Magi who came to offer homage to Jesus rest in three sepulchers in a "building that is square on the bottom and round at top." When seen from an airplane, an immense cross can be seen around the Tomb of the Christian Woman. This can bring to mind the Rose Cross or the eight projections of a wind rose that are circumscribed in a circle this way. For the specialist Léon Langlet, the motifs that support the cornice are not arches but spirals, and the decorative elements are neither acanthus nor lotus flowers but flames that frame triangles. Roses are found at the base of the capitals. It so happens that the four-petal rose is the symbol of an Egyptian sect. It reappears in the Rose Cross, that extraordinary secret society that once it fell from grace, gave birth to other initiatory brotherhoods.

The number 5—there are five doors on this monument—is the earthly number par excellence. It is the nuptial number for the Pythagoreans and is the reflection of that star that has a 72-degree angle between each point. The flaming star—or pentagram—symbolizes the all-powerful will toward reintegration. With the blooming five-petal rose, we sense the identical essence between the man of synthesis and the manifested God. The ten rays of the sefirot or the ten openings correspond to each of these branches. It just so happens that $10 \times 5 = 50$, and they are either the fifty doors of light or of the Intelligence that corresponds, according to Moses, to the fifty interpretations of the Divine Word. But human beings can only know forty-nine solutions; the fiftieth, the final stone, remains in the domain of God. The man that has regenerated under the sign of five can only be placed between earth and heaven—the square and the dome. This tumulus therefore places the collective man in divine synthesis. It is the mark of the androgyne. The Tomb of the Christian Woman could be one of the aspects of the Logos and the emblem of the grand arcanum (fig. 10.2).

The stone courses of the foundation number thirteen. This number comes up several times. Thirteen has a sacred value. There are twelve apostles around Christ; there are twelve knights around Arthur. Thirteen represents the number of perfection. But what are we to think about these mysterious marks carved on the stones?

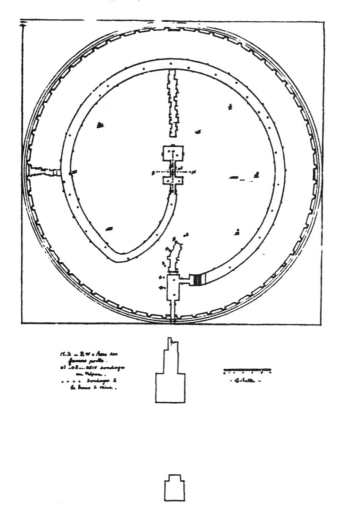

Fig. 10.2. The Tomb of the Christian Woman
Marcel Christofle, A. M. G. Editions

Marcel Christofle recorded these images and reproduced 216 of them. But these signs are too geometrical for them to be truly interpreted. Jean Brune, supporting the theory of Langlet, reproduced two of these signs with much more fidelity. For Christofle, they are the marks of pieceworkers, especially as the stone is always marked on a spot where it will not be seen. He deduced from this that the temple had nothing to do with initiation, as the marks were not readily visible. But can the message be decoded by just anyone? The multiple interpretations of sacred books, the hidden properties of the great pyramids demonstrate this desire to conceal from the profane the profound meaning buried by the builders. However, the marks of the pieceworkers, and more particularly those of the journeymen, are limited in number and come from one single crew. Their profusion at the Tomb of the Christian Woman is cause for great surprise, and it is often necessary to turn a stone over to find the mysterious sign. The problem raised by these marks has therefore not been resolved.

The peoples of antiquity held notions quite different from our own about what constituted spiritual values. For this reason we no longer orient our churches in correspondence with the four directions because we only know what is visible and material. The ancients, to the contrary, thought that waves, the telluric forces, had an effect on life. The person of the past knew magical activity, and this religious and incantatory message has often been preserved for us under the cover of other symbols. It would be a mistake to try to deny the symbolism of this ancient construction because we have lost its meaning. Everything in the Tomb of the Christian Woman takes part in reinforcing this idea of an initiatory temple: its low entrance on the east, its large underground passageway in the shape of a spiral, its stones oriented in the same direction as the fake doors, its rose emblem.

Léon Langlet did research on the interpretation of these hieroglyphic drawings, and it is to be hoped that his important work will be published. But in the images reproduced by Jean Brune (fig. 10.3)

Fig. 10.3. Signs from the Tomb of the Christian Woman
(based on the drawings of Jean Brune)

with the Y that is rising toward the sky and the double V, I see the principle of androgyny, the expansion of a reality that seeks to ascend toward the cosmic reality. Jacob's ladder makes it possible to reach heaven but also to go into the underworld. As for the other sign—is it the serpent of wisdom or the track of the lost path? Can this drawing of the labyrinth put us back on the right road?

In addition to this powerful symbolism, Henry Pamart has made some troubling hypotheses. He discovered the angle that the pole star makes with the horizon (360°34'30") in the angle of the isosceles triangle formed by the base of the platform and the center of the circle described by the first step of the ground level. While it is true that sometimes numbers are made to say too much, I am convinced that what we are dealing with here is a temple of initiation.

For his apprenticeship, the neophyte has to walk through a corridor that corresponds to one of the forms of the highest initiation. A lion and a lioness guard the entrance. These dreadful Cerberuses only allow those who are worthy to enter. There are reasons to be intrigued by the orientation and traffic flow in the passageway. Ordinarily the initiate follows a track that follows the curve described by the sun: from east to west by way of the south. Here the curve goes by way of the north, which means the center is on the left. It is therefore a reverse of the sun's course. In the Kaaba, where the Black Stone sits in a corner, one carries out the essential rite of *tawaf,* the sevenfold circumambulation, in the opposite direction of the hands of a watch, which is to say, in a trigonometric sense. It is possible to imagine that the neophyte is seeking the light, and he must yield to this encounter. But we do not understand why the door is placed on the east. By placing the door on the west it would facilitate his encounter with the regenerative astral body. Symbolically speaking, this retrograde walk means death. Does this mean to say that the man who enters the secret sanctuary must die to profane life in order to be spiritually reborn? The postulant must be continuously returning to himself. This retrograde walk is curious, because all movement in nature is dextrorsal. The sun revolves from left to right while keeping the center on its right, and the other planets follow the same law of rotation. The spiral of the univalves has the same orientation. The human being uses his right limbs more than his left limbs, and everything we create—staircases, corkscrews, screws, locks, watches, springs, induction coil wires—is in the same direction. But in the lands where the sun's revolution goes from right to left, even writing becomes sinistrorsal. The spiral thus remains in its biological and cosmic movement, which is most often dextrogyre.[11] The initiatory passageway in the Tomb of the Christian Woman complies with a clearly defined ritual. But it must also be noted that this spiral seems to be trying to withdraw into itself. In reality this circle allows access to the middle chamber through a sudden bend at one point in its curve. This idea of the circle is connected to the symbolism of the eternal return and uninterrupted movement.

After a series of passageways the apprentice can gradually make his way to the most secret temple, which, for some reason I do not know, is not strictly situated in the axis of the building. Does this mean that it is necessary to go beyond the immutable center to enter the definitive ether? For Léon Langlet, by going beyond the center, the adept does not attain the final goal of his initiation, so this can only be simply a stage of the initiatory process. This chamber only has one door, so in order to leave it the individual must retrace his steps. Gustav Meyrink, in his book *The Golem*,[12] puts his character Pernath through the same search. This return by the same path implies that the individual must go back through all the multiple states of his being, and this is simultaneously a return to the underworld and an elevation toward the Light.

The treasure that resides at the Tomb of the Christian Woman is most likely a spiritual and nonmaterial item. We will still be hunting for a tomb here for a long time and in vain. It is necessary to grasp the meaning of this orientation, this corridor, these stairs, these doors: a coffin would not contribute anything else. If this coffin exists—and I strongly doubt it does—it must be empty. The true value of this tomb resides in what we have already uncovered. It speaks to the spirit and not to our materialist sensibilities. It is necessary to have the courage to know that the tomb is empty while holding on to our faith. It is similar to La Fontaine's field, the one that contains no treasures but is itself a treasure.

Is the Tomb of the Christian Woman an isolated case? I have in mind the royal tomb located near Monkals in the Indus Valley, which is quite comparable to the one we just discussed.

I should also mention the Medracen located in the Algerian province of Constantine. It has the same silhouette as the Tomb of the Christian Woman but is more compact: it is only 60 feet tall and only 39 feet in diameter. It is also a terraced cone sitting on a cylinder adorned with columns. Its entrance on the east side is concealed by the joined stones of the third terrace. The Medracen only has a lone rectilinear gallery that provides access to the lone central hall. This chamber is 10.8 × 4.75 feet and contains vestiges of ocher wall murals and two seats. Finally, near the village of Haouret near Frenda, in the region of Tiaret, stand the Jedars, pyramidal tumuli raised over square foundations. The largest of them measure 158 × 147 feet. There are thirteen of them in all. On the cut stone we find the same marks as

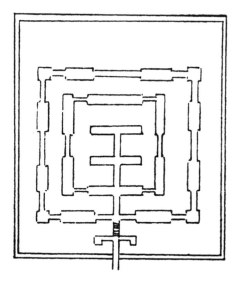

Fig. 10.4. Schematic outline of one of the Jedars of Tiaret
(based on Jean Brune)

those appearing on the tumulus of Tipaza;* the Jedars of Tiaret have passageways built in the form of labyrinths (see fig. 10.4).

The Medracen passageway appears too regular to me because it only leads straight to the goal—which is contrary to the initiatory quest. Only the chosen can therefore cross the threshold and by working his way through the obstacles make his way to the Holy of Holies.

Léon Langlet was of the opinion that this "so-called Tomb of the Christian Woman was in reality one link in an initiatory chain—the second degree—the first one having been crossed through the thirteen buildings located in the Jedar mounds, and the third one being the Medracen." It is in this last monument that we find the "middle chamber," the "Holy of Holies." Léon Langlet found a Pythagorean symbol, the *ascia,* in Tipaza. He also found the pentagram both at the Tomb of the Christian Woman and in the Jedars, and those roses we discussed earlier also represent the occult pentagram. A temple of Isis was discovered in Cherchell (twenty-five miles away). This makes the Egyptian influence undeniable.

For my part I believe that the Tomb of the Christian Woman is located, esoterically speaking, as the final stage. It belongs to the human scale, whereas the Medracen with its single chamber would represent divine consciousness, a consciousness inaccessible to human beings. But this rectilinear corridor reminds me of the Celtic-covered alleys that are always clearly oriented in an east-west direction and offer access to a sealed and illuminated chamber, just as the eye of wisdom illuminates the individual.† The Tomb of the Christian Woman allows the possibility of an earthly transmutation. It remains as an eternal becoming and allows us to attain a stage, a higher level of initiation.

In agreement with the outer shapes of these monuments we have just looked at, we find numerous tumuli in Etruria that are akin to the pyramids. The Cerveteri tumulus, located near the Etruscan port neigh-

---

*For Jean Brune, these mysterious signs could be runic letters that can be found as plentifully on the stones of the Sahara as on those of Scandinavia.

†This illumination is found on some menhirs and in ancient churches. The "third eye" permitted the hatching of the symbolism of the "hat" connected to the priests' tonsure.

boring Rome, is said to date from the seventh or eighth century BCE. It has a diameter of 48 meters and houses six passageways that offer access to chambers believed to be mausoleums. The Cucumella, a famous Etruscan tumulus of the Vulci region, on the left bank of the Fiora, is also circular in shape. Its underground chamber includes an inextricable labyrinth and a vast rectangular hall that has yet to reveal its secret. Could it be a royal mausoleum? But no tomb has ever been found there. Was it the scene of funerary honors? The Cucumella still remains quite mysterious.[13] In western Asia near the principal temple of Ur stands a massive tiered tower—the Ziggurat. A man-made hillock covers the ruins of a Hittite town near Hattusa; the defense of this capital was achieved by tunnels of audacious construction.

We should note again that the pyramids have yet to reveal all their secrets. The spiritual philosophy that presided over their construction is situated far beyond a sepulcher. For this reason it hardly matters if the tomb is empty.

Another relative of the dolmens I should mention are the poypes, mounds of raised earth that sometimes are 50 to 70 feet tall. They are found primarily in the region of Bresse, in Dombes, and on the Dauphin plain. Their shape is generally a truncated cone, but the butte of Ambronay is pyramidal. One of the largest is in Villars-les-Dombes (Ain), and a fortified castle was placed on it during the Middle Ages. No objects of interest have been found during any of the excavations undertaken there. Speculation about their purpose ranges from observatories to sacrificial altars. Charles Diot[14] has studied them in his capacity as a dowser. These mounds are apparently surrounded by four underground water flows, which form a quadrilateral that is oriented to the four directions.

The summit of the mound that has been leveled off certainly responds to an esoteric notion. For Diot, this terrace would be subject to oblique radiation from the four springs. This defines a center that commingles with that of the poype. This author also maintains that naturally occurring swastikas, formed by this radiation, travel through these mounds. The *tomelles* found in the Marne Department are also earthen mounds in which traces of funerary rites can be found. But as they are located quite close to each other, they must have been used for other purposes, perhaps like menhirs. Because so many of these tumuli have been removed, it is difficult to form any valid idea on their usefulness.

So we can now see that the monuments of antiquity had underground passageways that plunged the neophyte into the ambience of the cave and ensured he experienced the flow of telluric forces. We are going to revisit this notion with the labyrinth, but the Tomb of the Christian Woman remains one of the most astonishing cases. Study of it reveals a construction whose serene beauty reflects the world of harmony and proportion. Its passageway becomes the materialized symbol of a very exalted spiritual philosophy.

11

An Initiatory Passageway: The Underground Labyrinth

LIKE RENÉ GUÉNON, I consider initiation to be a genuine and uninterrupted transmission; its teaching in the form of an initiatory chain guides the neophyte from the outside to the inside, from the door to the secret temple, to the fixed and immutable point. This brings us to the idea of a path. It so happens that illumination becomes a personal possession, and the candidates who manage to reach the supreme center are few in number. This guiding path is therefore not rectilinear; it meanders often, and just when the individual thinks he is coming to the goal, the path suddenly turns in another direction, quite far from the place one wishes to go. The initiatory tests permit the young man to successively go through the stages with an eye to the restoration of his own being.

During these symbolic or virtual journeys, the neophyte seems to go astray at times. But his initiators are keeping watch, and he is constantly redirected, even unconsciously, back to the right path. Even in societies like Freemasonry and the Compagnonnage, and despite the great drop in their effective symbolic power, initiation refers to these initiatory ordeals as "trips." Most often the postulant's eyes are blindfolded and he finds himself in the darkness of the depths of the earth.

The initiations of the Compagnonnage once took place in the forest, at the edge of the sea, or in caves. Later, they took place in huts known as *cayennes,* or lodges.

All these initiations imply the idea of a selection. Not just any individual at just any moment in his life can all of a sudden become an initiate; placed on the path—which compels the idea that he was chosen—he does not automatically reach the stage of full awareness and knowledge. He can go astray, and retrace his steps—and we know that no one should ever look back.* These are all so many conditions that make initiation a real operation and a complete apprenticeship of life. Only the strong man will prevail; now stamped physically and morally, he will have command over his fellow citizens. There can therefore be several paths leading to knowledge, and it is not given that each individual will reach the final goal.

In an article titled "La caverne et le labyrinthe,"[1] René Guénon examined this subject. The cavern is the site of initiation, and the tunnel leading there, with its trials and obstacles, becomes a dark passageway for the neophyte, with incomprehensible twists and turns. But because this journey is long and sown with ambushes it allows for introspection without, however, any possibility of retreat, and it gives access to the secret temple and spiritual center where the "second birth" should take place. Total realization cannot occur until the individual makes his way from the outside, from the circumference, to the central point. He will then have escaped from the imprisonment of the cycles.

This passageway that connects the superior states with those called inferior has been given the name of "labyrinth." It includes an equal number of gains and losses. René Guénon describes labyrinths as external darkness, but this must be taken in the moral sense as it is characterizing a state of wandering that should end with the stabilization of the individual when he makes his way to the immutable point of the center.

---

*This theme illustrating female curiosity is rich in instances. In the Bible, the transgressor is changed into a salt statue. The symbolism of salt is also quite important.

In this same article René Guénon seeks the etymology of the word *labyrinth*. He discovers *labrys,* the Cretan double axe, but he also indicates that the word could come from *lapis,* meaning "stone."[2] Seen from this angle, we realize that the labyrinth of Crete answers this definition.[3] According to Pliny this was a tortuous, twisting, underground passageway leading to a central chamber where the Minotaur was imprisoned; it was created by Daedalus on the orders of Minos. Theseus only managed to slay this fabled creature thanks to the complicity of Ariadne.[4] Before Theseus, the unwary noninitiates never returned from their underground journey. Theseus grew from this trial and was able to emerge from it because he knew how to overcome a hidden force. All "quests" represent the same search because a spiritual thought persists beyond the physical deeds. The Minotaur represents less a monster than a necessary stage in the initiation, and his allegory deserves further development.[5] This god who is half bull and half man must be carved up so that his blood regenerates us. We find here the worship that is at the heart of bullfighting.

The Egyptian labyrinth was built near Lake Moeris. It is attributed to Petesuchus or Tithoës. *The Book of the Dead* mentions that the soul of the deceased, led by Anubis, travels through the labyrinth. With the help of a guiding thread the soul will find her way to the tribunal where Osiris is waiting with forty-two assessors (or judges). Herodotus, Strabo, and Diodorus Siculus all state that the labyrinth of Egypt contained three thousand rooms, and that located on the lower—underground—story were the tombs of kings.

Roger Caillois reports[6] that the first description of a labyrinth that comes down to us is that of Pliny in his *Natural History* (36.19.13). The maze at Heracleopolis in Egypt was built by Psammetichus 3,600 years before Pliny, and it was this construction that inspired Daedalus to build his own.

It is not just a narrow strip of ground comprising many miles of "walks" or "rides," such as we see exemplified in our tessellated floors or in the ceremonial game played by our boys in the Campus

Martius, but doors are let into the walls at frequent intervals to suggest deceptively the way ahead and to force the visitor to go back upon the very same tracks that he has already followed in his wanderings. . . .

The ground plan and the individual parts of this building cannot be fully described because it is divided among the regions or administrative districts known as nomes, of which there are twenty-one, each having a vast hall allotted to it by name. Besides these halls, it contains temples of all the Egyptian gods; and, furthermore, Nemesis placed within the forty shrines several pyramids, each with a height of forty cubits and an area at the base of four acres. It is when he is already exhausted with walking that the visitor reaches the bewildering maze of passages. Moreover, there are rooms in lofty upper stories reached by inclines, and porches from which flights of ninety stairs lead down to the ground. Inside are columns of imperial porphyry, images of gods, statues of kings, and figures of monsters. Some of the halls are laid out in such a way that when the doors open there is a terrifying rumble of thunder within: incidentally, most of the building has to be traversed in darkness. Again, there are other massive structures outside the wall of the labyrinth: the Greek term for these is *pteron,* or a "wing." Then there are other halls that have been made by digging galleries underground. The few repairs that have been made there were carried out by one man alone, Chaeremon, the eunuch of King Necthebis five hundred years before the time of Alexander the Great. There is a further tradition that he used beams of acacia boiled in oil to serve as supports while square blocks of stone were being lifted into the vaults.

The most famous labyrinths remain those of Lemnos and the sepulcher of the king of Etruria (in Italy). The island of Candia also contains several caves with deep galleries heading in every direction, with numerous false doors. Caumont is of the opinion that the labyrinths are the emblem of the temple of Jerusalem.

But whether it is the one of Theseus or the one in Egypt, the labyrinth includes several paths. The labyrinth is a snare, and someone who has gotten lost runs the risk of a disagreeable encounter at a detour from the corridor. A thread is necessary to find one's way again. In the initiatory tale of "Tom Thumb," this thread is contrived by means of white stones. One side of a Greek medal had the outline of a labyrinth carved on it on which two out of three corridors led into dead ends. We shall be seeing that in more recent labyrinths—Christian labyrinths—it is no longer possible to get lost.

Roger Caillois, in an excellent article on "the fundamental themes of Jorge Luis Borges," wrote in the magazine *L'Herne* that the maze can be imagined as a tortuous and interminable but obligatory itinerary in which "a single corridor is constantly suggested, although it is always curving and apt to give the impression that the person who takes it shall not be forced to retrace his steps. In reality it obliges him to cross over successively the entire territory covered by the labyrinth." The maze can also be considered as a place in which man is abandoned to his own devices within the complexity of multiple corridors. "Each segment of the corridor leads from a crossing and ends at another crossing, identical to the first one. The lost person is thus cast from one insoluble puzzle to the next. He has no means of knowing if the crossroads where he has ended up is not one of those he crossed through earlier. It is impossible for him to know whether he has made any progress or not, whereas in the constructions of the first type, there is always progress: the person who ventured into it will inevitably head toward the exit or, if he retraces his steps, toward where he started. This kind of labyrinth or artificial path is ordinarily viewed as an initiatory symbol of the pilgrimages of the soul in search of grace or salvation, the trials he must undergo in turn in an unchanging order.

Envisioned from the angle of initiation, the labyrinth should have three routes: one direct path that leads from outside to the secret chamber—but this corridor is rarely used, and rare are the chosen ones who attain knowledge directly; another path that makes its way to the central chamber after huge detours and many crossroads to pass through; and the third path leading nowhere, which is the way of the man who cannot be initiated; on this course go astray those who are unworthy of finding the spiritual center, the "invariable middle" in which the change of transfiguration tales place.

This notion of different paths can be seen in the work of Jules Boucher, who says that, first, the path that leads directly to the center is the Royal Way—"that of the mystic who manages from the first to attain the fullness of the initiation"; the second is the active initiatory path that is long and laborious; and the third is the false way, which leads nowhere. The labyrinth of the Masonic temple was replaced with the mosaic pavement with black-and-white square tiles. The mosaic pavement formed from the alternating black-and-white squares is "a regular network, made up of transversal and longitudinal lines that create a number of crosses."[7] After citing Ragon,[8] Plantagenet,[9] and Wirth,[10] Jules Boucher states that the virtual lines separating the rows of paving stones form the rectilinear path of the initiate. This is the esoteric path, which is "thinner than the edge of the razor." The narrow nature of this path—which is bordered by alternating black-and-white squares on one side—could have a connection with the path of the labyrinth.

The labyrinth of Saint Martin in Saint-Omer has an entrance that leads nowhere. It would be very interesting to analyze this subject further.

Marcel Brion wrote in a fine article: "the teaching we receive in the course of this walk, whose lessons are the stages, does not follow a didactic method: it advances in leaps and bounds with the suddenness and harshness of oracular revelations."[11] But clearly what is there "is a series of initiations whose sole reason to be is to lead us to the definitive initiation." Marcel Brion believes that it is death that dwells at the central point, but in reality this can only be a symbolic death; for in reality the individual must retrace his steps in order to personally pass on a part of the truth. This is the site of the second spiritual birth; the corridors of the labyrinth cannot receive signs because all outside contingencies no longer have any place here.

Recall the quest for the Grail: the Fisher King's castle suddenly appears to the knight who finds himself on the direct path, but because he does not know how to say the magic words the castle vanishes. Knights who appear worthy never find its entrance, and the paths they take lead them far and wide. Galahad, after some tortuous journeys on winding paths with many large detours, succeeds, through his valor and asceticism, to win the Holy Grail. A long path leads him finally to the most sacred place in the entire universe, since it contains the Blood of the Redeemer. In this same cycle of legends, Merlin is imprisoned in a maze by enchantment.

For reasons easy to understand, the underground secret labyrinth is replaced by a track that evokes the true dark maze. The labyrinth of the Catholic Church is placed flat on the ground. Made as a mosaic, its path is only symbolic. It is sometimes made from different-colored stones and enameled tiles. Because it is intended to represent the progression of the knight making his way to the Holy Land to defend the Holy Sepulcher, it eventually leads the faithful to the Holy Place.[12] All good will shall be rewarded. We are therefore in the presence of what is no longer an initiation in the strict sense of the word but of a form of encouragement that cannot fail to be crowned by success. This labyrinth became the emblem of the narrow and tortuous path, which, traveled on with Christian faith, will give access to heavenly Jerusalem.[13] Every man can win heaven if he so desires. This notion is summed up nicely by Abbé Auber in his *Histoire de la Cathédrale de Poitiers*:

> This labyrinth, which also bears the name of maze, meander, or path of Jerusalem, and which is embedded in marble upon the stone floor, presents in the middle of the main nave a series of complicated detours that appear symmetrical but are so mixed together by the combination of their lines that once one has gone inside them no exit can be found except by resolutely forging ahead on the path or by retracing one's steps.

Before analyzing the symbolism of this outline, I would like to point out that the labyrinth depicted in mosaic can only have an absolute value and meaning when envisioned in its subterranean expression.

While it is easy to find your bearing on a map, advancing through the telluric night is more akin to an adventurous quest. It is necessary to go into the darkness, down corridors with incomprehensible routes. Everything appears immense, unfathomable; the most courageous man is stricken with anxiety, for he is alone in a vast darkness, in which the sound of his footsteps echoes in the silence with a monstrous intensity.

Emile Amé reports[14] that according to Schmitt,[15] this was "only a puzzle for the workers." It is hard to understand the devotion surrounding such works if this is indeed the case.

Everyone during the Middle Ages dreamed of going to the Holy Land. In order to relive this long voyage, the individual would advance through the labyrinth on his knees, thus making it the path of Calvary, from the house of Pilate to the site of the cross: during the Middle Ages the labyrinth was a kind of path of the cross.

Despite the evolution of the mystical idea, we realize that the labyrinth continues to represent painful ordeals—most particularly those of Christ—and that in order to gain eternal life one must put oneself on the line. It is understandable why the labyrinth is called "path of Jerusalem." One also has only to look at the outline of this spider's web to realize how often the four branches of the cross appear quite clearly on it, with concentric lines that are simply the frame for a divine weaving.[16] The center is clearly the fixed and immutable point, and René Guénon has written the definitive pages on the center of the world. The labyrinth thereby remains a symbol of manifestation, and its multiple paths protect the access to this center that leads from the ephemeral to the eternal, and from the profane to the sacred; as a reduction of the universe it possesses infinite potential.

This is why the labyrinth can suggest the idea of time, as the man who is a prisoner of its dark corridors can travel the same route an infinite number of times if he has not found the qualifications of his regeneration, which is to say, if he has not found his Ariadne's thread. There is no end in the course of a labyrinth where the lost man wanders in circles, incapable of escaping his fate. He follows the same path that he already followed or the one he should follow. The individual is thereby the prisoner of a cycle, and these eternal rebeginnings imply the notion of a circular time in which all events reoccur at fixed and regular intervals, subject to an eternal return. As for me, I have mentioned that time cannot be represented by either an endless line or by a circle, which would imply a rigorous renewal of events. Instead I see it in the shape of a coil, a helix coiling around a crown. This extremely simplified representation makes it possible to better grasp these returns with shifts: the events remain similar but are never strictly identical. The crown could itself take a shape like that of a coil or spiral. I cannot extend myself any further on this theme except to say that it may be the very basis of our behavior.

The Compagnonnage, the order of trade guilds said to have been founded during the construction of Solomon's temple, has not been indifferent about the outline of the labyrinth. But we are right to ask what the Compagnons have retained of it. The strength of an initiatory association probably resides in the secret that is translated and transmitted in the form of a symbol that, once rediscovered, can only be explained and analyzed in the light of the high doctrine. But I think our time is too content about merely repeating the propositions of the occult quaternary: "Know, Wish, Dare, Keep Silent," while overlooking the true knowledge. The Compagnons du Tour de France have passed down signs and symbols without often knowing their value; Freemasonry drew from them but far too often altered their meaning. One has only to reread the issues of *Le Voile d'Isis*[17] devoted to the Compagnonnage to realize it is full of poorly digested repetitions. The Compagnons are happy to repeat when speaking about the labyrinth phrases such as "compagnonnic signature," "emblem of the memory of the ancients," and "anonymous homage," without clarifying the meaning because many other monuments would merit the same comments. All we find for a signature on the cathedrals built by the Compagnons is a first name with a descriptive word attached to it. The cathedral itself is another piece of architecture than the labyrinth, and the Compagnons also had at their disposal many other means for signing their works.

It is probable that architects such as Jules Gailhabaud and

Viollet-le-Duc, without being fully initiated into the rites of Compagnonnage, were familiar with the primary dogmas as they worked in close concert with the Compagnons du Devoir de Liberté. There they mainly learned the "tricks" of the trade and the procedures. The Compagnon is an excellent worker who will rarely comment in impassioned pages on the meaning of a symbol.[18]

It has been written that the labyrinth of the Compagnonnage represents a geographical circuit, the famous Tour de France of the Compagnons. This is only a second-rank symbol, as this two-dimensional labyrinth has never replaced the pilgrimage that continues to be followed on all the roads of France. This wandering journey is the basis for a moral discipline and development of professional expertise.

The Tour de France should end at Sainte-Baume. This is a ritual pilgrimage, as the cave is where legend maintains Mary Magdalene died and also where Master Jacques is said to have been murdered by disciples of Soubise. In reality this can be seen as a parody of the legend of Hiram. These two ritual deaths probably did take place in an underground temple, and it should be noted that the three evil brothers actually perform a cyclical murder. It is through this assassination that the body of Hiram will be found, and his spirit goes on to live in the thoughts of men, thanks to a veritable resurrection. With the redemptive blood of Jesus Christ and Hiram's acacia we rediscover the idea of the Universe-Man. Still today, the ritual of initiation into the Compagnonnage involves the symbolism of the labyrinth of Reims (fig. 11.1). The labyrinth most certainly expressed an idea whose meaning has been lost or altered. There is scarcely any likelihood that the labyrinth represents either the signature of the architect or his tombstone, insofar as many churches do not have this decoration but do possess the builders' marks.

The mosaic labyrinth of the thirteenth century is merely a copy of the labyrinths that were found in the Merovingian and Carolingian churches. Similar labyrinths have been found in Roman baths (in Verdes and in Loir-et-Cher).

What we can deduce from this is that the Compagnonnage has

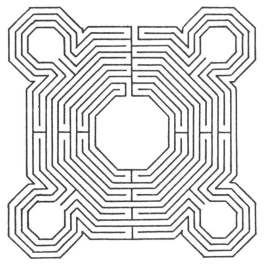

Fig. 11.1. Labyrinth of Reims (based on Amé).
It is believed to have been built in 1290; it was destroyed in 1779.

Fig. 11.2. Labyrinth of Mogor (Marin)
Pontevedra High School Museum

Fig. 11.3. Labyrinth of Tintagel
From Geoffrey Russell (R.I.L.K.O.)

Fig. 11.4. The symbol of Mother Earth for the Hopis
From Louis Charpentier, *Les Jacques et le mystère de Compostelle*
(Robert Laffont)

preserved a symbol in its rites that was Christianized but that must have been different originally.

We should recall that the Mogor stone, housed in the museum of the Pontevedra high school in Galicia, includes a very odd carved sketch, but the drawing is definitely that of a labyrinth (fig. 11.2). This stone dates from 3500 to 3000 BCE. But there are other megalithic labyrinths still in existence, one of which is preserved at the Dublin Museum. Geoffrey Russell has reconstructed the image of the one at Tintagel (fig. 11.3). They could possibly be objects for meditation, perhaps offering the possibility for advancement in subconscious or human thinking. It clearly seems that this image had an initiatory meaning for the Hopis of America (fig. 11.4). This is a fact that is confirmed by the legends that have come down to us.[19]

When the Compagnons du Devoir de Liberté asserted their liberal spirit and were being hunted down, they thought their sole chance of survival lay in integrating themselves among powerful individuals. They therefore turned to the intellectual elite, who gradually altered the Compagnonnage rite. Around 1459, the labyrinth disappeared, but the square and the compass took on a more important role. It is this sense that the labyrinth could assume the appearance of a collective signature, like an emblem. But the symbolism of the maze is on its own more important than that of a simple sign of recognition that could have been produced much more simply. The constitution that was created in Strasbourg in April 1459 strongly resembles the early constitution of Freemasonry that gradually asserted its moral authority over that organization.

Marcel Brion, while analyzing the thinking of Leonardo da Vinci, wondered about the construction of these interlaced designs, subtle mind games "in which it is necessary to follow the rigorous and bizarre progression of these intersecting threads."[20] But is the nature of this graphic diversion truly the same as the *azulejos*?* Marcel Brion notes that Albrecht Dürer had a predilection for these mysterious ornaments, whose artistic beauty can be akin to that of puzzles or even

---

*[Painted glazed ceramic tile work found in Spain and Portugal. —*Trans.*]

the arabesques of Muslim artists. Vasari believed they were a source of amusement for da Vinci; G. d'Adda believes he was making models for artists in lace. But Brion is of the opinion that these motifs are "the very portrait of Leonardo da Vinci, the projection of the circumvolutions of that passionate intelligence" who has seen "the initiation of the interlacing forms" in the middle of his imaginary domain baptized "Leonardus Vinci Accademia" (page 196).

And through the same expansion of thought, Mozart knew the labyrinth, as did Ulysses, who sealed the presents of King Alcinous in "a labyrinth of a variety of wondrous knots, whose secret he had been taught by the ingenious Circe" (*Odyssey* 8.443). Generally speaking, knots are used to represent the occult signs used to keep a secret.

Marcel Brion deconstructed the labyrinth starting from two primary motifs: the spiral and the braid. The spiral is the line that wraps around itself. In nature it can be found embedded in the shells of many crustaceans. This beautiful Druidic emblem is an optimistic motif because it is open. In complete contrast, the braid that closes itself off is a prison from which there is no escape. Marcel Brion sees in the labyrinth the inextricable convolution of the braid that leads into hopeless captivity, while the spiral provides comfort and salvation, as thanks to its open curve we are able to reach the inner chamber. But this explanation can only be imagined in consideration of the initiatory labyrinth, as the individual must choose his route if he wishes to make his way to the central temple where he must be reborn into a second life. From this aspect, the labyrinth of Theseus has a double spiral, and this lets us see the double axe René Guénon discussed while analyzing the etymology of labrys. It is also curious to find anew in Compagnonnage insignia—for example, the tiepin—the joining of two axes, a saw, and a compass with all these objects interlaced together. We see the double axe again in other trinkets. Theseus is therefore an initiate. The higher, spiritual man can only be born by immersing himself in the blood of the Minotaur—the sacred bull, the horned god—which implies a baptism of blood and fire. The Minotaur is the consummate animal: he falls only within the jurisdiction of the same law of harmony that dooms him.

This is why when Leonarda da Vinci decorated the vault of one of the two halls of the Sforza Castle by intertwining the knotwork with the trees, the painter was celebrating a spiritual and mystic life. We shall soon see what this octagonal system could represent. Similarly his *Bacchus* at the Louvre Museum is pointing toward the cavern of mysteries that no one can enter without Ariadne's thread. And the clump of columbine puts us in correspondence with the highest Hermetic tradition and the Johannite doctrine. In this way we again find the initiatory labyrinth in which the man must choose his path in order to reach the center. The perfectly apportioned trials lead to a redemptive transformation.

I just mentioned the octagonal design of some forms of labyrinth—this form was altered to become circular. It is the presence of the number eight that was dear to the Templars, but the Merovingians also constructed their baptismal fonts using the octagon.[21] However, the labyrinth must have an elliptical shape, and subsequently a rectangular one. I will not speak here of the description of Christian labyrinths, as this study has been carried out elsewhere; I can note for the record those of Reims, Amiens, Saint-Quentin, Saint-Omer, Chartres, Ravenna, Pavia, and Rome.

Many authors have been haunted by the myth of knotworks. The fantasy novel by Maurice Sandoz, *Le Labyrinth,* has no initiatory character.[22] In a short book, Jean Paris has shown the place occupied by the labyrinth in the work of James Joyce,[23] who more specifically wrote an autobiographical novel, *Dedalus.** Serge Hutin sent me an English story whose plot unfurls around a maze. The labyrinth here is in a garden and formed by cut hedges, but the initiatory meaning of it is very clear. The title of the story is "Mr. Humphreys and His Inheritance" by M. R. James,[24] which is supposed to be an extract from a late seventeenth-century book. It is the account of the adventures of a man looking for a jewel locked in the center of a labyrinth. This maze depicts the image of the world, and our life is more precious than the

---

*[The French title of Joyce's *Portrait of the Artist as a Young Man.* —Ed.]

most beautiful jewel. The key to this story appears with the motto: *Ad interiora morte.*

Marcel Brion has analyzed the mysterious impetus of initiating forces in the work of Hugo von Hofmannsthal.[25] This German author and contemporary of Rilke makes use of the initiatory experience that "uproots man from his fleeting conventions and ordinary spaces." His protagonist, Andreas, struggles with mysterious impulses born in the streets of Venice that sketch out a true labyrinth.[26] The initiatory theme penetrating the man and these various aspects are all so many mirrors that reflect the similar yet different passageways as they bring one closer or farther away from the sought-for objective, the cosmic sentiment of our universe. In *Das Bergwerk zu Falumm* Elis Frobom meets the Queen of the Mountain in a mine. He sinks deeper below the ground, aspiring to lose his personality and "to commune with the spirits of the metals." This is one way of rediscovering subterranean initiation with its vibration of telluric waves: it is complete contact to the point of integration with the Earth Mother.[27]

Roger Caillois showed in the admirable article I cited earlier that the principal key theme of Borges's work was that of circular time, whose projection cast light on the themes of the labyrinth and recurrent creation. "In turn those themes inspire symmetries and games with mirrors, systems of correspondences and equivalencies, and the secret balances and compensations that form both the structure and the substance of this writer's stories and poems." This is why Borges obsessively places the plot of his stories in a defined and circular space, the labyrinth, and in a time that is also circular. These stories include "Labyrinths," "The House of Asterion," "Ibn Hakan Al-Bokhari, Dead in His Labyrinth," and "The Garden of Forking Paths." This theme could also include "The Lottery in Babylon" and "The Library of Babel."

In Gustav Meyrink's book *The Golem,*[28] Pernath travels deep into the old Jewish quarter of Prague following dark and twisting corridors. He has to bend down and crawl in order to reach a room that is accessible by a staircase with eight steps that are five feet each. Meyrink calls this long underground passageway "the corridor of the Black School."

"Because strait is the gate and narrow is the way which leadeth unto life, and few there be that find it." In this secret sanctuary Pernath—a master gem cutter—is flooded by a clear light coming from the ceiling through a window with a grill. He suffers from the numbing cold in this room, and he puts on other clothes—those of the golem—in his fight against death. The Tarot card of the Magician is turned over. We are therefore witnessing the strange penetration of one being into another being, and through this splitting into two personalities Pernath becomes aware of the possibilities he holds within. This is therefore clearly a process of initiation with its underground progression, and we are certainly in the presence of several revelations of a German gnostic society, which could be the "Bavarian Illuminati" or the "Brotherhood of the Descendants of the First Light," which may have been known to Gérard de Nerval. We should note that Gérard de Nerval committed suicide on rue de la Vieille-Lanterne, still wearing his hat on his head, under the power of the number 13, the lunar principle.

Outside of amusements such as the garden labyrinths made from hedges or those of mirrors in fairs, the labyrinth, because of all the symbols it contains, continues to feed the reveries of poets and writers who pull from it, more or less consciously, a high metaphysical significance. The maze unleashes an enchanting power of mirage and vertigo, for the individual remains the prisoner of a spell. Events come one after another without any way to control them; the individual depends on something or someone, and this hold on the person keeps the reader's suspense and anxiety high. The extravagant labyrinth in the *Journey to the Land of the Fourth Dimension* imagined by Gaston de Pawlowski is an endless chain.

I have not spoken until now of anything but the means of reaching and entering the secret temple. The profane one who has managed to attain this immutable point thanks to Ariadne's thread, to outside assistance, becomes the Primordial Man, for he has been bathed in spiritual light. But to be fully initiated, he must return to the profane world in order to bring his knowledge there. He must return to the outside world, this place of darkness, since only material light can shine there, while in the central, underground enclosure a spiritual light is resplendent. But it is necessary to return by the same path. This is the cycle of death and resurrection and, as O. V. de L. Milosz writes: "The entrance is also the only exit; birth and death are one and the same passage of spiritual movement to physical movement and vice versa."[29]

The supreme objective can only be attained by human effort, and in this underground spot this simple worker unites with divine principle in order to return to earthly manifestation. It is necessary to know original purity and the reintegration of one's true nature in order to go back the way you came. After his slow ascension and dreadful torture, Jesus came back to earth. This earthly reincarnation after a brief sojourn in the depths of the earth is necessary. For in order to earn heaven it is necessary to suffer the passage to hell victoriously and to know how to cross through its eternal fire without being stricken by it.

In conclusion, the underground labyrinth proves the knowledge of telluric and cosmic forces. It demonstrates the rites of passage that take one from the ephemeral to the eternal and from the profane to the sacred. It is an initiatory passageway that gives access to a center, and its symbolism invites us to the reintegration of our entire being. We must now seek out the value of the crypt—another underground temple.

12

The Virgin of the Crypt, from Green to Black

THERE IS ANOTHER KIND OF LABYRINTH: the crypt. Dark, mysterious, twisting passageways lead to underground chapels: the Black Madonna appears in majesty and is associated with the cave. A typical case of this is at Saint Victor's in Marseille. Sometimes the statue extracted from its dank home stays in the choir, as in Saint-Roman-d'Ay, Rocamadour, Montserrat (the Morénita), and in many other places the statue has been moved so the faithful have easier access to her, but in reality the Black Virgin is enthroned in the crypt, the sacred cave and lair of mysteries, whose very form evokes the image of the primordial egg from which the androgynous substance is born. This place that allows the telluric forces to condense gives access to the true underworld, but in this heart of the world the eternally young and virgin Mother places the postulant back in his original setting with an eye to regeneration. Moreover, this sanctuary often takes a circular form like the earth, and this gives us Notre-Dame-la-Ronde and Notre Dame de la Rotonde (Rome). This thousand-year-old crypt is typically located in a sanctuary built on a wooded height, and a well is placed near the Virgin. The penitents probably immersed themselves in this miraculous water: "Truth comes from the well." In the variants of "Sleeping Beauty," the slumbering princesses stay in a well or a tower. The purifying water isolates one in the same way as the forest does and places things on the margin of the activity. The wells of Saint-Germain-des-Prés and Saint-Marcel possess healing properties.[1] Saint Justin Martyr deplored this practice, which he found sacrilegious: "They erect near spring the statue of the Virgin, who they call Kore and say she is the daughter of Zeus; this is an invention of demons" (*First Apology*, 64.1).

The black virgins come in the form of small wooden statues (from 12 inches to 36 inches tall). The virgin's robe most often takes the form of a triangle that flares out over her feet. The robe is sometimes decorated by vine stalks, blades of wheat, and allegorical plants. The hands of the virgins, which are often quite large, bring to mind those of the gods seen in cave paintings. Although a study of the Black Madonna does not fall into the bounds of my study, we should note that the statues are primarily found in France, Italy, and Spain. I have no intention of describing the black virgins and the locations of the one hundred fifty statuettes in France. I can only describe them from the perspective of their symbolic aspect connected with the underworld.[2]

The black color of the goddess can be intriguing. Some authors believe that the mutable quality of the wood—cedar or ebony—is the cause. But only the face and hands stand out against a lighter robe. Sometimes they have been painted: this coloration was intentional. Other authors then mused that a regional sculptor was trying to imitate a bronze patina, but this metal turns green, not black. Furthermore, we can state that such statues are extremely rare. The black coloration therefore indicates a very specific character. The power and holiness of the black virgins spawned a large number of pilgrimages, and being Caucasians, we can ask what this particular virgin represents.

The Holy Scriptures have little information about the Mother of Jesus, as she played only a fairly episodic role. In both the Scriptures and Islam the teaching is male. It was only much later that worship of the Virgin spread, and Christian iconography, seeking to make up for lost time, quickly became quite abundant. Mary's coloring should have been close to that of wheat and in the Song of Songs (1:5–6; and also 4:3 and 7:4) we read:

I am black but comely,

O ye daughters of Jerusalem,

as the tents of Kedar,

as the curtains of Solomon.

Look not upon me because I am black,

because the sun hath looked upon me.

The Kedar were a nomadic people of northern Arabia, and their tents, like those of the Bedouins, were made from goat fur.

For Lentulus, John of Damascus, and Nicephorus Kallistos—who all lived in the fifth century—Mary was probably a typical Palestinian, therefore not black.[3] The religious iconography respects the white face—a long oval (primarily in Spain); a thin straight, rectilinear nose; smooth, straight, not frizzy hair; a clearly delineated mouth; and fleshy lips. So why do we have the face of a white woman painted black for some unknown reason? This fact is all the more disturbing since during the Middle Ages a diabolical figure was designated as an "Ethiopian" or a "black,"[4] because the devil is black—but on the other hand, the pilgrimage of the Black Madonna enjoyed great favor at this same time.

If we look through the history of religion, we will see that black virgins existed in all parts of the world. Not all these goddesses who were worshipped during antiquity can be listed, but I can note here Isis, Cybele, Minerva, and Athena. We are also exhuming black Dianas and Venuses. Following Kali, the Dravidian Mahadevi found in excavations on the banks of the Indus appears black, as does the black Demeter of Phigalia found in Arcadia. This goddess is associated with an extremely important wheat cult in the mysteries of Eleusis. All these goddesses represent the Earth Mother, a fruitful being who remains chaste; the womb from which all things come and to which all things return. Demeter and Ceres reign in a cave. The Annunciation took place in these same conditions, and the angel Gabriel developed the higher faculties of Mary, the regenerated Eve. We have looked at the symbolism of the sacred cave; the crypt represents the same thing. Isis is representative of all female deities: as the land of Egypt impregnated by the Nile and the sorrowing wife of Osiris, the god dismembered by Typhon, she gives birth to Horus:

> I am she that is the natural mother of all things, mistress and governess of all the elements, the initial progeny of worlds, chief of powers divine, Queen of Heaven, the principal of the Gods celestial, the light of the goddesses: at my will the planets of the air, the wholesome winds of the Seas, and the silences of hell be disposed; my name, my divinity is adored throughout all the world in divers manners, in variable customs and in many names, for the Phrygians call me the mother of the Gods; the Athenians, Minerva; the Cyprians, Venus; the Candians, Diana; the Sicilians, Proserpina; the Eleusians, Ceres; some Juno, other Bellona, other Hecate; and principally the Ethiopians which dwell in the Orient, and the Egyptians which are excellent in all kind of ancient doctrine, and by their proper ceremonies accustom to worship me, do call me Queen Isis.[5]

Isis, Osiris, Horus form the most perfect trinity; this symbolism brings us back to the meaning of the three pillars, Wisdom, Strength, and Beauty, which, through the interpretation of the sefirot of the Kabbalah, definitively represent the divine manifestation. In Celtic symbolism, the yew is compared to Wisdom, the oak to Strength, and the birch to Beauty. I leave it to the reader to explore this point more thoroughly, for here we again discover the "three rays" or the "three cries" of the Celtic creators.

Isis was known in Gaul;[6] a statuette of her sat at Saint-Germain-des-Prés.[7] Cardinal Briçonnet had it destroyed in 1514.[8] According to Witkowski (*L'Art profane à l'Église*) a statuette of Isis was also enthroned at Saint-Étienne Cathedral in Metz. This approximately eighteen-inch statue was a bust of a naked woman: her skin was red and the drapery surrounding her waist was black. A similar statue is also said to have existed at Saint Étienne in Lyon.

This may be where we should search for the idea of the curious unpublished novella by Jean Giono: *Entrée de la vièrge noire* (Entrance of the black virgin). A plowman turning over his field discovered the statue of a naked goddess, a pagan deity symbolizing physical desire. According to Christian-Michel Felder (N.R.F., 1938), this work is akin to *Lyrisme cosmique,* which is Earth, the Universal Mother. Giono often found inspiration in cosmic life, and this song of the world and Dionysian experience led to *Serpent d'Étoiles* (Serpent of the Stars). We should not forget that Manosque* owns what may be the doyenne of our black virgins, Notre-Dame du Romigier, found in a blackberry patch in the sixth century, then discovered again buried in the ninth century (a sitting virgin about 24 inches tall).

Until 1610, the church of Pennes (Bouches-du-Rhone) kept a bas-relief depicting Cybele. It so happens that Cybele, according to Fulcanelli (page 53), was worshipped in the form of a black stone that had fallen from the sky. Semele, a mortal virgin who was the daughter of Cadmus, king of Thebes, and spouse of the god Zeus, was also black. The placement of the black virgins often coincides with places where the Holy Grail was sought, or with the land of the Cathars, or with the major monastic schools (Orleans, Ferrières, Chartres, Montpellier). Egyptian statues have been discovered in Clermont-Ferrand, and in Nuits in the Côte-d'Or region.

Initially hostile to any conversion of pagan images, the Catholic Church later began pursuing a policy of tolerance. The Church did recognize, though, that the adoration of the Black Madonna came from the ancient worship of Isis. But before the blessing and Christianizing of the pagan sanctuaries, how many of these statues were burned? Just as the menhirs were torn from the ground, pagan statues were stoned. What we have at present are a few survivors that have been Christianized. Christianity had to accept the ancient cult, and in 431 the Council of Ephesus decided that Mary was the Mother of God.

This eternal and supreme Mary, the goddess of all eternity, is part of the Uncreated Realm. The Christian Virgin was not able to wrest her supremacy from her entirely.

---

*[Giono's home was in Manosque. —*Trans.*]

Isis probably took the place of an unknown virgin; the Black Madonna and Mary were installed in the same places. Notre-Dame de l'Épine (Our Lady of the Thorn)—a strange building in Champagne—possesses a Virgin of the Bush. This majestic basilica near Châlons-sur-Marne dominates the Champagne plain. A well exists on this hillock, but the virgin is not an exact copy of the earlier one. According to ancient documents, her robe flares out over her feet, and I remain convinced that the pilgrimage of earlier times came to pay homage to a black virgin. This is a good example of how Catholic worship developed its ritual out of pagan beliefs they could not eradicate.[9] The incarnation could only take place in the womb of a virgin; virginity is a sacred and sublime state. Joan of Arc had a divine mission, as her virginity could be proven. Maternal virginity appears clearly in India, Mexico, and Africa. The young girl is impregnated by the breath of God, and the children are the sons of the sun. The devil also knows how to seduce virgins. This is how Merlin and Robert the Devil were born.[10] In order for the child to possess all qualities, the mother must be doubly sanctified, which is to say that she, too, must be born of a mother without stain. The theme of an immaculate conception can be found in Maya and Addha-Nari (India), Isis (Egypt), Myriam Astaroth (Hebrews), and Mary (Christians), and this is how Krishna, Jesus, and Horus were born.[11]

The black virgin appears to come out of Celtic tradition. The venerated stone cannot be cut; the wooden statuettes have only come down to us in scant number. Because we hardly know anything about this civilization, historians have stated that there is no Celtic art. Camille Jillian has spoken of the "clumsy-handed" Gauls;[12] Ferdinand Lot judges them to be "barbarian philosophers, but philosophers all the same," and he summed up his opinion about their art in fourteen lines.[13] It was not until April 1955, on the occasion of the extraordinary exhibition of Gallic art at the Pedagogical Museum in Paris that people found themselves surprised by the power of this highly stylized art that is only interested in the essential, the line, and possesses all the power of magic art. Our childhood was still cradled in Roman civilization, by "the miracle of Greek art," which in reality led to a dead end. What Celtic art that has come down to us displays an amazing artistic sentiment: an art of synthesis that could only belong to a lineage of artists who transgress the "finite" in order to evoke the primordial. I am also thinking of the extraordinary discovery at Vix and at the museum in Châtillon-sur-Seine that contains so many important pieces. Along with this mandatory visit it is also necessary to see the treasure at Carnac Museum and that housed in the museum of Saint-Germain-en-Laye. All of this art represents the feminine and the godhead.

The virgin is of all eternity. She existed before the creation of the earth;[14] she is elementary matter and the rootless root that is envisioned in its nonmanifested aspect and in its manifested aspect. This higher form of the feminine was also included in the androgynous Adam. In the Mosaic text it is said that God created the first Adam with the projection of his own substance and gave him life with his contact, and that later the Eternal One took Adam's volitive sensibility to make from it his companion. This is how the two poles—positive and negative—were separated by the will of God. This echoes the works of Saint-Yves d'Alveydre, Fabre d'Olivet, and Guaita.

She was called the Mother because she is the crystallization of a millennial hope.[15] She is the passive substance, and God, the vital Spirit, impregnates her in the Universal Action. In the Tantric form of the Hindu doctrine, Purusha and Prakriti are two poles of the manifesting activity, the substance and the essence, the creative duality. Prakriti is the principal substance, the undifferentiated substance. For the Kabbalists, she is the supreme mother, and for the Gnostics "Our Lady of the Holy Spirit." Shakti is awareness of being, a consciousness that is both dynamic and static. She is the manifestation of all that is manifested, the realized substance. She is Maya, the Great Mother, the Divine Mother. Here we find Astarte, Isis, Ishtar, the Asian Kwan Yin, and the Virgin Mary. The Black Virgin is the negative and female aspect of Brahma. God, the uncreated active spirit can only exercise his power on something passive: this creation therefore becomes as pure as God but foreign to his substance while emanating from him. The

Virgin, the Mother is the spouse of God, but she is still the substance of the universality of things. While she is passive before the uncreated Being, she is active for us, and it is in this sense that we pray to her in her sanctuary.

Analogously, Adam is formed from the Earth, and Aïscha or Eve pulled from the man's very substance remains in an inferior state. The generator of all things, this virginal and fecundating element produces the cohesion and determines all the evolutionary phases of substances. The virgin makes fruitful the seeds in the womb of the earth; she presides over the germinations, and the cosmic mysteries develop in her womb. We come to the notion of the superior Mother reigning over the depths.

The black virgin has the color of the beginning of the Great Work, and "all the black virgins analogically teach this truth that beneath the ground is hidden 'the mineral light' at the deepest depths of the vile and despised, but not despicable body, *nigra sum, sed formosa*."[16] In this way these virgins are bearing the light of the world, and their bellies glow with a resplendent sun (especially in Spain). This earth made fertile by the inner fire becomes the Immaculate Conception. The miraculous birth follows the nonmanifested desire and the universal passivity.[17] A world is born from this union, which is itself living matter. In the *Zohar* (3.50b), it is said that the Matrona serves as an intermediary for the world above to communicate with the world below (and reciprocally). She is the perfect mediator between heaven and earth. Born from this cosmic order, in the divine manner, is the process and birth of Jesus, who, moreover, incarnates the world as the "word is made flesh." This is again an instance of the law of mutation and analogy. We are in the presence of the intelligence principle, the universal intelligence, consciousness in the pure state. "The Virgo of the zodiac is the sign of spiritual redemption," writes Wirth.[18]

Osiris and Krishna are black gods, as this is the color attributed to the spouses of universal life: Ishvara in India is the mate of Prakriti, El Elion in Syria is the spouse of Tonah, and Iod in Israel is the spouse of Hevah. Zeus also appears as a black god. The creation of a negative aspect, the symbol of impurity, can appear quite simplistic. However, it is said that the raven was once as white as snow and was turned black by Apollo's curse because he had told of Coronis's infidelity. All colors are involved in the composition of pure light. Black symbolizes the primordial matter, the element of Earth. "Matter is not innately evil; it is merely the last degree of life that emanates from God."[19] Manichaeism established the equivalence between matter and the darkness that reigns in the secrecy of the cavern, but it seems difficult to subscribe to the malefic aspect of a universe created by divine thought; it is surely better to accept that all contributes to achieving Unity. Nor can I subscribe to the observation made by Huysmans in his book *La Cathédrale:* "Black, the hue of error and nothingness, the signature of death." Nor can I accept Victor Hugo's sentiment: "Evil is the material. Black tree, deadly fruit."[20] It is necessary to stop making a distinction between the mirror and the object: we must understand that all is connected and inseparable, that everything goes into the formation of Unity, and we are thus aware that nothing can be negative because we have sublimated the evil forces. But we can only attain this whole consciousness after we have rejoined the Supreme Center.

On the human plane black can represent evil, but alchemy shows us the effort of matter's ascension toward light and redemption. This is what India teaches us, where the yogi who has achieved the final liberation is clad in black. What should we think of the black Christ carved from oak in the cathedral of Saint-Flour? The black Christ of Lucca was the subject of intense worship during the fifteenth century and with the Christ of Wurzburg can be considered as the husbands of universal life. Blackness, with the cosmogonic Trimurti, represents the primordial earthen matter. This stage precedes regeneration; in China, as the emblem of sovereignty, it especially represents the color of deliverance and the ending of a cycle. Subsequently it became the color of negation and sorrow; it no longer symbolizes anything but pain and the loss of a loved one. When it is considered as an emblem of mourning, its true meaning is occulted. Queens throughout the Middle Ages wore white when mourning as the principle of conservation. But Anne of Brittany dressed in black at the death of Charles VIII.

The sacrifice of black animals—and primarily dogs, the guardians of underworld dwellings—was mentioned frequently in the *Iliad* and the *Odyssey*. This served to pacify the god that ruled over the empire of the dead. The black ram that has had its throat slit subsequently plays a part in a series of malefic activities, such as the Sabbath with its black mass and retinue of witches under the dominion of the Great Black Goat. However, according to Plutarch, Osiris is a black god, Isis dressed in black, and the priests covered the golden bullock with a linen slipcover dyed black. The bull of Heliopolis, Mnevis, sacred to Osiris, was black. According to Herodotus, the Egyptian priests would accept no victim for immolation on their altars whose bodies had any black hairs. Their inspection was quite meticulous. In the Rig Veda, the horses of the sun are black,[21] and the Vedic priests stand near the hearth of Agni with a black horn in their hand. In China, this color represents the feminine principle.[22] The Zhōulǐ considered it to be the emblem of sincerity; the emblem of Chinese sovereignty would be a piece of wood or a stone that was often black. In his human form the Mexican god Tezcatlipoca is represented by a body consisting of a black stone. According to the Ramirez Codex the priests on the god's feast day blackened their faces, and their costumes were similar to those of the idol.

I could cite quite a few more examples, but the symbolism of the color black always targets the underworld deity. Black can represent the color of deliverance, the culmination of a cycle with a deceptive appearance, but we are touching on another mystery here.

So we should not be opposing white to black and good to evil but concentrating more squarely on the chthonic worship of the fire petrified within the rock. This worship is that of the black virgin in the Rosicrucian Hermeticism that says it is necessary to descend into the earth to find regeneration. Earlier I noted[23] this commentary by Fulcanelli in which "Mary, of the lineage of Jesse," means that she comes from the race of sun and fire. But she is also the root, which is to say, the principle and the beginning of everything. This allows us to grasp Fulcanelli's assertion that the black virgin "represents the matter on which the alchemist must work." It is the "Hermetic symbol of the *virgin earth,* which the artist must choose as the *subject* of his Great Work. It is first matter in mineral state, as it comes out of the ore-bearing strata, deeply buried under the rocky mass" (*Mystère des Cathédrales,* 58). Perhaps black is sacred to the gods because "these benevolent deities go down into the kingdom of darkness to bring to them those men that are regenerating."[24] Black therefore indicates the stage that precedes regeneration.

The Saintes-Maries-de-la-Mer, at the uttermost tip of a bewitching place that is the only one where the *sansouire** exists, does not possess a Black Madonna, but a mysterious servant of the Marys called Black Sarah. Sarah appears to me to be quite close to the black Shulammite who is also primordial matter. The fortified church at sea level contains a crypt that, according to Mistral, is "the mecca of the entire Gulf of Lion." A miraculous freshwater spring appears in this salty lagoon. Mary Salome, Mary Jacob, Mary Magdelene, and Lazarus set off on a vessel without sails or oars and landed on this desert shore.[25] Excavations were ordered by King René in 1448 that unearthed some bones. One must attend the pilgrimage of May 25—as well as the one of October 22—to get a sense of the medieval atmosphere, which combines a perfect display of devotion with strains of the amusement park and the charity bazaar. During these three days the Gypsies remain in the crypt continuously; some even eat there. The priest has trouble maintaining order in his church, but the "Holy Sarah, pray for us" echoes there with extraordinary power. The guardians, mounted on their small white horses, enter the sea surrounding the holy relics. If I am stressing this point, it is because I think this ceremony must be seen as the survival of an extremely important early rite. Isis was also paraded about on a vessel. Furthermore, the immaculate Virgin, the mediator between the Father and the Man, wears the blue color of the wave. She is called Marie Stella, the Star of the Seas.

---

*[The salted and flat lands typical of the Camargue region. —*Trans.*]

It is written in Genesis that the Spirit rested over the womb of the waters; this is where we find the similarity between the Virgin and the Waters, as in each case the Holy Spirit presides over the supreme act by resting over the immaculate creature, the Virgin or the Waters. The primordial Waters, vehicles for the thought of God, remain pure and incorruptible. Christ, the fish, resides in the womb of his mother, and Notre-Dame de la Délivrance, near Bayeux, was known in the sixteenth century as being "of *yvrande,*" which in Celtic means "the water border." The worship of the Saintes-Maries-de-la-Mer confirms for us that we are in the presence of a goddess of the fruitful earth,[26] but contrary to the other regions the worship of the Virgin could not be established: the Gypsies claimed Sarah. This remote town at the edge of an abandoned plain where there long ago was no farming perhaps did not permit the Catholic Church to prevail over the customs of the many Gypsies lingering in the region, primarily in Tarascon, which possesses an odd Virgin installed near Saint-Étienne-de-Grès (Château-Moulin). She only resides in Tarascon for forty days, a very symbolic number: this Virgin then wears forty dresses.

Faithful to their tradition of entire tribes coming to worship this pagan idol each year, they drink at the miraculous well where outside of all Christian control these Gypsies perform ancestral rites. Guénon, in an article entitled "Le Compagnonnage et les Bohémiens" (*Le Voile d'Isis,* October 1928) explicitly states that the Eastern Gypsies or Zingaris do not take part in this pilgrimage. The election of their queen also takes place in this crypt. The Gypsies claim that the Sarah dwelt in this city before Christianity, and we can therefore connect the Black Virgin to a very ancient form of worship.[27]

Marseille no longer possesses more than one Black Madonna in the crypt of Saint Victor's church. The people call it the Bouéno Mèro Négro, but its name is "Notre-Dame de Confession." There were once three Black Madonnas in Marseille, one of which was located in the Heveaune Chapel that was demolished in 1850. The other was in the Notre-Dame de la Garde chapel.[28] Saint Victor's is at the end of rue Sainte. Let's take a more detailed look at this beautiful ancient statue, which is full of nobility. It is hollow and carved from walnut and stands 28 inches tall. The seated virgin is holding her child on her left knee. In her right hand she is holding a scepter and is wearing a three-flowered crown on her head. Beneath her azure mantle she is wearing a green dress. Jesus is clad in green; their faces, feet, and hands are black. The excavations investigating this strange crypt have not yet been completed; initially this cave overlooked the old port. A well, which is now filled in, sits close by. It should be noted that green wax candles burn around the Black Madonna. On the day of Candlemas, February 2, the subterranean image is solemnly displayed. Pilgrims carrying green candles escort the black queen in her green garments. "Bavettes," small breads baked in the shape of the saints' boat, are sold at the exit. This parade still takes place today. The same devotion is given to the Black Madonna of Murat, Notre-Dame des Oliviers, whose lamp is only fueled with olive oil. On her feast day—Candlemas—she is clad in green and carried by butchers. The children dedicated to her wear green, and her canons wear a camail with green trim. This church has no miraculous spring or crypt, but the formerly prosperous hamlet of Bredons with its oppidum and vast cavern once owned a virgin, all trace of which has been lost. It is possible to imagine the transfer of that statue from Bredons to Murat. The abbey of Jumièges celebrates the Festival of the Green Wolf—June 24—with a procession that also uses green candles.[29] But the festival of Candlemas, the major Celtic festival, was celebrated like the festival of Saint John and, in the Armenian Church, featured the renewal of fire. The faithful lit their candles from the candles of the church in order to exorcise the air and brought them back home to protect their houses from thunder, storm, and tempest.[30] The flame therefore represents solar virtue and is beneficial. For Papus it was living matter, and this is why one must not stop this life by blowing on it. The flame must be smothered by depriving it of oxygen; breath generates the life of fire.

We can wonder about the meaning of this new color that has appeared here: green. Isis was sometimes called the green goddess, and Cybele wore a green cloak. As a gateway to the East, Marseille was able to preserve an Oriental tradition quite easily. Let's hunt more carefully for the symbolic meaning of this consecration.[31] Green is often considered to be the color of creation because, according to Revelation (4:3), the Eternal One appears at the center of a green rainbow, just as Vishnu reveals his presence in the third sphere.[32] The Spirit of God therefore enters the central zone of the earthly Trimurti, whose sacred nature was symbolically represented by green. This is how green became sacred to the deities that represent the union of good and evil—like Janus, Saint John the Evangelist reflects the light of the Logos; it is therefore a reflected ray. Osiris assumed a dark appearance in the underworld to judge souls, but when he welcomed the adept and presided over rebirths, he was green. Isis and the marine gods assumed the same color choices. According to the *Book of the Dead,* a large green jasper scarab and a similarly colored stone had to be placed inside the sarcophagus holding the mummy.[33] The Peruvian god Pachacamac was green, and the Incas revered emeralds. Victor-Émile Michelet saw this Venusian color as that of ardent vitality.[34] The same notion can be found in the work of Jacques Duchaussoy, for whom green was a light bearer between the names Christos and Chlorus (green).[35] From this it is easy to see why only candles of green wax were burned in front of the Mother of Christ.

It so happens that four colors are each assigned to the four elements: fire is red, air azure, water green, and the earth is black. Frederic Portal [Des coleurs symboliques] (page 122) believed that the symbols of initiation at the first grade were the colors black and green: "Black is reminiscent of the primordial waters or chaos, just as green depicts creation." However, we should not overlook what Dom Pernety had to teach in the preface to his *Mytho-Hermetic Dictionary* of 1787: Our water takes the name of the leaves of all trees, and of the trees themselves, and of all that is green in color, in order to deceive the foolish.

Rama, in the first stage of regeneration, appears green when he fights the giants. According to Pausanias, the Greeks worshipped two Venuses, one was celestial—green—and the other one was earthly—black. The green Venus was born from the womb of the primal waters, and this color is also sacred to Poseidon and to the Norse goddess Freya. This symbol of regeneration and springtime was used to represent the cross that thereby became the symbol of hope and charity. Green was much used by the Arabs: the Koran regards it as the color of initiation, and white and green are still the colors of Islam. Green, white, and red are the national colors of Italy, but they are also the three colors of Beatrice. They can still be found in the Compagnonnage (carpenters' guild) and in the high grades of Freemasonry. For these reasons, emeralds possess miraculous healing properties and the virtue of hope.

Muhammad adopted this green of sanctity and wore a green robe. According to the Koran (18:29–30) the true servant of Allah would be adorned in Paradise with gold bracelets and clad in green. The ovate, a member of the second degree of Druidism, wears a green robe just like Elijah. One of the four central sefirot of the middle pillar is green: the supreme principle, Kether, is represented by black; Tiferet, the intelligible cause, is white; Yesod, eternal activity, is red; but Malkuth, cosmic receptivity, appears in yellow when spreading light and in green when manifesting as an eternal, creative substance. We know that these metaphysical numbers—sefirot or enumerations of the divine aspects—provide one of the keys to the Kabbalah. Based on the results of the experiments of Laville and Croanda, Louis-Claude Vincent concluded that life was triggered in water and its first form was that of green algae.[36] Gustav Meyrink wrote a strange initiatory novel, *The Green Face,* in which, after being split into two, the chosen one attained eternal life. Goethe gave us *The Green Snake,* because the universal spirit manifests in that color: it is "the Signature of the World Spirit in the three kingdoms of nature." We should also note the childless green emperor in fairy tales who lives at the other end of the world, where he successively welcomes his three nephews. Saintyves cites a German tale from the principality of Naldeck in which a man chases a green hare that leads him into the lower world where a giant's castle is located.[37] We should also connect all the many legends featuring green birds to this story. Old Catholic liturgy gave a much greater place to the color green. Its use of that color is now much more restrained.[38] The immortals of the Académie Française dress in a deep green. In the profane world, slang is called "the green language." Crude expressions are used by individuals initiated into the same concerns when they need to communicate their thoughts without those around them understanding. All of these green rays serve as a veil over the "vitriol of the philosophers." Claude d'Ygé has recorded countless notes on this coloration,[39] of which the Green Lion inspires Khunrath's enthusiasm in his *Amphitheatrum* (third level, CLIV; sixth level, CCXIV).

With alchemy, we should not overlook the fact that the volatile blood of the *green lion* fixes the blood of the *red lion*. The Cosmopolite states that in the work "there is this single green lion that opens and closes the seven indissoluble seals of the seven metallic spirits, and who torments the bodies until they have been fully perfected by means of the firm and long patience of the artist."[40] This is the Vitriol of Basil Valentine. In the third figure of the *Golden Fleece,* the philosopher is dressed in red beneath a purple mantle and is wearing a green cap. He is holding up a flask that contains a green liquid. Jean Reyor also had questions about the color green.[41] He made the comparison between the emerald that corresponds to Saint John and the stone of the Holy Grail, the translucent substance that fell from Lucifer's brow. He also gave thought to the Emerald Tablet that provides the text of the wise and the credo of the alchemists[42] and quotes Nicolas Flamel: "Adorn the chest and shoulders of the goddess of Paphos: this will make her quite beautiful and she will leave the color green to take on a golden hue." But Jean Reyor would have done well to mention those rare stones—like the callaïs—green stones that are quite similar to turquoise, which have been found beneath the dolmens of Brittany. Pendants of the same nature have been found in Brittany, the South of France, and Portugal. It so happens that this stone could only have been mined in the Caucasus. This is yet another indication that the relationships between the peoples of this time were quite extensive. We should not forget the oft-mentioned famous tin road. But this green stone must possess some very singular qualities to have been carried all this way from such a remote land. A strange legend that comes from the Incan empire allows us to connect the legend of Parsifal to that of Atwalpa.

In 1845, a certain Gaetano Osculati, a Neapolitan adventurer, set off in search of these fabled cities alleged to house the treasures of kings. On October 1, 1847, a police expedition under the command of a Lieutenant Ximenes found five corpses. On top of one of them was Osculati's account inside an old rum bottle.[43] In Cajamarca, Osculati says he was brought into the presence of a reliquary housed in a crypt. This reliquary held the "green goddess," which he managed to steal. This is how Gaetano Osculati's journal ends:

> I will pass on to whoever passes by the secret of the green goddess, this secret that cost me my life. . . . Here it is, taken from my cartridge pouch and radiating in the sun of all its facets. Here is this fabulous goblet hollowed out of a single emerald that thanks to which the supreme Inca captured the power of the stars. It is the largest emerald in the world. It takes both my open hands to hold it. It is cut in the form of a pentagonal bowl. It is sacred and it is magical. It made it possible to move mountains, but it could not save the life of the foreigner who stole it. . . . I am alone, my eyes are clouding over. I shall soon no longer have the strength to write. The key word, the magic word, is *umina*.

This green virgin that lived in a crypt and was worshipped in the form of a goblet carved in an emerald casts a new bridge between Europe and America. But their god Kon Tiki had already come to them from the east accompanied by powerful red-haired white men.

"Green" still characterizes the greatly coveted isle, the residence of the solar god, the Supreme Center. This green isle is often identified as Vardhi, "the aspect of Vishnu's Shakti" (and more specifically in connection with his third avatar).[44] The "green Erin" is used to define Ireland because its hero, Brenos [Brian], son of the supreme god Dagda, wore a green cloak. Fairies and nymphs wearing green robes appear there quite often. The pre-Columbian Mexicans worshipped the god Tezcatlipoca in the form of a black obsidian statue whose navel was formed from a green stone.[45] As it happens, in the theory of the chakras a green ray floods the abdomen. It is concentrated on the solar plexus, associated with emotional feelings. The ten rays of the umbilical chakra alternate between red and green, with a preponderance of green rays, which thereby revitalizes the liver, kidneys, and intestines, and the entire digestive tract. Through the association of ideas, this brings to mind on the one hand the mysteries of the first initiation and on the other this extraordinary solar ray.

During total eclipses of the sun, astronomers have noticed a light and a focal point of special light, a focal point placed outside the sun. This light, which distinguishes itself in the form of a nimbus or crown, has been called "coronal light." Spectral analysis of this light was performed by Huggins, who discovered an undefined green line. This is the line that is called 1474 on the Kirschoff charts. This extremely bright color is green. I wrote in *La Symbolique du feu* (The symbology of fire) (page 62) that the alchemists maintained, based on traditional sources, that the sun was a star with obscure rays. The Rig Veda and Saint Hildegard spoke of a black sun: they maintained that heat and light were caused by the shock of the vibrations against the gaseous molecules of the earth's atmosphere. After the initiatory theme of Osiris, it is necessary to read this extraordinary text of the genesis of the world contained in the Bharawabja.[46] Professor Picard wrote me on October 26, 1958, to let me know that the "sun is a hot body that radiates heat and light; that at 1 mile high we would even suffer from its heat; it is naturally the sky that, observed in the stratosphere, appears dark." Other scientists, to the contrary, believe that the cold of the stratosphere is not caused by the sun. Major David Simons ascended to 20 miles in August 1957; the sky became blacker and blacker, and the wave frequency increased; their wavelength diminished in accordance with Planck's law. Commander Carpentier reached 13 miles on July 17, 1958, and the shadows were deep black. On April 22, 1958, Audoin Dollfus observed that at 8 miles high, the temperature was minus 600°.

But "if the sun was a ball casting light on interplanetary space, we should be able to glimpse the illumination of space behind the limit of the cone of shadow, which was a maximum seven thousand kilometers [4,350 miles] at midnight: when all space was black."[47] This engineer also noted that "examination of the solar photosphere revealed that its immediate borders, in space, were deep black," whereas this spot should have been, conversely, dazzling bright. For J. P. Boucher,[48] a dark sun is factually possible but currently unverifiable, as all our observations through the atmosphere use instruments that are based on light. After numerous experiments and observation, Louis-Claude Vincent, in collaboration with Dr. Jeanne Rousseau, concluded that the light on earth comes from the electromagnetic illumination of the solar ionosphere. The sun was therefore a cold and frozen astral body; the true sun emitted no more heat than it did light but sent out electromagnetic waves. We are therefore seeing here a phenomenon of ionization, and all takes place as if it were in a neon tube because "the sun moves in a spiral around equipotential electrical circuit of the galaxy, which is perpendicular to the magnetic axis." The real, black sun, located at 93,000,000 miles in a place of absolute cold, emits electromagnetic rays at a very high frequency that would cause on the tip of the solar ionosphere a luminous image situated around 500,000 miles away; the energy would be maintained by the equipotential currents of the galaxy around which the sun moved in a spiral. This light would break down into heat (reduction of the frequency) at the moment of the rays' impact with the earth. This is how, according to Louis-Claude Vincent, we are only seeing an image of the sun through our atmosphere.

On the other hand, scientific knowledge informs us that the surface temperature of the sun is estimated at 6000° centigrade, that the atmospheric envelopes surrounding the sun have temperatures that climb toward the exterior and vary from 20,000°C in the chromosphere to more than 1,000,000°C in the corona. Scientists like H. Bethe and Carl von Weizsacker demonstrated in 1938 that the sun received its nuclear energy through a series of reactions—the carbon cycle—with a transformation of hydrogen into helium through the catalytic activity of carbon and nitrogen. It has been calculated that the sun consumes one hundred million tons of hydrogen every second and that it would take approximately 40 billion years for the sun to exhaust its stores. As it happens the sun has only been burning for around 3 billion years. From this standpoint, the energy emitted by the sun would be due to the incessant transformation of chemical elements and not to a phenomenon of ionization and waves.

I have no desire to take a position in this debate of two opposing theories but only wish to point out a traditional aspect that is connected to the formation of our world. It is very puzzling to find the same correspondence in ancient texts: Alchemy also speaks of the "black sun." "For the eyes of the Sages see nature in a different way from common eyes. As, for example, the eyes of the commoners see that the Sun is hot; the eyes of the Philosophers, to the contrary, see that the Sun is cold, but that its movements are hot."[49] So this is no longer some coincidence or gratuitous opinion but a disturbing fact. It is also possible that they were speaking about this second sun, an invisible astral body located at the second focus of the ellipse, opposed to the blazing sun we are familiar with. In traditional thought, when our current sun vanishes, the second will come to life and become luminous.

According to the laws of themodynamics, energy degradation, Planck's law, and Curie temperatures, it would appear that an infrared ray emitted by a heat source located millions of miles away and orbiting through the cold reaches of space would have to possess a much higher frequency for it to arrive at its destination hot (L.-C. Vincent).

Found behind this dark disk is a blazing white, translucent light, one ray of which is green. This can bring to mind the legend of Gwenwed, the "White Mountain," spoken of in Druid religion. It is truly curious to note that the hymn of the Isha Upanishad is akin to this vision of coronal light:

O Sun, everywhere present, Son of the Lord of Creation, command your rays to withdraw their light. Remove the Veil so that I may look upon His Face. His Face veiled by your gold disk. For the one that is there, that Being, is myself.

How could this not bring to mind Meyrink and his study of the initiatory splitting into two seen in *The Green Face?* But when we learn that astronomers have recorded that coronal light enraptures whoever gazes upon it, we immediately think of Galahad studying the mysterious emerald, and we sense the strange, ultrashort telluric wave that surrounds the Great Pyramid, which belongs to the sector of negative green.[50] This is the integral quality of light, the embodied light that is the Light of God. The Logos said: "I am the Light of the World," and this ray that shines in the middle of immense spaces was considered as the matter during the crafting of the Philosophers' Stone. Beatrice, according to Dante, wore a white veil and a green cloak, and her dress looked like a flame: these are the garments of light.

Extensive study of religions and the great laws of the universe show that ancient civilizations were quite advanced in their understanding of the formation of our world. We know next to nothing about the cosmic and telluric powers. Some readers might smile on hearing me talk about the black sun. They are welcome to stick to the prevailing official point of view, but I have no desire to write a scientific or technical book. I want to restrict myself to this field of symbol and inspire my readers to reflect on the ancient laws that may appear paradoxical, impious, and absurd. Yet haven't we also noticed the monumental errors that have managed to slip into the so-called positive theories over the course of each century? Nor were these scholars devoid of all good sense and sincerity. Through an intense spiritual elevation and revelation the great initiates were able to incorporate an almost divine understanding. While we should attempt to attain spiritual understanding and become better beings, there are still boundaries that are not permissible to cross: "A little light is illuminating, too much light is dazzling."

This correspondence between the light and the black gods clad in green needs to be pointed out, but we also need to remember that the Black Virgins represent a form of initiation. By their underground location near a spring and a grove surrounding a peak, they symbolize the higher underworld goddess, the Mother, from whom all forces and energies are born and to whom they all return. This is how the Black Virgin transports the light of the world; and the world made fruitful by inner fire becomes the Immaculate Conception. The miraculous birth follows upon the nonmanifested desire and universal passivity. The Black Virgins stand for the cavern, the telluric night from where all things are issued, because you must die to one life in order to be regenerated into another life, and as Apuleius cried out: "I neared the boundaries of death." This Virgin that gives birth illustrates the eternal feminine, the Mother Goddess who has assumed the names of Venus and Ceres, but especially that of the dark and maternal Isis. The latent force descends into the depths of inertia, into the primordial earth matter with the Plutonian power. Later, this sign of a higher baptism—black—became the color of mourning and carnal death. Already the spiritual symbol was being occulted and concealed. In this aspect of regeneration, green floods the third heavenly sphere, after red and blue. Green is the color of vegetation and creation. It is that strange green ray that is connected to spring water. Because it is coming from the star of life it irradiates the initiator. It is worth noting here this strange association of a black sun and its green ray located in the most transparent form of light. But like the dark gods, the Black Madonna, the agent of telluric and magical forces symbolized by the snake, governs the ultra secret temples and initiatory centers, because her power as a subterranean goddess commands Life.

13

The Telluric Reptile
and the Spiral

AS GUARDIAN OF THE EMPYREAN REALMS the serpent is coiled around the genitor stone in all the Mithraic representations. This reptile that embodies the active principle is essentially mobile; even coiled in sleep it is ever ready to strike. The snake therefore represents the soul of movement, and this preeminent telluric animal is the personification of Mother Earth. I am only planning to analyze it here as the mysterious force of the earth.

The snake appears in all religions but does not carry the same meaning in all of them. For the faithful of the Catholic Church it is the tempter who offered the forbidden fruit to Eve. For Oswald Wirth[1] this serpent represents astral light; it is "a beneficial guide as long as human malice does not disturb its primitive instinctiveness." We should in fact recall the bronze serpent conceived by Moses inspired by God in the book of Numbers (21:6–9), and in John (3:14–15) that only had to be gazed upon by anyone bitten by a snake for the person to live. L. Charbonneau Lassay[2] then compares the serpent of Moses with Christ on the cross, and Kipling writes that the bite of the old blind snake is not fatal (*The Jungle Book,* vol. 2). Jacques Duchaussoy in *Le Bestiaire divin*[3] demonstrated the inevitable problem of the dualism created by the opposition of the water snake to the fire snake. This sacred animal represents life, and the Greeks attributed healing powers to it.[4] The Ligurians, by comparing it to a stream, had a fertility rite in mind. Generally speaking, the ouroboros—the serpent that forms a circle swallowing its own tail—signifies the indestructability of life and the rebeginning of all things. The snake heals and ever restores.

In its positive aspect, the serpent can combine with the bird. We have an example of this with the Quetzelcoatl of ancient Mexican traditions, and Saint Matthew counseled people "Be ye therefore as wise as serpents, and harmless as doves" (10:16). In Mexican folklore the eagle battles the malefic snake. On the Pallene Peninsula—in Phlegra—the blood of the crippled Ouranos spurted from giants with serpent legs and reptile heads. This equivalency between snakes and giants can be seen again with the great Midgard serpent who is nothing other than the metamorphosis of the colossus Urcaguay: the Incan god of underground treasures who has the head of a stag and who wears small gold chains on its tail. Jean Doresse[5] reports that in the pharaonic legend *The Castaway's Tale,* a sailor is given welcome by a giant gold-ringed serpent. This kind monster saves the seafarer when the island sinks beneath the waves so that the living may not stumble upon it. It is therefore a paradisial island and, according to Doresse, the islands of Ethiopia—the Hanish Islands—mean the "Serpent Isles." The Egyptians designated Ethiopia as the land of NHS, which likely has a connection with snakes. Papus, in a similar spirit, sees in the name of Isis the dominion over the serpent (S) by the divine science. Saint Anne Catherine Emmerich describes[6] the chalice carried by the apostles. Inside there is a snake, a bunch of grapes, and a grain of wheat that should be placed between a yellow apple and a vine stalk. The Adamic earth created from this mud gives birth to the golem, the man that is given life by a kabbalistic spell (according to Gustav Meyrink).

The guardian serpent emerges from crevices in the ground to deliver the oracle of the Pythia, and in Olympia the voice of the goddess emerged from an abyss. Gaia, personification of the earth, presided over the most famous of oracles in Delphi, where her servitor assumed the shape of a snake. This spirit of invocation figures in the story of

Samuel.[7] Saul consulted a seer in order to question Samuel. This woman had a "python" spirit, and by using her as his intermediary Saul caused the spirit of Samuel "to rise toward him." The kingdom of the dead is therefore located beneath the earth. Many times the sacred text said: "You shall not suffer a witch to live,"[8] which implies that consulting the prophetic python was not acceptable.

The Great Serpent, the guardian and protector of the city, lived in the temple where the Athenians offered it honey cakes.[9] It guarded the tree of the Hesperides, and in the form of a cobra, this snake is also found at the foot of the Hindu Aśvattha. It is likely also the guardian of the tree of life, but the serpent Nidhogg gnaws at the roots of the Scandinavian ash Yggdrasil. We also have the dragon at the foot of the linden that Siegfried has to kill.

The "wife of the serpent" deserves a very extensive analysis, as we find this motif in the most ancient Mexican, Assyrian, and Babylonian monuments. Zeus transformed into a snake in order to seduce Pherephatte, and in the mystery that is illustrated by this rite, it was said that the bull was the father of the serpent and the serpent the father of the bull. Saintyves noted the variants relating to the worship of the snake god in Orphism. In reality, the fertilization of the serpent is akin to a rite of initiation and guarantees eternal life.[10]

The snake can rejuvenate itself by changing its skin. The onion shares this same kind of symbolism of renewal. According to Greek tradition, snakes love fennel, which has the wonderful power of restoring youth. This spirit of possessiveness and keeping fit also represents the keen desire for realization, and this takes us to the notion of Buddha when he describes the "Wheel of Life" on which a green snake is coiled. Faust also connected the serpent to the wheel of the world and turning away from the luminous void.

Goethe would reuse this image in his story *The Green Snake*. This animal swallowed gold stones that made it luminous. He revealed the fourth secret of the Old Man whose lantern spreads clarity in the midst of the darkness. This resplendent serpent allows souls to cross from one bank to the other, and when it makes a gift of its life, its body transforms into sparkling gems that become a bridge. It so happens that in Celtic esotericism, the serpent along with the rainbow stands in for that over-turned goblet and that boat that with the Trimurti could be used as a vibrant, aerial path for going from one bank to the next. The gods make use of this bridge, which was one of the themes Meyrink used in his book *The Green Face*.[11] But in order to be able "to swim to the other side" and become a member of that eastern community of the Paradā, it is neces-sary to have a traveling companion, which brings us back to the notion of the androgynous individual. I should also note that a legend in Sologne indicates that all the snakes of the land gather together each year to pro-duce an enormous diamond that reflects the colors of the rainbow.[12] This same symbolism can be found in both Celtic and Hindu thought.

But the serpent that emerges from the earth, and creeps and twists like a dancing, swirling flame, symbolizes the vital fire enclosed in mat-ter. The serpent represents the blood sealed within the earth fertilized by the crippled Ouranos: here the broken god or king returns to the earth for the purpose of fertility. This is a sacrificial process in which a human being gives the generating fire back to nature. According to Boehme, this astringency is desire, the root of all condensation, the salt of the alchemists and the "fire of nature." Fire is found in a latent state inside the stone and gives it its consistency. This fire with its spiraling shape is within the human being. This fire of Hecate, of the shadowy life, animates the blood. We have the "serpent of fire." There are certain energy centers in our body that bear the Sanskrit name of chakram or chakra, the word meaning "wheel" or "rotating disk." These centers of etheric matter are in a state of rapid rotation. C. W. Leadbeater writes that "the serpent of fire called *kundalini* in Sanskrit is the manifesta-tion on the physical plane of one of the greatest universal forces, one of the powers of the logos. This force would be similar to a liquid fire when it leaps through the body, and the course it has to follow is similar to the rings of the serpent."[13]

This is why Kundalini, the dozing and latent cosmic power and divine energy in the *muladhara* chakra, and which the yogi can awaken, is depicted in the form of a snake: it is "the preeminent sacred animal of all the traditions, and which, according to the Christian Scriptures, predicted Christ when Moses raised the cross topped by a serpent to heal the tribes that he was guiding through the desert. The symbolism is universal. All of Asia as well as the ancient Egyptians represented divine energy in the form of a snake."[14] Concerning this, Marques-Rivière cites a very curious text of the *Yoga Vasishta* (6.80.36 and *ff.*) that describes this Kundalini:

> The center in which rests the goddess has a circular form like a vortex or a whirlpool, or as half of the syllable OM. This center is present in the body of all creatures, gods, demons, animals, fish, birds, insects, and so forth. The Goddess rests in a form that resembles a coiled serpent, put to sleep by the cold. Kundalini twitches gently and continuously and is extremely delicate, like "the flesh of the plantain." Kundalini is the greatest and ultimate Power that organizes the life of all living creatures. Like a furious cobra, it pulsates continuously with a hissing sound. Its mouth is opened from above.

Prana is the vital link between the coarse body and the subtle bodies. Prana animates the linga sharira [etheric double], which corresponds to the "astral snake of kabbalistic tradition." Prana can give the kiss of life: the teacher electrically recharges the body of the adept. We should take from this that Kundalini is a force in an embryonic state.

Leadbeater and Marques-Rivière have provided an outline of the nadis—a tubal network belonging to the subtle body—based on the centers of force in the individual. Leadbeater maintains that seven of these principle centers exist, while Marques-Rivière claims there are only six. I have reproduced the circulation of the chakras (see fig. 13.1) in the human body from Marques-Rivière who writes (page 39):

> It is incontestable, for example, that the caduceus erected in the place of the sex organ on the Baphomet-like idols and the Sabbath goats is a debased representation of a highly devalued initiatory knowledge of the Kundalini force.

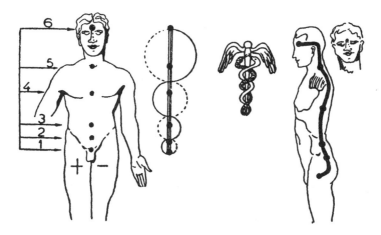

Fig. 13.1. Course of the nadis, after Marques-Rivière, Le Yoga tantrique
(Paris: Éditions Vega, 1938).

In India the course of the nadis in accordance with the plan of
the spinal column is called the Brahmadanda or Brahma's staff. For
Leadbeater (page 33), the activity of these circulatory forces is obtained
by the three stages of initiation "sought by Freemasonry at the moment
when the Elder creates, receives, and constitutes." But this "staff of
Brahma" brings to mind the vertical axis, the world axis that we see
also in the caduceus around which the two helical lines coil in opposite
directions. The caduceus can also lead us to the Stone composed of two
substances, one wet and the other dry, one volatile and the other fixed.
This projection of subtle currents implies the presence of two contrary
and complementary principles, the dual action of the single force, of
the androgyne. This cosmic force, with its two directions of reversed
rotation, comes into play in the symbols of the yin and yang and the
swastika.

As Élie Lebasquais[15] writes, the two colors of yin and yang in the
end only figure as a unity, as in the way that inhalation and exhalation permit life. This Taoist esotericism that figures in the I Ching or
Book of Changes thereby contains the male and female principles. By
combining them three by three, they obtain the eight magical trigrams
or Bagua (Pa Kua), the essential principles of the universe. We should

forcefully stand up against this notion in which all life would be divided between good and evil. The full day consists of both day and night, two variants that are equally necessary. Manichaeism did not make a radical division of good and evil, but it noted them as two aspects with the same purpose. The myth of the Dioscuri again shows us that nothing can be separated. The helix of yin and yang (fig. 13.2), the swastika (fig. 13.3), and the double spiral (fig. 13.4) are closely connected.

They show the nondiscontinuous movement of the "multiple states of universal existence," the two principles of male and female, and they are clearly the representation of the androgyne with his two parts differentiated but not separated. Similarly one of Janus's two faces is turned toward the past while the other looks into the future. Guénon[16] defined this set of cycles of universal manifestation in which the ouroboros represents "the indefinite quality of a cycle." The serpent can coil around

Fig. 13.2. The I Ching
(with depiction of the yin-yang symbol)

Fig. 13.3. The swastika   *Fig. 13.4. Double spiral*

the tree—of the world or of knowledge—and around the polar mountain. It can head toward either higher states or lower states—these two beneficial and malefic aspects will eventually resolve into a single state. Eugene Baillon sees the letter *I* of the angel's alphabet in the double spiral, and its number is ten, which is the sign of manifestation.

All of these circles of individual destiny have a center, and according to René Guénon, it is in this point that all oppositions are reconciled and resolved. The synthesis of all the contrary terms is established there, and their center is "the fullness of activity, since it is that of the principle from which all the individual activities are derived."[17] The spiral representation of an undulating movement depicts a very strange outline, as at the reverse end of the circle the center is connected to the circumference by an unbroken line. In the drawing we can perceive two complementary movements, one going from the circumference to the center, the other from the center to the circumference. This is the dual movement of the heart that gives breath its rhythm. We manage to grasp why in the initiatory quest, in the passageway of the labyrinth, the man must go from the outside to the inside, then retrace his steps on the same path. Man can be merged into a spoke of the cosmic wheel: the center is identified as heaven and the circumference as the earth. The pole—the world axis—stands at the center, and this canopy and floor makes us think of the cosmic chariot of Hindu tradition. Yves Millet sought out comparisons between this spiral and the forms of nature,[18] and he established some ingenuous relationships between the spiral of the snail and acoustical problems. The snail has a shell that takes the form of a musical spiral, whose radius grows following a geometrical—and not arithmetical—progression so that when we vary the polar angle, we find the geometrical progression $p = {}^n 0$. Maybe we can now grasp why Venus was born in a conch shell, a deep cavity, vessel, or receptacle whose shape is that of the spiral helix, and also why the ancients used the buccina. But here we are touching on the rhythm and unfolding of the cycles inasmuch as we are finding the primordial sound. We shall again return to the symbolism of the bowl and the cave.

G. Beltikhine, in an article titled *L'Horloge cosmique des Templiers*

(The Cosmic Clock of the Templars),[19] sees in the four-centered spiral the four ages of the ancients in the relationship of the arithmetical progression of 1, 2, 3, 4, known under the name of the tetrad: added together they create the 10 of the divine Tetraktys. By taking two diametrically opposing spirals coming from a common center, Beltikhine produced the drawing of the Tai Chi (fig. 13.5), the concept of balance and fullness. This construction reveals that "beneath the appearance of two principles reunited in the formation of a third, four elements are hidden—the four simple opposing spirals out of a common center— whose tangible nature always remains concealed by the manifestation of the principles it supports."

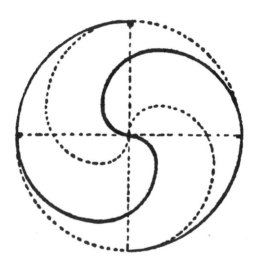

Fig. 13.5 The Tai Chi

This is how all these representations of an undulating movement whose image is stationary have been symbolized by the crawling movement of a snake, which can also stand for the seismic movement. This pulsing—which gives birth to the logarithmic spiral—is connected to the Egyptian Kneph. According to this tradition, the serpent that inhabits the waters produces eggs through its mouth. "The serpent as well as the system of concentric circles, is at bottom the emblem of the same ideas as the Philosophical Egg, symbol of the universe and symbol of alchemy."[20] This water-dwelling snake brings to mind C. Laville's theory according to which life forms in water when molecular hydrogen, carbon dioxide, and nitrogen are present. Under the action of photons (the energetic factor that creates sustained oscillations), in the presence of a catalyst, the silica (microcrystal with a piezoelectrical effect) plays the role of an amplifier (transistor) and establishes a whirling field: this is the vibratory movement of life. The whirling lines of courses of least resistance take the form of a helix. Pauling even demonstrated in 1954 "that the structure of living matter was formed by polypeptides arranged in helical cables."[21] This law can be seen again in the movement of all the planets that describe spirals. The electromagnetic effects they create have an effect on human behavior. In the spiral of the earth, one revolution corresponds to a terrestrial year: 20 to 22 of its revolutions coil around one revolution of the sun. The spiral of the moon, for which one revolution corresponds to 29½ days, or 12 revolutions, 4/10 of the moon per revolution of the earth (1 year) and 248 to 273 revolutions around 1 revolution of the sun (20 to 22 years). For L.-C. Vincent, the generators of the perigees and apogees represent, in the upper—or negative—part of the solar spiral, the annual maximum of negative and ultraviolet solar rays (winter solstice), and the annual maximum of positive and infrared solar rays (summer solstice). The sketches of Louis-Claude Vincent are, from the spiraliform perspective, quite useful for understanding these phenomena. We thereby rediscover the harmony of the universe, and it is quite likely that the forces of gravity, the harmonization of planetary revolutions, the lines and feelings of humans are due to electromagnetic laws. This brings us to the notion of perpetual motion and the great breath of ether. According to Faraday, Maxwell, and Hertz, the vibrations of ether are electromagnetic. The Egyptians knew this symbol well, and the decorations on Neolithic Chinese vases also include the spiral.

By combining the serpent with the egg, we come to the enigmatic representation left by the Druids, and meticulous study of the alignments of Stonehenge and Carnac and the various drawings on the menhirs can teach us much. One of the most beautiful spirals is carved on stone in the collection of the Dublin Museum. The journeymen stone carvers would make a pilgrimage to Saint-Gilles-du-Gard to admire its spiral staircase supported by a ringed vault climbing around the newel. But with the Orphic traditions, our thoughts also turn to either Khnum the potter, who modeled the egg of the world on his tower on the banks of the Nile, or to the egg of Brahma, whose seven shells are the seven spheres. The cave of Mithras is identical to the egg whose lower half is the earth and whose upper half is the sky. The egg of the Celts has comparable qualities.[22]

The catacombs of Egypt and Chaldea, as well as the underground crypts of Thebes and Memphis, all take on the name "the passage of serpents." The Mexican demigod Votam passes through the "hole of the serpent" and the Voodoo altar is dedicated to a snake god.[23] The hierophants, Druids, and Mexicans called themselves "Sons of the Serpent." The Egyptian scholars met in the Brotherhood of the Serpent, and Jesus recommended to his apostles to be like serpents. The inner man must shed his old skin to become the Son of Wisdom; he has to enter the earth indebted to the electromagnetic forces that preside over the cohesion of matter. The snake, the emanation of light, represents elevation as cosmic manifestation. This reptile only crawls because of a divine curse, but this evolutionary force associated with mental grace is transformed by perfection. Here we have the symbol of the two columns, one of time (Boaz), the other of space (Jachin).

This is why in Hindu symbology the serpents are the guardians of spiritual truths and occult powers. To be "teacher of the serpent" is to become the possessor of secrets.

The serpent that answers to cosmological symbolism characterizes the premanifested involution and modality of the Universe. This reptile haunts the whole of the occult science of the Middle Ages;[24] child of the fecund earth, guardian of the threshold and the cave, this dreadful force, subject to the power of God, can be the representation of good or evil, values that stem from the same common tree. Coiled around themselves, the image of eternity, the two snakes of the caduceus through their apparent antagonism illustrate the great law of analogy, this correspondence with the tablet of Hermes. For Apollo to become the slayer of lizards, it was necessary for harmful activities to correspond to the obscuring of the primordial center of intelligence, and evil then took its place in the darkness beneath the surface of the ground.

Everything living grows beneath this image of the spiral, from the solar system to the evolution of a leaf. Through this law of harmony, everything proceeds by progressive cycles in our three-dimensional world, natural progress cannot follow a straight line, and the circular path would be the equivalent of an eternal rebeginning. For life to exist, evolution has to take the three-dimensional path, a spiral that always advances by turning and rising: the spiral twists in the ether.

14

The Temples in Caves

UP TO NOW I HAVE ONLY envisioned the cave from the initiatory angle, but in life other, less metaphysical problems can hold our attention. Even in the profane literature these large underground cavities with their mysterious darkness, unknowable depths, noises, and waterways have attracted man's attention while causing terror and superstition. "For the caverns are dark and the essence of these forces is mysterious."[1] And caves are indiscriminately dubbed the caves of fairies or the devil, even if the word *cave* is not intended to designate an underworld chapel.

Many tales maintain that caves were the first human habitations, though they have no foundation for such a claim. Schoolbooks have illustrated these fables and thoroughly brainwashed young minds with images of humans wearing animal skins leading completely brutish lives. J.-H. Rosny the Elder gave birth to a complete literature featuring bandy-limbed men with bestial jaws and thick skulls living lives ruled by a collective fear. Historically, the Cro-Magnon men, with their prominent brows, were large and well proportioned. While I have no desire to revisit a subject I explored in *La Symbolique du Feu,* I must concur that the cave could have served as a temporary haven during epidemics, wars, devastations, and great cold snaps, but generally speaking, human habitations were erected in the open. There are caves in India with spacious chambers, which belong more to the regime of the troglodytes and thus do not fall into the cycle of the true cave. Easter Island also has grottoes that can be entered by long underground passageways. It is here that the souls of the ancestors reside.

However, it is said that the Germanic tribes dug underground passages in which they placed manure. They were used as a refuge during the winter months and as a storehouse for their harvests. Aeschylus wrote in 470 BCE that the first men "slid into the earth like skinny ants." Edouard Utudjian reports[2] that—based on the accounts of Diodorus Siculus, Strabo, and Plato—the inhabitants of Crete, Sardinia, and the Balearic Islands dwelt in caves. In the *Anabasis,* Xenophon drew up a picture of their life in which we see the growth of chickens, goats, sheep, and cows. This seems to be more an imaginary tale to me, as in reality life is hard in an actual cave. It is a dank home that causes illness and a dulling of the senses. It is easier to believe Pomponius Mela when he writes that the people of Tauric Chersonese in Crimea took shelter underground because of the harsh winters. Vitruvius and Quintus Curtius also appear to have underground refuges in mind. The dwellings of Ulfion, near Lake Victoria Nyanza,[3] and those in the Dordogne region fit these requirements, but none of them are deep caverns. Caves that were used as refuges during wars and natural disasters are quite numerous. We should make a special note of the curious caves of Jonas near Saint-Nectaire, in the Puy-de-Dôme region that are said by oral tradition to have been embellished and transformed by the work of several fugitive Templars. We should include the "baumes" of Provence in this telluric rite.

The abbey of Mont Saint Michel, created in 709, wanted to establish a pilgrimage similar to the one founded in 493 at the foot of Mount Gargan in southern Italy. Saint Michael was worshipped at the mount in an underground church. To reach this deep cave, one must descend some ninety-six stairs. This cave is known as "Hell's basement window." But in reality, this subterranean oratory with its thirty tapers was not created by Saint Aubert because this location with its very distinctive properties had already been known to the Druids. Thus, before "the mount" became the site of a pilgrimage, the subterranean temple there was a site of worship.

J.-H. Rosny the Elder has also shown the underground struggle of man in *La Guerre du Feu,* while Jules Verne described a utopian journey in his *Journey to the Center of the Earth,* which must have also served Norbert Casteret as inspiration in *La Terre Ardente.* Jean Doresse[4] found throughout Ethiopia "fantastic galleries hollowed into the rock. The churches of Lalibela were entirely concealed within their vast excavations; they were delved from the stony ground." This author established a connection between "the pharaonic temples of Abu Simbel, the Indian caves of Adjanta, the Buddhist monasteries in the cliffs of Dunhuang and Kyzyl in Turkistan, and the numerous cave churches in the vicinity of the ancient Caesarea of Cappadocia, admirably studied by Father Jerphanion." These churches are arranged in a circular pattern, or on the octagonal plan dear to the Templars. They generally have three doors oriented to the east, north, and south and contain three enclosures. Traditional values therefore presided over these constructions, which are shown all the more clearly by the fact that at the center of this *qedest* is a square chapel that is closed in every direction. It is the preeminent holy place. This sanctuary is known as a *maqdas.* I have touched on the matter of the triple enclosure elsewhere.

The caverns were also home to nonreligious rituals. According to legend the Frankish judges delivered their verdicts here. The Holy Vehme, the formidable secret society founded by Charlemagne in 772 and recognized by King Robert (1404), had to fight against magical activities. Based on the engravings, those charged were placed bareheaded with their eyes blindfolded before this secret tribunal to await its verdict. In reality, the Vehmic courts were located in cities.[5] With the Cathars, the caves provided the final refuge for the good folk, and we can recall the drama of Ornolac-Bethlehem where the Pure were imprisoned.

Generally speaking, the cave was used as a spiritual sanctuary, since magical or religious rituals took place there. For Frazer, in *The*

Golden Bough (1:73), magic came before religion. I think that it is difficult to separate these two modes of thought, as religion by definition is an act of magic. Because the cave was cramped and confined, a larger space was sought to permit the gathering of larger groups. The forest met these conditions: the sacred grove reproduced the dark and closed arrangement of the cave. The Cretans formed enclosures planted with trees for this purpose, and we have already looked at the symbolism of the tree. In order to render more tangible the mystery released by the natural cavern, humans thought to improve on it: hence the birth of cave paintings.

This matrix of treasures, this burial site, this cave that offers access to the underworld became the place for divination and prophecy. Salomon Reinach had this in mind when he analyzed these frescoes and their ritual character.[6] Man creates the *volt** that should act on the dark forces of life, the celestial forces, or the telluric forces. These totemic talismans attract cosmic forces whose benefits should spill out over the tribe. These cruciform signs and symbolic drawings appear in red and black, or as in Australia, over a reddish background. This color comes from clay colored with oligist iron or iron peroxide, but what is most surprising about it is its extraordinary preservative powers. Sometimes the drawing is outlined in black (manganese dioxide), these mineral salts were mixed with animal fat and crushed charcoal. This red color is much like that of blood, the life principle. It is the color of the first zone of the Trimurti. Edelstend de Menil investigated this power of red in his *Études d'Archéologie:* the Romans covered the bridal bed and the path taken by the newlyweds in red. In India, the bride must sit on a reddened bull's hide; and in the bouquet of the French provincial bride we find a red carnation. All of this is intended to denote the life force.

But this color that defies times can also come from animal glands. Currently something called the "bitter stone" is used for dyeing; this is a red stone with strong coloring potential that is found in the diseased

---

*[A magical talisman, often in the form of a small clay or wax figure. —*Trans.*]

livers of some members of the family *Bovidae*. When we think of cattle being sacrificed it is not ridiculous to think that our ancestors may have extracted this stone at those times. This coloring agent can also come from the gland of a mollusk. The Phoenicians would catch these shell-fish, open them, and take out the glands. The liquid was then placed in a lead vessel over a gentle flame, then clarified. After ten days cloth was dipped into it and then exposed to sunlight. The initial violet color would then transform into purple—this purple of Tyr is not a scarlet red but is the color of coagulated blood. And ancient authors have written how in Tyr the workshops and dyehouses exuded a pestilential odor.[7]

Drawings transformed the natural cave into a temple: often the animals depicted there appeared to be wounded by an arrow. These totems could have an effect on the lives of animals. In the first stage the human took care of them so that they would multiply, and in the second the hunter would catch them. What we are seeing here is therefore a magical and ceremonial act, an act of incantation and enchantment. This can appear quite plausible when we know that the magical act possesses a sacred and divine nature whose meaning we have lost. It cannot be compared in any way to the magic performed by modern charlatans. We should see in it rather a heightened religious sentiment.[8] Furthermore, all of South American literature features animal-men. Our ancestors would therefore have been animals. What we are seeing here are the remnants of a cult.

These drawings appear in very remote spots that are poorly lit and only accessible through very narrow passageways. We can rightly ask ourselves why such decorations exist in these secluded areas; was it the solitary action of an artist or a magician, intended to serve an individual? On the other hand, Paul Le Cour notes that these drawings do not always have a food connection, as tigers, eagles, snakes, and scorpions appear among them.[9] They would therefore be "the symbolic representation of attributes of the deity."

In American, French, and Spanish caves, the bison—a kind of bull—occupies a place of pride. Plutarch mentioned that the altar of the temple of Delos was equipped with horns, as were the Hebrew altars. In the biblical text of Habakkuk (3:4) it is written: "And his brightness was as the light; he had horns coming out of his hand; and there was the hiding of his power." And in the Psalms (75:10) we read: "All the horns of the wicked also will I cut off; but the horns of the righteous shall be exalted." Moses wore horns, rays of light from concealed knowledge. The horned god Cernunnos was connected to the idea of abundance. In the Trois-Frères cave in the Ariège region of France, the head of a masked man is crowned with antlers of a stag or reindeer. Osiris's head was adorned with a crown in which the symbolism of horns was obvious. The pharaoh wore the same headgear, and Alexander the Great, following his fabled conquests, adorned his clothing with horns in order to clearly show the divine nature of his royal position. Michelangelo envisioned a horned Moses (housed in the Basilica di San Pietro in Vincoli—Saint Peter in Chains), and Theseus was obliged to slay the Minotaur, a fantasy being with dangerous horns. It is impossible to completely list all these representations,[10] but the number of horns increases so as to create a veritable hierarchy of the beings invested with them. The supreme gods have seven horns, which brings to mind the seven-branched candelabrum that illuminates the world. The Gauls honored Cernunnos the horned god on their helmets—the horns later were replaced with wings. In the Catholic Church, the Lord is represented by the ram, the preeminent horned animal who figured prominently in the old religion. Then the ancient pagan god became commingled with the devil; in 1305 the pope accused the bishop of Coventry of paying homage to the devil in the form of a sheep. In the Middle Ages the devil became an entirely perverse being that had two horns and presided over the Sabbat. Far from being a sign of mockery, the horn signifies a sacred nature; it represents strength, power, and royal authority.

In 1879, de Sautuola revealed the frescoes of Altamira, which started everything moving. In 1895, E. Rivière entered the Mouth Cavern (Dordogne); and in 1896, Deleau revealed the existence of the carvings of Pair-non-Pair (Gironde). The German ethnologist

Leo Frobenius[11] collected many rock drawings around 1896. He rightfully states that these were not elementary drawings at all but admirable frescoes. The extraordinary mastery they reveal gives the strong impression of an advanced and educated society. The graphic representation is based on the notion of the sacred: Paleolithic man went straight to what is essential in art; that withering of the being did not yet exist. The drawings of Marsoulas (Haute Garonne) were discovered by Regnault in 1897. In 1901, Breuil, Capitan, and Peyrony reproduced the cave drawings of Combarelles and Font-de-Gaume (Dordogne), while in 1906 Molard revealed the prestigious fresco of Niaux, near Tarascon-sur-Ariège. In 1933, one of the largest collections of prehistoric paintings was discovered: the frescoes of Tassili.[12] Thanks to Henri Lhote we have the reproduction of an extraordinary museum that shows us that the Sahara was fertile once upon a time. An Egyptian influence can also be detected there. The wonderful drawings that illustrate the caves of the mountain chain east of Ghat (Sahara) idealize a troubling prehistoric race: men with white skin and blond hair.[13] As for Lascaux, where the rite is closely observed, the great chamber of the bulls is called the "Prehistoric Sistine Chapel." These drawings of feverish movement and an exceptional transfiguration are sometimes located in spots that are almost inaccessible, in nooks that a person can only slip into with a great deal of trouble.[14]

While the Pythagorean basilica of the Porta Maggiore was only revealed thanks to a partial collapse of the Rome-Naples train line, we can still find rich decoration in the new Christian catacomb discovered on the Via Latina in 1956.[15] Should this inexhaustible legacy make us think that these churches were reserved for a small elite, hence the idea of an initiatory center and a Christian esoteric doctrine? For Byzantium, art implied a deindividualization, a deliverance from the human condition to the benefit of the divine. The execution of a portrait therefore tended more toward a symbol than an illusionary resemblance of a moment. Chinese art is placed under the dominance of the symbol. Egyptian art is distorting because the idea was more powerful than the physical aspect, whereas Greek art, to the contrary, tackled the idea of physical perfection, often to the detriment of the intellect. Greek statuary is beautiful but it is no longer suggestive of spiritual life like Egyptian, Hindu, Peruvian, or Celtic sculpture.[16] This is therefore why, under the impact of an abstract thought and an absolute artistic value, our elders were outdone by an art that sees perfection in stylization. This is an art of absolute purity, and it is the fruit of perfect observation. It inevitably produces an effect on our civilization that is increasingly focusing on spiritual issues. Our era is much like the ancient civilizations: the public races toward the manifestations offered by millenarian art, and our young artists immerse themselves in them, for, in accordance with a natural law, the evolution of art aims toward an abstraction that remains in a positive, human form. When I say abstract art, I am not thinking of the modern art that is incorrectly called "abstract art," but which would be more appropriately called "nonfigurative art." I am thinking, to the contrary, that Egyptian art—with its stylized silhouettes, the bust placed full face with the head in profile—was an abstract art because in evoking a feeling it represented a mental abstraction. We could therefore say that all figurative art whose purpose is the expression of an idea or a plastic value through an infinite number of other values is innately abstract.

The spirit of this multiple life, with its profusion of forms, finds itself illustrated in the oldest sanctuaries. Odette Viennot[17] has noted the hieratic postures of the famous temptation of Mara executed by Buddhist artists. Among other cave temples, we should make note of those of Ajantā and Ellora, whose sculptures sanctify the glory of Shakyamuni, but among Paleolithic and Neolithic caves we should also note the cave of Pech Merle in the limestone rich region of the Lot.[18]

The caves and their decorations do not fall into the category of a gratuitous art. They represent a human desire and aspiration. We do not know how our ancestors lived, but these drawings created with an astounding mastery are proof that a civilization existed. We have forgotten the divine and the sacred, and it is difficult for us to imagine a world different from our own. This sanctuary puts us on the trail of a totem, however: one of its magical aspects remains with the Black Virgin, with the underground temple, that matrix cave of Mother Earth who gave us our life and will take us back at its end.

15

Burial Caves

THE WORD *GROTTO* COMES FROM the Latin *crypta,* meaning "crypt." This underground vault of the church once served as the sepulcher for martyrs. Orbigny analyzed this kind of cave in his *Dictionnaire d'Histoire Naturelle* (article by Desnoyers). The grottoes of Arkalokhou (3000–2100 BCE), of Canaris, and of Psychro were used in Cretan worship, but I am only envisioning the burial rites outside the general worship of the dead.[1]

The man of the Lower Paleolithic era shrouded his dead and powdered them in red (often with hematite). A stone was also placed under their heads. The same rite existed during the Mousterian era as the body was interred beneath the hearth. During the Neolithic era, the cave became a veritable tomb. After the body had been deposited inside, the entrance was walled off.

As for initiatory rites, artificial grottoes were created if natural ones were not available. "Peking man" (*Sinanthropus pekinensis*) is presumed to have lived in the cave in "Chicken-Bone Hill." This civilization knew the use of fire, and for around five thousand years used quartz crystals in their tools. The same ritualistic thinking erected the dolmens and covered alleys and tumuli. The corpse was not laid flat as in our time but in a curled position with the knees drawn up to the chest and the limbs pressed close together. The individual was thus returned to the earth, his nurturing mother, in a fetal position. Some authors have written that this was done in order to prevent the dead person from returning to the world, as he had no business concerning himself with the affairs of the living. This reasoning implies that the dead individual wanted revenge on those who had the privilege of remaining on earth.

In a civilization like that of the neomatriarchal farmers, burial was performed in two stages. It was necessary to wait until enough flesh had come off the skeleton so that the skull and long bones could be put in the appropriate place.[2] Skulls allegedly possessed supernatural powers. They presided over the major holidays and over the rites of initiation. Masonic writers have said that the skull placed in the chamber of reflection frightened the postulant and showed him the vanity of all things. I see an older rite within it: it is a guide placed by the side of the neophyte whose magical power attracts the motivating souls that reside in the celestial spheres to come to it. The arrival of a spirit allows for a palpable perception to take place.[3] These souls of an intermediary world, with their ethereal visions, liberate us from our heaviness, and the individual becomes open to new spiritual notions. He discovers the notion of imagination, prophetic inspiration, and even that of visions. This inner illumination can be achieved by means of initiation. The initiations of current secret societies have lost too much of their power to provide a true illumination.

The dead man has been revered in all eras, not only because he is the remains of a cherished being but also because he represents a power with which man must find conciliation. The dead receive offerings and human sacrifices. The royal tombs of Tutankhamen and the kings of Byblos have left undying monuments to posterity. Thanks to these complicated and luxurious rites we can manage to understand the vanished civilizations better.

The Etruscans believed in the immortality of the soul, and they placed their tumuli shelters (with cave drawings) in the region of Viterbia, at Cerveteri in Tuscany. The two primordial events of life on earth—birth and death—do not belong to the free will of a man because the end of one cycle necessarily coincides with the beginning of another. The yin-yang symbol allows us to recover this metaphysical identity. The caterpillar and the butterfly appear to be two distinct beings, and yet one comes from the other, the chrysalis being merely a figurative death.

Juvenal indicates that while men are burned after they die, children are buried. By incinerating the corpse, one delays the cycle of earthly lives, but by placing it in contact with the earth, its reincarnation is activated. For Mircea Eliade,[4] placing the body at the site of its birth will spare its former owner long torment. The patient regenerates by entering into contact with the ground. This is the custom of the Hurons and Pygmies, as well as the Greenlanders and Swedes, and can also be found in the Laws of Manu. Knowing this, it is easy to understand why the cave is given the body of the deceased. As the preeminent site of the first birth it is regarded as the womb of Mother Earth.

According to Genesis,[5] Abraham buried Sarah in the cavern of Machpelah, in the land of Canaan, and Joseph buried his father Jacob there. In Jewish belief, after his death man becomes a shade, and this form without substance descends to the Scheol, a dark cavern that is located beneath the ocean in the depths of the earth. It should not be confused with the Christian hell. The heavy doors of this underground only open under the influence of magic words: "Have the gates of death been opened unto thee? Hast thou seen the doors of the shadow of death?" (Job 38:17). The dead live inside the earth, and in the first book of Samuel, when the Witch of Endor summons the shade of Samuel at Saul's request, it is definitely from the depths of the earth that the former king emerges. We find a parallel between the secret Egyptian and Orphic doctrines in the Book of the Dead, as well as with the mysteries of Eleusis, centered on those of the beyond and the afterlife. For this reason the Egyptians buried their dead on the banks of the Nile in hypogea. The images of seventy emperors—or solimans—are collected in the galleries of Kaf Mountain. But after the hypogeum—or crypt, a tomb for one individual or several members of a family—we find catacombs and common graves. Strabo (*Geographia* 17.1) mentions the pagan catacombs of Alexandria; those of Rome contained some six million individuals. These important necropolises had lengthy galleries such as seen in Naples and Syracuse; the one in Paris measures 177 miles. This vast underground network sometimes has several stories; the corridors widen to form rooms transformed into chapels. The dead rest in elongated niches that have been dug into the walls—called loculi. Sometimes a plaque with the name of the deceased seals the entrance. The dead are not always buried in Spanish cemeteries, but placed in a thick artificial wall that has been made higher. Probst-Biraben has noted[6] that Gypsies, Jews, and Arabs wash the corpses while they wail litanies as they ritually pace around the body. It so happens that "the first group of journeymen who came from Syria and Palestine to France passed on to more recent initiates, who were not of Eastern origin, these mortuary rites." In Petit Morin valley, funerary caves hollowed out of chalk have been found. Fernand Niel told me that these caves were concentrated in the commune of Croizard in the canton of Montmort (one in Courgeonnet, three in Croizard). These Celtic grottoes resemble the generally accepted design: a king of the Gallic underworld was depicted as a man wearing a wolf skin and armed with a mallet and accompanied by a dog.

This is how the crypt took the place of the sacred cave: hollowed into the rock it first served as the tomb of a saint, then that of a martyr;[7] the cult was celebrated in these catacombs. Churches were raised over these sites, and saints continued to be buried in their underground chapels. The basilica of Saint Denis houses the bodies of dead kings. The basilica was initially a place where businessmen met and was used for court sessions. This rectangular building, separated into several naves by rows of columns, then became the principal church of the city.[8]

The entrances to many burial caves have been oriented to a specific direction. The dead man benefits from very favorable cosmic influences. The orientation of the necropolis was scrupulously observed by the Egyptian, Hindu, and Muslim peoples. The monument was sited in accordance with the four cardinal points, which determined the placement of the center where the deceased would lie at rest under the influence of the number five, the symbol of mastery. The building would be marked out by placing four points at each corner; in other words, sixteen perpendicular and level boundary markers—or landmarks—

which with the center makes the number seventeen. The orientation (five) and demarcation (seventeen) of the construction give us a total of twenty-two. This is a value we see in sacred alphabets and in the Major Arcana of the Tarot. The cornerstone therefore becomes the masterpiece of the building because, subject to the law of numbers, it enters in the creation of rhythm and harmony.

This temple of the final dwelling possesses an agreement of measure of the constituent elements to each other and to the whole. This is why the architect considered it to be made in the image of the manifested cosmos. The tomb, like the cave, serves as an intermediary between Heaven and Earth as imagined by the Royal Art; the grave therefore spiritually receives the expression of a higher truth. This secret instruction reveals itself esoterically, but I must think that the luxury, beauty, and proportions of the construction reveal nothing but their outer appearances. Feng shui not only determines orientation but specific placement, the nature of the terrain, and the most favorable day for the burial. We can consider mummification in the same spirit, as well as the burial of the dead person in the midst of the living, with the cemetery located around the church or in the center of the village. This way the deceased continue to take part in collective life—invisibly. This encourages the reintegration of the individual's soul into another body, and because it has been spared difficult tribulations through this reverent treatment, the dead individual usually prefers rebirth as a member of his former family.

The tumulus—which is sometimes as much as fifty feet high—often tops the grave, thus burying it—the tomb is located in the middle of the tumulus. This is the case with the royal Scythian tomb near Nikopol in the great loop of the Dnieper. The king, with his head toward the setting sun, rests among several sacrificed servants and horses. The dead person is laid to rest with his head toward the sunset so he can see the rising sun in the east when he rises during his resurrection. In imitation of the natural cave in which Jesus was laid to rest, monolithic churches were built. The three underground churches of France are located in Aubeterre, at Gurat in Charente, and at Saint Émilion in Gironde. They are rather scarce temples. It seems that only the ability to erect them was a criterion. These churches dating from the eleventh or twelfth centuries are not oriented. The nave of the church Saint John in Aubeterre measures some 60 by 37 feet. Its vault, which is 55 feet tall, rests on octagonal columns. This odd monument became the communal cemetery in the nineteenth century. The church of Saint George of Gurat, carved in a cliff of the Lizonne valley, is much smaller. Its nave measures 40 feet by almost 20. Its barrel vaults are some 25 feet high. The church of Saint Émilion is 120 feet long, 65 feet wide, and 65 feet high. This powerful construction is lit by a round hole pierced in the vault. I must finally mention the underground church of Hautes-Isle near Mantes, which has been carved in the limestone and contains only a single nave that is 70 feet long with a barrel vault that is 26 feet high.[9] In the Sierra de Guadarrama, the underground basilica of Cuelgamuros is the Spanish national monument reserved for those who died in service to their country but that has numerous additional galleries issuing from its main underground hall. I will end by noting the buried church of Saint Pius in Lourdes, a church that has nothing to do with mortuary worship. This vast edifice, built under the direction of the architect Vago and M. Freyssinet, our famous French engineer, can hold up to twenty thousand people. This underground church, which is oval shaped—the form that framed Christ on the tympanum of ancient cathedrals, as well as the shape of the fish and the emblem of the first Christians—measures more than 650 feet by 250, equaling a surface of 162,500 square feet; the master altar is located in the middle of the basilica and raised up almost 6 feet.

In conclusion, what we can take from all this is that burial originated as an initiatory ritual: by burying the dead person in his or her nurturing mother, he or she is permitted to go more quickly to a new life. This is why the dead person must be oriented. We are only in the presence of part of a funerary ritual, but the crypt remains a duplicate of the cave; it reflects the primordial cavern in which all are born and to which all must return, but it is also the place where humans must sometimes work, and where they conceal their activity.

16

The Underground Factories

IN THE DEPTHS OF THE EARTH, man hides his activity; he works safe from prying eyes in discretion and safety, but his workshop here also benefits from telluric currents and waves that facilitate and embellish his task. The lower deities of this world reveal themselves, and their alchemical knowledge helps the blacksmith: the subterranean spirits have, for the most part, a pronounced taste for metallurgists.

The Dvergrs of whom the Norse Eddas speak have influenced German traditions, especially the *Nibelungenlied*. These dwarves skillfully craft enchanted weapons; while they are quite wealthy, they can also be quite wicked. The sword Durandal was forged by one of the disciples of the greatest craftsman—named Veland, Wieland, or Volundr—and Mime, the horrible dwarf, forged the sword used by Siegfried to kill Fafnir, the hideous dragon. The dwarves or kobolds of Germany haunt caves and other dark and lonely places; they are often compared to ants. Perhaps because will-o'-the-wisps can be more easily seen close to mines, the legends cite numerous spirits that guard these riches with jealous zeal. The Harz region of Germany, in Hanover, is particularly enchanted. A black cow (West Africa) or even a human being (Malaysia and other Eastern countries, Peru) is immolated in honor of this terrible guardian who may be appeased this way. But whoever touches the sacred treasure first will die immediately. According to Kircher, the Tyrol is infested by little demons, but Bernard Palissy rejected those convictions: "Those who say and have written that harmful spirits kill the men inside the mines have erred," which did not stop the mines from ceasing operations in the sixteenth century because men no longer wished to work in them, and, according to Claude Magnus, apparitions are frequent in the demon-haunted mines. Out of fear and not scorn, antiquity sent convicts to work in this dark world; in Galatia, in the Sandaracurgium Mountain, the miners there were paying for their past misdeeds (Strabo, 1.12.3).

But while these capricious dwarves, who were magicians and prophets, these black, hairy, stocky, frizzy-haired creatures with wrinkled faces and muffled voices have no liking for men, the Breton *teuz,* like the elves of Scotland and Iceland, establish contact with miners and help them with their work. These elves are extremely beautiful. One might think that the physical strength of these gnomes is limited, but their magic cloak that makes them invisible also gives them the vigor of twelve men. Quite disciplined—they have a king: Laurin, Alberich—they group together to marshal their efforts. These little beings can be malicious, mischievous, and teasing, like the pygmies of Alsace or the little miner from the tales of the Nièvre region, but they are indulgent.[1] The most famous German gnome from this category would be Rubezahl—the Spirit of the Mountain—but he only torments the wicked. There are many deities who reside underground in Finland, such as the god of iron, Rauta-Rakhi. In Japan, we even find a god of wealth: Daikoku. In France the patron saint of miners is Saint Barbara.[2] But in reality the knowledge of metals was first taught us by the Dactyls, the first miners, who were enchanters.

According to both Diodorus Siculus and Apollonius of Rhodes, metal was discovered in Phrygia, and the first attempts at forging took place there. Vulcan, the inventor of everything concerning the working of iron and copper, gave birth to the Cabiri. Vulcan essentially remains the god of the earth's inner fire and the god of volcanoes. He later became the god presiding over metallurgical operations. The Cyclops connected with Vulcan only worked on behalf of Olympus, creating the weapons of Jupiter and Poseidon's trident. With the blacksmith god, the Uranian Cyclopes Brontes, Steropes, and Arges created Zeus's thunderbolts, Apollo's bow, and Athena's breastplate. At the request of Thetis, Hephaestus forged invulnerable weapons for Achilles. Vulcan, the most deformed and ugly of the smiths, wed the perfect creature: she who stepped ashore on the banks of the Cythera from her seashell and whom the Naiads called Venus.

In the organized activity of this underworld, outside of the *Iliad,* the *Odyssey,* the *Aeneid,* and the *Thousand and One Nights,* we learn that Odin owes his spear to Gungnir, and that Thor also gained his symbolic hammer from these dwarfish master craftsmen. They were also responsible for Freyr's golden boar and magic ship. Sif received from them her beautiful golden hair and Freya a necklace whose rings enriched their owner indefinitely. Vulcan's children, the Cabiri, did not work in their father's forge; they followed the trail of the Dactyls, without, however, taking metal out of the earth. They were the missionaries of Rhea, the daughter of Uranus and Gaea, out of Phrygia into Samothrace. While Strabo devoted a chapter to the Dactyls in his theological research, and while Hesiod composed a poem in their honor, Rossignol[3] has shown that the only difference between the Dactyls, Cabiri, Corybantes, Curetes, and the Telchines were their names, and they all fell into the same class of spirits. These "metallurgists" worshipped Vulcan. They forged weapons but also created tools good for working the earth. When one of the Cabiri was murdered by two of his brothers, the cult that surrounded his death created an initiatory ritual in which this allegory formed part of the mysteries. Near the underground palace of Enoch, Adoniram—according to the admirable story by Nerval, *The Story of the Queen of the Morning and Solomon—* placed his forges and foundries underground. According to these *Nights of Ramazan,* Adoniram went down to this palace located at the center of the earth after his temporary setback.

This sanctuary of the secret fire, with its master Pluto, brings us close to the alchemist whose workshop is underground. Here we see anew the Earth and its maternal womb, the heat that gives life to both heart and stone, and the Fire that engenders. But "that which germinates burns; that which burns germinates." The mine becomes the place where metals grow. According to the Arabic book of Teifaschi (thirteenth century), and in agreement with Aristotle, "the earth and water brought to a state of smoky or vaporous exhalation or to a state of dry exhalations that first form fusible substances and metals, and next produces stones." Palissy shares Pliny's opinion (*Natural History* 34.49) that the galenite mines of Spain would be reborn at the end of a certain period of time. "Metals grow in the mines."[4] A similar theory by Daubrée appears in *La Génération des minerauz métalliques dans la pratique des mineurs au Moyen Age.*[5] Metals form in the depths of the earth just like the planets in the sky through the power of Light. Ores are classified as male and female, and Paul Sébillot (*Les Travaux publics et les mines,* pages 406–10) has shown that mines could only be discovered by divine beings who are therefore asexual. The mines of northern France, Belgium, and China were only unearthed with the help of a fairy;[6] Saint Piran became the patron saint of mines for much the same reason. The opening of a mine therefore involves religious ceremonies (Paul Sébillot, 421) because we must show ourselves as deserving the favor of the spirits that live there.

If I may stray for a moment from the subject at hand, I would like to speak, echoing Mircea Eliade, of the initiatory ritual of these admirable smiths who had a perfect mastery of fire. This would inevitably lead us to the sacred nature of the trade and to alchemical research. And so with Novalis, for whom "the miner was a reversed astrologer; the miner is the hero of the depths prepared to receive the gifts of heaven and exalt joyously far from the world and its miseries." This initiatory ritual still can be glimpsed in the rites of the Compagnonnage. In the quarries of Anjou, the reception of the Compagnon is called the *guêtrage* because the new worker is given gaiters [*guêtres*] to wear. The highest grade is called the "hewer," he who has perfect mastery of the craft. The foremen are called the "masters of the mountains."

Some factories are installed underground today. The spectacular excavations of Sweden provide a haven from the danger of atomic war, reduce the evaporation of gas by storing it underground, and facilitate climate control and consistency of light in these factories. It was most particularly evident in the hydroelectric centers where the length of the pressure pipes had been greatly reduced. Edouard Utudjian has studied the effect of the underground on organisms;[7] atmospheric pressure increases and air temperature increases by 1° centigrade for every 108 feet. Humidity intensifies, and the absence of light causes eyesight to atrophy, the skin to lose pigmentation, and the red-corpuscle rate to fall, while reducing muscle strength. The underground factory therefore has some serious drawbacks. On the other hand, tunnels (under mountains, rivers, and the sea) and transport routes and the Paris subway system offer numerous material advantages.[8]

To return to the investigation of initiatory matters, we can ask ourselves how the ancient workshops were illuminated. Phosphorescence is a possibility, but phosphorus is a dangerous product that oxidizes rapidly in air, where it can spontaneously combust. It may have been used in water, where it continues to burn after being lit. In the presence of mercury, through dual decomposition, it becomes black phosphorus. But neither its illuminating power nor its conservation nor its use (for example, mercuric oxide) can be improved this way. Sulfides—particularly zinc sulfide—were very well known by ancient peoples. They are naturally luminescent and give off a very bright light at a very low level. To restore this light, they must be exposed to another light source. Given radiance by daylight they can be used in the form of mirrors or movable wands. These sulfides do not oxidize and last quite long, provided they are not touched. In order to avoid altering them they can be left in place, and an artificial light source, such as a torch, can be used to recharge them. The sulfur will then reflect a bright and nonsparkling light. However, without having studied the light emitted by these things in lumens in order to determine the likely surface, it does not seem that this was the bright light used to illuminate the corridors of the initiatory temples; furthermore, we would find traces of the combustion from torches on the walls. The ancients also knew the use of translucent materials that allowed for light to spread. There were alabaster statues in Egypt that would serve this purpose, but this procedure does not allow for illumination, which moreover can be caused by the passage of ultraviolet rays through specific paintings: ceric oxide and thorium dioxide are luminous, and I am leaving out the petroleum products that the ancients were known to use in the form of gas and naphtha for the presentation of the mysteries. Mirrors could also have been used in certain specific cases (direct access by refraction of the light source). But it is probable that the Egyptians knew a form of electricity. Remnants of electric batteries that were used to gild copper have been discovered in Ur in Chaldea. For Louis-Claude Vincent, the Ark of the Covenant, made from acacia wood and covered with gold plating on both sides, had a kind of antenna with its cross and large crown, thereby making a perfect condenser. Maspero, the director of antiquities in Cairo, was actively searching for this Egyptian lamp. This sums up all the conjectures made on this subject, but we should keep in mind that no trace of combustion or conductive wire have been found in the ancient monuments. Perhaps the Egyptians knew how to harness the energy of the atmosphere in the form of certain high-frequency cosmic rays, but we have to admit that we still know nothing of the source of their blazing light.

The underground workshop therefore remains the privileged place where nature passes on its power: the smith is inspired by the magic act, the dwarves hoard wealth; but we always come back to the quest of a spiritual realization. This factory and this mine took part in the symbolism of the cave and the initiatory temple, for they put man in contact with the hidden powers, the forces that allow him to attain his second birth.

17

Conclusion

WE HAVE REACHED THE END of a long journey, and there still remains so much to say! Numerous notes await completion, and there are many other examples that deserve citation. But we must preserve the essential.

What does this underground world truly represent, this world of gnomes and elves, this resistant world upon which we live and in which we take root like a tree? All definitions turn vague, and we perceive that man is prisoner of a definite universe that he does not know. To recover the substance of Eden this seeker takes the labyrinth, a symbolic path, whose steps and risers are so many stages of purification. In this world of anguish and darkness, the individual becomes aware of his nature because he has lost all assurance and all pride. Through divine grace he has found the low, dark door, but although his chains have not yet fallen, he shows a pair of clean hands. The veil falls, and in this central chamber the illumination comes down into his heart. But to understand the mysteries, to attain the higher states of being, one must go down into the center of the earth. One must bury oneself in matter by going beyond the cavern that represents the site of the first death and the second birth.

All the texts cited—whether religious or profane—expound a ritual that activates the symbol. For in reality, there is nothing material about this underground journey: its subtle, psychic nature causes a spiritual elevation in the individual that can be carried out in the initiatory ceremony. But are there many initiates who entirely understand this lengthy allegorical progression, those stages to cross through, those purgative states described by Argos in Dante's *The Veil of Isis*?

The door opens beneath the polar mountain, Mount Meru, the mountain of Purgatory. As shown by Dante, we are then in the presence of the unknowable Highest and the Luciferian crystallization. This center of the earth makes it possible to reflect all spiritual influence. The postulant emerges from it in a state of glory. If he resumes his path through the labyrinth, he now knows where he needs to go; his footsteps are no longer hesitant. The maze that served as a means of ritual defense against profane influences becomes an energetic symbol. During this ascension the initiate can recapitulate all states from his crystallization in the mineral to his present situation. Then the waters of Lethe will erase memory of all things, but by drinking at the second fountain the individual will be purified. After an effective, Hermetic labor, this king of the world leaves the cave and leaves the cosmos through the opening at the zenith. This pierced vault reflects the solar core and cosmic light. Those who cross through it bear a crown on their heads, as in a novel by Meyrink. But this door, placed in the world axis, has this singular Stone for its keystone, the cornerstone and the gateway of the gods. That individual who finds himself beyond Heaven and Earth, who has vanquished the Wheel of Transmigration, becomes immortal.

All these trials, this entire long quest for the mineral realm and multiple states also leads to philosophical understanding and the spiritual liberation of the soul. The cave, the place of theurgic meditation, offers the enigma of the Lost Word. Here the Mother, the maternal virgin who dwells in the telluric night, is invoked. The chain of initiates goes until this matrix, for life is born of Death. "The chain of initiates restores and passes on the elements of the sacred tradition." This is how the Black Madonna bequeaths us a complete message, inasmuch as within this kingdom of shadow where water and stone reach their just culmination and where the tree slakes its thirst, the Magna Mater radiates a dazzling green light.

Current initiations, despite the loss of documentation and the abandonment, forgetting, or ignorance of many customs, unfold symbolically at the center of the earth. They preserve the desire to keep the lower door secret: they conceal the entrance to crypts, necropolises, and temples; they make access to them difficult, insurmountable, and terrifying. The path of silence has veiled all these notions since earliest antiquity and the allusions of Plato, Socrates, and Plotinus only give us a vague view of the Eleusinian Mysteries with their trials by the elements and their glorification of the ternary. But we also find there a few clues about the harmony of the spheres and about the rhythm that is the very essence of life.

Villiers de l'Isle-Adam writes: "I do not teach; I awaken." I would like to make this beautiful thought my watchword, for in reality every symbol can still present itself under many meanings depending on the personal grade or spiritual aptitude of the person envisioning it. Can we truly attain this truth that by nature is solely unique? Apollonius of Tyana teaches us to distrust ourselves, how we think, and how we see: "A thing is never created or destroyed: it simply becomes visible or invisible."

Contrary to the spirit of equality and uniformity with which our society is imprinted, this book wishes to give the individual the possibility of going beyond him- or herself. The comprehension of the problems I have discussed here can allow other minds to manifest and become better and, as I said earlier, become more forgiving. By opening the latent possibilities slumbering in every human being, we have to be able to win through the externalization of the craft. This is no longer a utopian dream, as we find here the Compagnonnage, an extraordinary movement that only addresses those young people pursuing a manual craft. We have to take into account their powerful spiritual elevation and sense of honor to better understand their skill. I have seen apprentice carpenters in their velvet "trousers" joyfully working on large geometrical sketches that many engineers would have looked upon as a chore. Creating in joy and in full awareness is the way to achieve a more perfect realization. Submitting one's thought to the traditional teaching is an invitation to self-mastery and offers entry to the universal will.

Through this spiritual discipline the individual release of our intentions coincides with the universal emanation. We go beyond our habitual limitations. Through correspondence between the inner and the outer, the work comes to life and can no longer be superficial; the journeyman then achieves his masterpiece because individual awareness permeates all that he does. This full realization of the individual clearly appears in the creative artist who, with his or her synthesis of the material and the spiritual, which, under the influence of a shock, a second state, and inspiration of an otherworldly order, manages to create an intense work. But an era produces very few artists worthy of the name.

The energy that commands all remains the Spirit: without spirit the artist cannot create. Modern Western science has also realized that this vital principle gives life to material progress that brings satisfactions but not happiness. The most recent discoveries, increasing at an anguish-causing rate, have not yet managed to put us on the path of our own world. Professor Hurzeler, curator of the Natural History Museum in Basel, maintains "that there have been at least ten million years when beings similar to men and different from anthropoid apes have been alive." I am convinced of this, but we know next to nothing about any of this series of civilizations. We do not know nature and the great universal forces, and yet traditions bring us, through texts that look different, the same spirit of truth.

I have perhaps spent a disproportionate amount of time discussing the Vedantic scriptures, but the Hindu tradition remains one of the forms closest to the primordial condition. Many others have been altered over the course of time. The human cycle deforms these cycles; the Celtic figure is akin to the Eastern structure that repels us with its incomprehensible names. Unfortunately our own heritage has left us little by way of written records, as teaching was oral for the most part. We are therefore obliged to refer to the Hindu Gnosis, without seeking to attribute it a supremacy it cannot have. I have looked at what could be universal in each religion, for each holds a large portion of the truth. But truth is not Christian, nor is it Jewish, Hindu, or Masonic; it is only Truth.

It is necessary to venture through the dark shades of an unknown world to conquer the truth. It is necessary to penetrate the essence of things and, in accordance with the words of Saint Augustine, "Let us therefore so seek as if we should find, and so find as if we were about to seek" (*De Trinitate*, 9.1). He who seeks cannot be deceived, and while for some reality can only be conceived in the sense of the physical world, the creative imagination also has a true value. Becoming initiated does not mean restricting oneself to the effort of incorporating doctrine. Henry Corbin, in his very great book that represents a great sum of knowledge, *Creative Imagination in the Sufism of Ibn Arabi* says this: "We must have the courage to look into the bottom of the tomb if we are to know that it is indeed empty and that we must look for Him elsewhere. The greatest misfortune that can befall the shrine is to become the sealed tomb before which men mount guard and do so only because there is a corpse in it. Accordingly, it takes the greatest courage to proclaim that it is empty, the courage of those able to dispense with the evidence of reason and authority because the only secret they possess is the secret of love that has seen."[1] We have to transcend our own nature in search of an ideal that is acceptable to all men of good will. Paradise is truly on Earth; it is the exact reflection of knowledge; to be in Paradise we have to attain our full freedom.

We should avoid hoping that thought or intellectual effort will allow our integration into understanding; thought remains a mental mirror and external value. Reason allows a rift to appear between mirror and object, between subject and object, and the association of ideas scares us because we are scared of our own reflection. Only Spirit allows us to unite together in the All because "the All takes part in all and it comes from all." Intelligence does nothing, but only Beauty, the engine of love, will put us on the direct path. In a few words Raoul Auclair in *Le Goéland* (no. 77) expressed a high initiatory wisdom: "Light enlightens but too much light will cause blindness just as too much noise causes deafness."

This entire quest of the underworld, with its descent into hell, its long initiatory path that assumes the shape of the labyrinth, the revelation of its square chamber bathed in a white and greenish light in which sits the Black Virgin, only represents a process that leads to the mystery of the absolute, but in this place we can once more become integrated into the divine Unity.

MAISONS-LAFITTE, 1973

PART TWO
•••
The Cavern

18

Preamble

THE CAVERN! Such a vast subject that is difficult to define with any precision, as its definitions are many and varied, covering everything from natural caves—whose strange and seductive beauty has been revealed by the spelunkers—to the underground shelters dug out by the hand of man.

There is something intriguing about the underworld. The imagination may be possessed by this world because of the fairylike wealth of some of its caves, the noises that echo there, or its sumptuous expanses. The most legendary beings live in these realms in the company of spirits that should only be faced with the greatest caution because treasures are buried in the depths of the earth. These treasures can be guarded by giants or by dwarves with supernatural powers. The cave is also the basement window of hell.

In the glow of torches, these vast halls glisten with the fires of all those crystals sparkling like diamonds. The human being bows down before such a luxurious and fabulous scene, with so many bewitching things that are a source of constant wonder. The individual is compelled to show his respect but also his fright. And yet, as Gaston Bachelard noted in his book, *Le Psychanalyse du feu,* there is in people "a need to penetrate and go inside things, inside beings."

I am not planning to provide a census of all the caves in France here, though my country does possess a large number. But these natural riches deserve a mention since they have been developed for tourists who visit them by walking along narrow ledges or riding in boats, surrounded by the twinkling of mysterious secretions.

Everything comes from the earth, and to the earth everything returns. Corresponding to the place of the first birth is that of burial.

With this premise, we shall scan several aspects of this underground setting, while noting that humans do not live inside the grandiose décor of the natural cave. They stay on the threshold of "prehistory's Sistine Chapel," and the rock offers them shelter. Yet sometimes they do descend deeper, and in these almost inaccessible regions they have drawn their dreams and their magic desire for dominion. In this site of enchantment and possibly initiation, we can find astounding wall paintings that show a surprising amount of technical mastery in both the line and the conscious observation of an environment that an individual depicted and symbolized.

To reach this site where worship was given not only to fertility but to the ancestors, it is necessary to get down and crawl to get through this narrow gate. The postulant must be able to cross this threshold that stops the rash person who has not prepared himself to receive.

Michel Random writes that

the narrow way was, for our ancestors, the one that led to the most sacred part of the cave. Communion with the gods had to be earned by a difficult progression, symbol of the transformation of the individual and his necessary regeneration at the approach of the sacred.

It cannot be otherwise even today. The way is always very narrow and the path equally difficult. There is no "prodigious dialogue with the gods," as René Huyghe rightly notes, that is not also a prodigious dialogue with the invisible. From the very time of its birth, Art has been holy magic.[1]

Our image of primitive man has totally changed. It is recognized today that these wall paintings are essentially religious and that at the base of every religion is a cosmic notion that serves as the starting point for ceremonial magic, then for the mythology with its cortege of tales and legends.

In his *Natural History Dictionary*, Orbigny made a connection between the crypt and the cave using the cells of the catacombs where the early Christians buried their martyrs as an example. From the hypogeum, which means underground construction, a burial site was established, the crypt—*kryptos*—which represents, however, what is hidden inside the earth. What we actually find in the burial rites associated with the dead individual placed in the ground, in the caves, or beneath the tumuli that represent the Sacred Mountain is the conviction that the spirit survives from the carnal remains that break down in the ground. The dead person in the primordial cave indicates the path to the living person who has yet to awaken to a higher stage of consciousness and the exchange that takes place between Heaven and Earth. The individual meditates and prays near the grave; the dead individual has withdrawn from everyday life but is taking part in the apotheosis of a sublime life and therefore purifies this place, which becomes a sacred enclosure. Thanks to these underground chambers, these chambers of reflection, Moses, Pythagoras, Hermes, Orpheus, and Hiram were plunged into darkness and came back to life in the dazzling light of the revelation. Jesus himself descended into the depths of the earth for three days and drew from it the ascensional power that led into the sky.

Jesus was able to cross through the underground fire without being burned. Other heroes and heroines whose names I cannot resist citing went down into this infernal zone: Izanagi, Ishtar, and the chthonic Artemis exhibited their dignity this way, and through their heavenly ascension these individuals earned infinite bliss.

According to the ancient authors, Hell is connected to our world. For Cicero the souls of the dead were summoned out of the numerous holes that riddled the hills among the sacred groves bordering Lake Avernus in Campania. For Strabo, the cave of Acherusia in Heraclea, sacred to Cybele, is also one of the gates to the underworld. We have to know how to reach this passageway if we wish to experience the middle chamber that offers regeneration. And yet, if we are to believe

Ossendowski, this supreme center of knowledge has been hidden for six thousand years. It went underground into hiding at the beginning of the Dark Age.

Perfectible man must demonstrate his desire to improve himself; he must transcend his inner nature by blending his mind with matter.

It is necessary to know how to battle the Minotaur, even if we are forced to resort to artifice, because it is necessary to emerge from the chaos alive and rediscover the light of resurrection. Cerberus, the monstrous fifty-headed dog, the dog Garm of Germanic mythology, sought to stop the most intrepid adventurers with their brazen voices. It is necessary to know how to enter the labyrinth and go probably astray there, in order to find, like a chosen one, the strait and secret gate. In the underground central chamber, thanks to a baptism of blood, the predestined individual will become the initiate who will find spiritual realization.

So here we are in the initiatory passageway, the one that leads the individual from outside to the secret chamber, that room that is decorated in such a way that its drawings and symbols will permeate the person who has been accepted into the mysteries and who knew how to cross through the narrow neck of the lower door. Symbolically speaking, the individual dies inside the mountain and, in this matrix, takes part in the mysteries of nature and the concert of life. The individual is born a second time in the womb of the earth, Mother Earth. Since the dawn of time his emotions have made him draw on the walls of the cave. He worshipped nature, his gods, and the Mother Goddess who is ever beautiful and fruitful.

Cave art has left some moving testimonies. The sureness of the line and its plastic beauty move us. I will speak in greater detail about the wealth of such art we can find in France, but it should be noted that in all other parts of the world—whether in Asia, Africa, America, Europe, or Australia—we find, tangibly from the same era, the same drawings influenced by what this very observant individual saw in the world around him. Although these civilizations are quite far from each other, and there were no known relations between them, the ambience is similar, and all these drawings share a close kinship.

The same holds true for the mother goddess who is honored in all civilizations, housed in the deep cave where water seeps from the rock and feeds the thin threads of water that snake down the walls. The tempter animal is always cited here as crawling and slithering through these "snake holes," which is the name given to these narrow passages all over the world, although this reptile does not live in this deep underground environment. The serpent is, however, associated with the worship of the mother goddess, the virgin of the underground who passed on her worship to Mary. The enigmatic goddess who dominates the labyrinthine force is often enthroned in a green setting. This woman retains the memory of virginal life and its magnetic power.

The miraculous statue of the Black Virgin was still held in high esteem during the Middle Ages, while with the path of the serpent one can access the city that bears the light, the mysterious Luz that bathes in the celestial blue (and one representation of which can be found above Lourdes).

We really need to talk about the dwelling achieved by man in this world of the cave. We need to replace the image of the brute bestial figure emerging from his lair for that of a more subtle individual who was seeking protection against the elements, such as the cold, rain, hail, or fierce sunlight. This individual was able to enlarge the natural cavity and dug it out of the crumbly rock on the hillside, or even level with the ground.

Whether shelter, house, or a means of defense against bad weather and other dangers, these troglodytic dwellings are called "underground refuges" by Adrien Blanchet and have more recently been referred to as "retrofitted underground spaces." We should mention some carefully crafted dwellings that are comfortable homes and form part of veritable underground cities. Some of our contemporaries live in these houses, and these cave dwellers are no different from any other Frenchmen. There are educated people who benefit from what nature gives them, such as the archaeologist couple the Lists, who live near the cave with the sculptures at Denezé-sous-Doué. The paths pass over their house and barn and when one of their family members dies, they "raise him into the ground."

When nature is more miserly, man can use his intelligence to build something like a cave, such as a hut with a protective roof, but he has lowered the celestial vault to his level; and thus the dome was born. Other constructions have been erected—tumuli, mounds, dolmens, pyramids—all answering to the same need for protection and a place to hide. Everywhere associated with the dwelling we find the sanctuary.

I will not examine the metal extraction works that use mining techniques that have been expanded to include the search for solid, liquid, or gaseous fuels. However, folklore has given us moving stories in which man has asked the earth or its people—whether elves or giants—to not treat him with hostility, for he is not seeking to mutilate or murder his mother the Earth, but only to extract the products he needs from her. For the metals are born and live in this nourishing belly just like the man cast from red clay who is fated to return to dust. I will not discuss this mysterious world and the beings there with supernatural powers that defend its natural riches. And yet if an accident should befall any worker in the underground world, it would be because he failed to honor these subterranean spirits sufficiently.

Nor have I any intention to talk about urban constructions such as sewers, cisterns, reservoirs, drilling sites, or the creation of underground aqueducts, train tunnels, and highway tunnels. I am not going to discuss the works of the National Center for Scientific Research [CNRS], which has been performing experiments since 1948, in the Moulis Cave near Saint Girons, in the crafting of various concrete structures as well as on the diet and development of animals—all the mysterious fauna of the underworld.

Although experiences of caves are likely among the oldest adventures of mankind, and they have given life to powerful and rich legends with this descent into the hells, I am only going to give a brief mention of the joy of the explorer; an impassioned and intoxicating game for those who venture into an unknown and grandiose world that only gradually reveals its beauty. Homage should be paid to the geographer

E. A. Martel, who has paid a key role in revealing a wealth known only to a few regional amateurs. This pioneer is responsible for the creation of the science of speleology. Among these bold men, another deserves mention, Robert de Joly, who was the founder of the Speleological Society of France.

That is the theme of this study that seeks to reflect the universal spirit of the cavern, a place of habitation and protection that became that of a secret temple. The human being regenerates in this maternal belly, and we end up with the most intense form of spirituality, inasmuch as in the most remote and least accessible of places is where the initiatory ceremony unfolds with all its symbolic input.

The real common thread of this approach is the strange continuity or practices and beliefs from prehistory into the eleventh and twelfth centuries in a Middle Ages whose thought was centered on the problem of life and death, and a symbolism that we have an increasingly harder time verifying. It is moving to realize that the oldest remnants show that the caves preserve the history of our ancestors who believed in another life; remnants that show the same concerns and conscious desires have remained with modern men.

It is clearly this permanence of the human spirit that is raised up this way; this is clearly where we find the chain of our tradition.

19

The Cave on
the Earthly Plane

AS AN EXCELLENT OBSERVER, prehistoric man noted that many animals—both birds and mammals—dug their dwellings. Insects, in the interest of their communal lifestyle, created vast irregular constructions with tunnels, chambers, and numerous exits.

The natural needs of humans and animals are both subject to the same imperatives. The human being who found shelter at the entrance to natural cavities copied those things the animals he saw there did that seemed most clever to him.

Caves are created by the action of water that causes the rock to crumble: they can be more or less large. Based on the findings of our excavations, humans settled at the entrance to the shelter, benefiting from the natural circulation of the air and the light of the sun. Sometimes they would use branches or stretched hides to partially close the opening on the spur of rock, and sometimes they enlarged the natural space. Humans rarely occupied the deep caves: dark and dank, they caused respiratory problems, and it was difficult to keep a fire going. These deep cavities were places that were left alone, but as we shall see, these remote areas were given a décor that inspires dreams.

When nature failed to offer him a natural shelter in a cliffside, man would use this terrain by digging a hole in the ground and using the vertical rock wall as part of his underground dwelling, which remained hidden in the landscape of the plains. Like animal burrows, these dwellings had a number of emergency exits. The mole's lair is a circular chamber—the keep—in which seven or eight converging galleries meet. The troglodyte houses built this way on flat plains would appear later—starting in the ninth century.

If it were impossible to settle in the cliffside caves, or dig one in flat terrain, an artificial hill would be constructed with rooms built inside. The use of troglodytic habitations is well known throughout history. Following the Norman invasions and pillaging, many religious communities fled toward central France. For example, in 932, the monks of the Plélan-le-Grand monastery fled the coming of the Norman chieftain Rognvaldr and made their way to Pithiviers, where they placed the skull of their holy king Salomon III. There are also the movements of the Plecit religious community, who left a bone of their first abbot, the saint Gudwal. There are countless cases like these, and it was mainly in underground refuges where they sought to hide from the cruelty of their enemy.

The very famous line of the Chemin des Dames crossed through numerous galleries, one of which is the immense Cave of the Dragon. The Germans turned it into a barracks, lit by electricity, with dormitories, stores, and an infirmary.

This protection has often proved to be an illusion. It has been a common practice since antiquity to smoke out those seeking refuge. Adolphe Badin in his book *Grottes et cavernes* (page 135) recorded the sad incident in 1510 when several brutal soldiers from the rearguard of the French Army commanded by Chevalier Bayard smoked out the inhabitants of Lungara. More than two thousand perished, much to Bayard's despair, and he ordered the guilty men hung. The same author (page 137) also describes the Chittor cave in India, which was the theater for the tragedy in which Princess Padmini sought refuge there with thirteen thousand women to escape the ferocious conqueror Allauddin. They intentionally set themselves on fire and died.

Fortunately underground havens have also been used by peaceful dwellers, as shown in this passage by Jacek Rewerski.

Troglodytism is therefore as old as humanity, and, like humanity, it is universal. The nature of the belowground terrain determines but does not limit it. In North Africa it was developed in limestone regions, in the Middle East (Petra) in sandstone, in Anjou in the tufa, in Cappadocia, Turkey, in the volcanic tuff, and in the loess in China! The spatial distribution of troglodytism seems to correspond to the logic of a certain climatic zone, for the bulk of troglodyte dwellings across the world occur between the temperate and equatorial zone with the maximum amount of development in arid zones and around the Mediterranean basin. It would therefore appear that troglodytism is a dominant phenomenon in regions with hot, dry climates. The underground habitat provides effective protection against both the heat of day and the chill of night. Another reason why cave dwelling developed in these areas more extensively is due to the lack of forests.

Even today, there are several million human beings living in caves (natural or man-made), not only in Africa and Asia, but in Europe (Italy and Spain) and in France where there are still some "cave dwellers."[1]

Edouard Utudjian, a great expert on the underground world, in 1960 estimated that there were some twenty-five thousand cave dwellers living in France, particularly in the Anjou region.[2] Adrien Blanchet did a survey of 1,200 underground refuges in 1923. As of now there are about 2,000.

There are points in common shared by all the cave dwellers of the world. The limited number of rooms ensures their multiple use, and their openings are small. Their ceilings are crude vaults, and their irregular shape is often round with more or less elliptical or Gothic arches. The floor is often covered by a layer of clay or dirt, which is sometimes colored red, and the walls are sometimes coated to make them smoother. When the rock allows it, the dwelling can have several floors, and a wooden floor can be created with beams and joists. The staircases, which are often quite steep, are straight as a ladder and rarely spiral. They can be made of wood or carved directly out of the rock. The temperature is usually a constant 53° to 59°F. It is therefore a fairly pleasant setup that can have some large rooms equipped for meetings or parties. They can also include chapels. In addition to the money saved on heating, there is also a lack of expense for building materials—cave living is quite ecological.

I should also add that these subterranean refuges all over the world have low, narrow corridors, which are often equipped with sliding or rolling doors for sealing the entrance. Inside of the more or less square rooms, benches carved into the walls make it possible to rest and even sleep there. Lookout posts, with seats, are placed at strategic locations, near a bottleneck. Generally, people are only able to travel through them single file, so they are quite easy to defend. These locales are aerated, often by tubes that communicate with the outside while being well hidden. The arrangement of these underground homes is quite complex, apt for leading astray any foe who seeks to enter them, in addition to the passageways that are quite narrow or steep. Everything is created with defense in mind. Adrien Blanchet in his *Souterrains refuges de la France* notes (page 45) that several underground quarters were equipped with a kind of acoustic installation between the rooms: curved narrow pipes, which are small in diameter (0.1 mm), thereby precluding sight, have been found in various sites (Deux-Sèvres, Vendée, and so forth).

Countless groups continue to seek out these mysterious underground settlements. For example, in the Velay region, Boudon Sharmès, who has broadcast his message by publishing eighty-two accounts, entered an underground city that was a mile long. His friend, Lucien Ughetti, who still lives in Saint Étienne, told me about some of their discoveries. Some places have been sealed off by order of municipalities alarmed about the safety of their citizens. No survey of them could be performed. The ground beneath our feet still contains a rich legacy that will be quite difficult to identify.

CAVE DWELLINGS IN THE CLIFF

Anyone who has visited the French countryside, primarily the valleys bordered by cliffs, has probably seen houses carved into the very rock. The sites bordering the Seine, Loire, and Rhone rivers are numerous and varied, and sometimes even luxurious. They are not only the homes of the poor but also the dwellings of the well-off and even aristocrats. The castles of Souzay-Champigny of the Vignolles between Saumur and Montsoreau are richly decorated both inside and out.

I would also like to just mention the village carved into the cliffside of Haute-Isle, not far from the village of Mantes, but I will speak at greater length about its monolithic church later.

Troglodytic refuges can be found all over the world to a certain extent. Along the Niger River in Africa, the Bandiagara cliffs, as well as those of Matmata in Tunisia, are inhabited. Underground refuges such as Pettenau, Ering, Hurn, and Unterwesterbach are famous in Bavaria, but the French caves of Petit Morin have also left moving remnants. The most gripping are the cave dwellings in Turkey. Tupsa, the former Van, has funerary chambers in its artificial mountain from 900 and 800 BCE. Anatolia has preserved the oldest constructions. Cappadocia, which has a very uneven terrain some ten miles from Caesarea offered all kinds of possibilities for refuge. For example, Çatalhöyük is said to have been founded around 6500 BCE. These isolated, pyramidal rocks, which are typical of Ürgüp, can also be seen in Uçhisar. The dwelling is carved inside the cone-shaped stone trunk. The valleys of Zilve and Gavus have the greatest concentration of these underground constructions. The underground city near Nevsehir could hold 60,000 people.

There are also some amazing cave dwellings like these in France, such as the caves carved in the 70-foot-high cliff overlooking the Gironde and the ocean at Meschers-sur-Gironde (Charente-Maritimes, Royan). Protohistoric remnants have been recovered here, and the Protestants found shelter here during the Wars of Religion. Currently there are fishermen living here, and some commercial establishments, such as restaurants, have been opened.

But it is the Calès caves of Lamanon in the Bouches-du-Rhône region that undoubtedly house one of the most important underground cities. Its 12-by-16-square-foot rooms superimposed in the cliff are connected by ladders and staircases carved into the stone. Benches, beds, seats, nooks, ovens, cisterns, and mangers can be seen there. This hodgepodge of dwelling places is so vast that it brings to mind the dwellings of Cappadocia. These homes allegedly housed Neolithic peoples, followed by the Celts, and, more recently, French peasants.

The Jonas caves near Cheix in the Puy-de-Dôme, form a very odd troglodyte city. Made with human hands, the rooms are placed one atop the other in stacks some 130 feet high, with exterior and interior ladders connecting over sixty rooms. Cisterns were used to collect water. According to oral tradition, fugitive Knights Templar took refuge there and stayed there for some time. They are supposed to have converted these caves, which are in fact quite mesmerizing.

There are habitations of the same kind near Jonas in the Chaud de Corent above Martres de Veyre. This area that was once occupied by the Romans also produces an excellent wine. Similarly, the fortress of the town of Domme, which overlooks the Dordogne, is an enormous rock outcrop riddled with caves and galleries. In 1280 this castle belonged to Philip III (Philip the Bold), and after their arrest in 1307, the Knights Templar were imprisoned here. Numerous examples of their graffiti have been found. This also brings to mind the troglodyte houses carved by men in the cliff of Brantome. A scene of the Last Judgment was carved in one of its rooms. The hill of Lamouroux (Corrèze-Brive) also possesses twenty-four artificial caves: a five-story village has been contrived here on a façade of almost 1,000 feet.

Saint Peter's Mountain in Maastricht on the border of Holland and Belgium has a vast network of underground galleries. The island of Malta has megalithic cities that are highly interesting. The one located near Sasa Paula proves the existence of agrarian life: there is a bed carved in the rock as well as nooks for cheese and bread, and there are stables.

CAVE DWELLINGS ON THE PLAIN

Anjou, the most important center for cave dwellings in France, is quite distinctive.

In a large region above Angers, near La Doué-la-Fontaine are quarries from which "Mousseau"—tufa stone and shell marl, both fertilizers—were dug out. Contrary to what took place in the Dordogne region, where troglodytism was for the purpose of refuge, what we have here are veritable underground properties: farms with houses, sheds, stables, and sheepfolds. Jacek Rewerski (page 15) writes:

In the southern part of the Saumur region, both quarries and cave dwellings exhibit a singular character—they are buried vertically in the rock, a fact that is relatively rare even worldwide (an exception is Matmata in Tunisia).

The Douesian plain developed a very distinctive kind of lowland troglodytism (vertical), directly linked to the exploitation of a different stone than tufa, although it is still limestone: shell marl.

They began their construction by digging a trench about three feet wide. The wall builder then dug into the falun while following a convex then concave line to make a vertical descent either to where the rock layer was exhausted or when an underground aquifer was reached. The width of the gallery was calculated on the depth of the excavation so that the proportions of the vault could insure the maximum stability of the building (the height = 2.5 × the width). Actually, no visible change can be seen at the vault level. It should be pointed out though that the extraction of shell marl is more recent than that of tufa and erosion has therefore been at work for less time.

Two uses of the stone are possible here: shell marl for treating the fields or for roadworks and for building material to accompany the massive stones that are used. In this last case, the results are rectangular-shaped cavern courtyards and quarry entrances in the form of "bottles," converted into housing.

With vertical troglodytism, we are dealing with a rural habitat that has many attached farm properties (in contrast to the hillside settlements).

The access to the habitat buried in the prairie is made by a steeply sloping single path (the *courdouère*), which leads to a courtyard located on average twenty-five feet below the fields overlooking it.

Each square (the courtyard of the caves) can contain several homes, and each home most frequently consists of one room with a large fireplace near the entrance. The fireplace often includes a bread oven lined with a smaller fruit oven (for prunes). As in the cliff dwellings, there are lots of nooks that are used as closets, with the largest ones reserved for cradles and beds.

Above and between these "cavern courtyards" snake the small streets of the village, the sole evidence on the surface of a human settlement, except for the church and several chimneys sticking out in the middle of the fields, and the *jittes** used to transfer the harvest (most often grapes) into the caves.

Photos taken from the air give us a seemingly disorganized image of the vertical cave settlement, which does not have the symmetrical structure we are used to seeing. . . . In a conglomeration like this, the streets and paths circumvent the cave courtyards. The framework of the site is not created by the network of connections but by the troglodyte space.

In his doctoral thesis on the Angevin anthropokast, Jacek Rewerski added this:

The large-scale troglodyte settlements in Anjou seem to have appeared in the early Middle Ages, close to the hillsides along the Loire between Gennes and Montsoreau. This may correspond to the use of probable shelters carved out by the Loire over time.

Toward the later Middle Ages and especially the Renaissance,

---

*[Low stone stacks. —*Trans.*]

there was a full expansion of troglodyte settlements that was closely tied to the flourishing exploitation of underground quarries that were dug deeper and deeper into the tufa cliffs.

These quarries were responsible for the renown and prosperity of the region by offering employment, substantial economic impact (export), but also for the prime material of the local "aerial" constructions. Lastly they offered access to a vast hollow space that could be developed for habitation.

The Anjou region possesses a great variety of these creations, some of which are open for visitation, such as the ones at Rochemenier, Denezé-sous-Doué, Grésille, and Doué-la-Fontaine with its zoo. But by traveling on the Loire River it is possible to see Gennes, Cunault—close to its impressive Romanesque church—Souzay-Champigny, Trèves, Dampierre, Chênehutte-les-Tuffeaux, and Saumur.

Among the troglodyte dwellings excavated in flat terrain that are similar to those in Anjou, I should mention the underground dwellings in Tunisia at Matmata, Toujane, Hadege, Tchine, Beni-Aïssa, and Tamezret. A circular or sometimes rectangular pit with a diameter of around 12 feet would be dug into a mound. This pit would go down 15 to 35 feet. At the bottom, a horizontal gallery offered access to the plain and to livestock. Living quarters and stables were crafted around the pit: the main chamber would be oriented toward the east.

In China, urban cave settlements are highly developed in the province of Shaanxi. The houses are also hollowed out around the pit, but the central patio, which is open to the free air, is even larger. It is often 30 by 75 feet and is a little under or over 30 feet down in the Loyang region. The houses are connected to these courtyards.

The ventilation systems have been the subject of much study, and it is also necessary to consider the distribution of light, which is reflected off whitewashed walls after passing through perfectly placed portholes.

Let's return to France with the town of Provins in the Seine-et-Marne department, which has an underground city. Long corridors lead into vast spacious rooms that are around 15 feet high. The vaults are supported by numerous columns, which give the visitor the impression of being inside a temple. Some galleries are open above the others, and it is likely that these arrangements were created before the medieval era. Symbols have been found on the walls: geometrical shapes, circles, and suns as well as fish and heads. Some of them were scratched into the surface and others added. It is hard to form an opinion about the meaning of these marks.

The underground beneath Paris contains some of the largest open spaces in the world. The three and four floors of rooms and galleries found here add up to some 190 miles in all, to which the subway and underground parking lots need to be added. We are all familiar with the catacombs where the skeletons from Parisian cemeteries, particularly the Charnel House of the Innocents, were deposited.[3] The entrance to the immense galleries of the Tombe Issoire is near Place Denfert-Rochereau. A command post for the French Resistance that was 80 feet below the surface was established here between August 19 and 23, 1940, by Colonel Rol-Tanguy, the regional head of the Ile de France.

The caves of Passy beneath the hill of Chaillot—also used for mining stone—were given a place of honor during the 1900 Paris Exposition. Pignare, the director of the restaurant at the Eiffel Tower, installed his wine cellar and mounted painting exhibitions here that attracted much attention. But there are many other caves, such as those in the Latin Quarter or in the nearby suburbs, such as Meudon.

The Office of the Inspector General of Quarries was created on April 4, 1777, to oversee this entire subterranean domain.

The troglodyte village of Naours in Picardy (about 10 miles from Amiens) deserves a quick description. This refuge that is buried some 100 feet below the surface, with its high 6-foot corridors, is an impressive construction. There are nooks for oil lamps over its 125 miles of tunnels; it has twenty-eight galleries, three hundred chambers—ranging from individual rooms to lodging for large families. Each cluster of dwellings has a public square with a fountain—six in all. This veritable refuge city has false doors, guard posts, and ambush sites. The chimneys emerge aboveground far from the habitations, and sometimes even into the chimneys of houses built on the surface. It seems that this underground city was used between 1340 and 1792. Father A. Danicourt restored it in 1887. The Wehrmacht occupied it in 1943. This city has been classified as a national historic monument and is open to visitors.

The site of Lamouroux in Corrèze consists of eighty rooms distributed over five stories.

In Turkey, I can mention the underground cities of Kaymakli, Derinkuyu housing 20,000 inhabitants, and Özkonak, where numerous levels have been discovered (up to seven). This city includes corridors, staircases, air ducts, squares, and streets. A number of defense systems have been noted: large millstones can seal the passageways near the lookout posts, which are equipped with sound ducts for speaking with visitors. Several of these cities could likely hold 60,000 residents.

We find a number of remarkable settlements in Spain that range from cliff-dwelling installations to those that are truly underground. In Murcia province after Cúllar de Baza, we have the great Iberian necropolis of Tútugi; near the Gypsy quarter of Albaicin near Granada, we have the vast underground network of Sacro Monte with its fascinating views; between Granada and Almeria, Guadix offers us a strange underground city whose houses are arranged in squares of nine. The "barrio of Santiago," also inhabited by Gypsies, has a population of around 40,000 inhabitants. To live here the community must agree to accept the would-be resident, so no one can occupy a dwelling without the neighbors' consent. These dwellings are on the hillside overlooking Guadix. Along the path of this magnificent Spanish cliff we should note the Nerja Caves, the village of Cuevas de Almanzora (9,000 inhabitants) to the south of Puerto Lumbreras with their whitewashed façades merging into an extraordinary landscape.

The Crimea also has some underground towns (Inkerman, Tepe-Kermen, Mangup, and Katchalene). The country of Georgia (and Russia) has some similar installations between Moscow and Vladimir.

There are immense temples in Ellora, India. At Inudzuka, Japan, we have the "Hundred Holes" or "Hyakuana," which, like many other such places, contains many narrow low tunnels. Comparable installations can be found in the Hokkaido and Honshu Islands. There are also similar constuctions in Arizona (Flagstaff and Rio Mancos), and the Rio Verde. The underground chambers near Santa Fe are often circular, with domed ceilings and floors of beaten red earth. Their walls are often painted. In addition to the Yucatan, Mexico also has such caves in the cliffs of the Sierra Madres near Jalisco. Religious ceremonies have been performed at the San Pedro mine in the state of Chihuahua.

NATURAL CAVES

France holds the greatest number and variety of natural caves, which are true wonders of nature. Fifteen thousand caves have been listed by the French Federation of Speleology (130, rue St. Maur, Paris 11). Professor André Leroi-Gourhan has written this about the geographical circumstances and formation of caves:

> The majority of the caves of any substantial size were formed during the Secondary Era of limestone's Jurassic stage, in the thickness of the banks formed by the sediment of shallow seas where developed large coral reefs like those of the Antilles or the Australian coast today. The presence of this limestone explains the situation of caves in France, which draws a backwards Z from Bayonne to Montpellier, from Montpellier to Angoulême, and then from Angoulême to Arcy. There is then an irregular line that runs from the Belgian Ardennes to Monaco by way of the Jura and the Alps.
>
> The creation of the caves is the result of a variety of actions whose exact interplay has not yet been completely elucidated but which are connected overall to two phenomena in which water plays a major mechanical role. The first is the erosion or wear caused by particles, sand, gravel, and pebbles carried by the water. This is the predominant cause for the opening of the large underwater channels and, generally, while the cave is still buried beneath the level of the valley

during the time the water is working like a "pressure pipe." This erosion is extended during the period when the cavern has been opened by the subsidence of the valley and water is still circulating in the galleries, but it only affects the channel bottom at this stage.

The corrosion or chemical wear plays an accessory role during the erosion stage but becomes more important once the walls are exposed to the open air. Rainwater and condensation charged with carbonic acid attacks the limestone walls and causes them to dissolve. Streams of rainwater flow directly into the chimneys and cracks. The condensation of hot air that circulates in the galleries is much larger than previously imagined. It provides a constant volume of water that is sufficient for dissolving a part of the carbon in the limestone, which then crystallizes in the concretions.

Not far from Paris, some hundred caves have been listed in the region of Arcy-sur-Cure; the valleys of La Cure, the Yonne, and the Serein were carved out of limestone.

Let me cite several famous caves in France. They go from the simple "Dog Cave" in Royat where a layer of carbon dioxide persists at ground level to the Cave of the Maidens or cave near Ganges in the Hérault valley, where a cable car takes visitors 300 feet below ground. Its immense hall, the "cathedral," with its spectacular stalagmite, "the Virgin and Child," is given special lighting thanks to a modulator console. A midnight mass is celebrated here with choirs, and the ballet *Salome*, interpreted by Ludmila Tchérina, was filmed here for television.

Then there is the Gulf of Padirac! It is in the Lot region, not far from Rocamadour. This is the most famous abyss in France: it is a pit that is 250 feet deep and 100 feet in diameter. Its colossal size makes an impression, but so does the harmony of its proportions. Then there is the hill of Chaillot, where E. A. Martel created dioramas for the 1900 Paris Exposition. After the initial works by Martel (1899), Guy de Lavaur and R. de Joly continued the exploration of the underground river 325 feet below the surface. The visitor travels 1,900 feet of the 8,000 feet of the cave in a boat. A troglodyte restaurant has been installed here where four elevators are in service transporting an annual 250,000 visitors.

The sinkhole of Orgnac (Ardèche) houses the heart of Robert de Joly (1887–1969), who discovered this immense cave where visitors also descend by elevator. It is an overwhelming landscape in which everything is of gigantic proportions.

Another hallucinatory setting: the Armand sinkhole in the gorges of the Tarn River (La Parade-Lozère). A train on tires takes visitors between the four hundred pillars of stalagmites, some of which are 100 feet high. This discovery is due to Martel and his foreman, Louis Armand.

The caves of Bétharram in the upper Pyrenees have been a constant magnet for visitors since 1888. There they find magnificent crystal columns; an extremely high, vaulted ceiling; an underground river; and 9,000 feet of tunnels. The arrangements for tourists are quite remarkable. There are cable cars, electronic information posts with a commentary in six languages that have excellent sound quality, and very good ventilation, which all add up to a comfortable visit to a magical place.

Many other countries have caves that are equally compelling. The Han caves in Belgium receive a large number of visitors. The longest cave in the world is in Switzerland: the Hell Hole has 50 miles of galleries that makes it even larger than Arizona's "Colossal Cave," which only has 40 miles of them.

CAVES WITH SCULPTURES

The cultural legacy of humanity was enlarged by the civilization of the Upper Paleolithic era. These men lived in caves, but they also built round huts girded with stones—like Villerets in the Massif Central—or with mammoth bones—like Mezhyrich in the Ukraine.

With their new tools the people of that time cut and engraved the rock. They also created harpoons and awls and invented the needle. Red ochre was used, primarily for tombs, for which funeral rites were extensively developed. The people of that time carved, painted, and sculpted.

It is the Paleolithic art between 18,000 and 8000 BCE that is the richest and most moving: the man knocked down by a wounded bison, transfixed by an arrow and spilling its entrails—from the Paleolithic period at Lascaux—and our thoughts wander to the bison sculpted in the clay of Tuc d'Audoubert. But in the Lion's Head Cavern in the gorges of the Ardèche, materials have been found from the artists of 18,000 years ago who had finished painting a cow, a stag, and some ibex heads. On the ground there were some shards, spots of paint, and charcoal, because a good light source was needed in this realm of darkness.

It is in fact in the deepest part of the cave, in its most remote and hard to reach areas that these artists left their mysterious messages in an art that was poorly understood for a long time. When these overwhelming discoveries were first made, dignified scholars cried fraud and refused to believe that these great artworks were ancient. They were stubbornly convinced that our ancestor the caveman had limited intelligence and was more animal than human. He had a low forehead and was narrow-minded and stupid compared to us. Suddenly he had become our contemporary and our brother, and his artistic notions are quite close to our own. The artistic beauty, the sense of movement, and the precision of its crafting all indicate a civilization with a love of beauty. This dexterity is evidence of the mastery of a developed world that expresses life's mystery. All of this underground decoration sends us into raptures and moves us deeply.

We know of three major production centers in Europe. There are some astonishing affinities between them, if not to say between them and the rest of the world as well. Is this from knowing how to observe nature and the sky from any point on the planet? Is the same reflection we see here due to the understanding of the laws that govern us? These three European centers are located in Russia and the Ukraine, then the central Danube region—future headquarters of Celtic culture— and finally primarily in southwest France (Dordogne and the region beneath the Pyrenees).

The Eyzies-de-Tayac (Dordogne) is definitely the world Paleolithic capital. The entire Vezère valley contains archaeological finds of the highest importance. The Madeleine cave in particular contained an 11-millimeter ivory amulet of a hyena resting near a human skeleton (National Antiquities Museum). In the Moustier shelter in 1908, Hauser unearthed the skeleton of a Neanderthal man from a layer dating back to the Mousterian era. Then in Loussel, in 1991, Dr. Lalanne discovered a limestone slab on which two figures, and then three mother goddesses (called Venuses) had been carved. One of them carved in the round on this ocher limestone clearly symbolized their fertility. In Cap-Blanc, Lalanne discovered a 50-foot-long frieze depicting bison and steers—all mesmerizing models enhanced with red ocher. In the hamlet of La Mouthe, in 1904, Rivière discovered the first engraving created by prehistoric man at the same time as the painting in the cave of Altamira in Spain was being discovered.

Still in the vicinity of Eyzies there are three hundred wall carvings in the cave of Combarelles, in which Father Breuil (1877–1961) worked as a young prehistorian.

The elegance of the sharp line is also found in the Paleolithic era paintings in the Rouffignac cave (Dordogne-Eyzies). The depths that can be attained by the human mind can be seen in its frieze of mammoths. The drawing at the cave of Pair-Non-Pair in Marcamps (Gironde) is less precise.

The etchings of Teyjat (Dordogne) are clearly highly skilled masterpieces of primitive art. In the cave of Villars (Dordogne Brantôme), with its extremely beautiful stalactites, we can see among thirty wall paintings one that depicts the scene of a man confronting a dangerous animal—here a bison.

Human representations are few in number. However, the cave of Marsoulas (Haute-Garonne-Salies) has, in addition to the amazing bison composed from the juxtaposition of large red dots, human faces both from the front and in profile. We should also look at the clay statues, the bear of Montespan (Haute Garonne, Saint-Gaudens) and the sexual symbols, often male, about which Leroi-Gourhan spoke. But it is at Montesquieu—Avantès (Ariège Saint-Giron) in the cave of the Trois Frères that we find two male and female bisons modeled in clay, as well as footprints and most significantly that mysterious masterpiece, the Sorcerer. Stratified prints of human feet can also be seen in Niaux (Ariège), the famous cave that with Altamira and Lascaux are the three caves with the most beautiful paintings. The fullness of the composition and the preservation of the works that date back to 12,000 BCE reflect rigorous observation and exceptional mastery.

A serpent appears in the cave of Russan (Gard-Nimes), and the figures of prehistoric animals have been preserved in the cave of Vallon-Pont-d'Arc (Ardèche). In Bouzies-Bas (Lot) the cave of Pergouset was studied by Leroi-Gourhan. There among several animals a human silhouette can be seen whose head has been replaced with a bison tail. Among the Aurignacian-Perigord paintings of Cougnac in Payrignac (Lot-Gourdon), which are from 15,000 to 10,000 BCE, we can see several humorous depictions of human beings. And what is the significance of the 10,000- to 12,000-year-old human footprints that can be found at many places, such as Cesseras (Hérault)?

But it is also Lascaux that overlooks Montignac-sur-Vezère (Dordogne) that was discovered in 1940 and to which Father Breuil went running. A flood of visitors came to see it, and films were made. Then it was seen that microscopic algae were attacking these paintings, and it proved necessary to reproduce these prestigious frescoes in a new reconstructed cave.[4] There is no more that needs be said about the beauty, design, and mastery of the art. The "Chamber of Felines" has been justly admired by our contemporaries, who can no longer judge prehistoric man as a lowbrow, narrow-minded individual, a kind of barely evolved animal. The same is true for the cave of Niaux (Tarascon-sur-Ariège) from 10,500 BCE, a veritable museum, with its depictions of bison, horses, stags, and ibexes.

The temple cave of Pech Merle (Lot-Cabrerets) reveals the profuse diversity of reliefs painted some 15,000 to 20,000 years ago. These Aurignacian hunters used bold, bright colors to depict mammoths, bison, and horses; their linear skill is quite precise, but there are also those stalagmite mounds that look like women's breasts. The pointillist horses are surrounded by the naked handprints and footprints of a man and a child. Father Breuil wrote that Pech Merle is "one of the most moving monuments of Paleolithic pictorial art." Bison also are in the artwork found in Loubens (Ariège-Foix).

A sensational discovery was revealed in 1990. While exploring the rocky inlet of Sormiou (between Cassis and Marseille), a scuba-diving instructor, Henri Cosquer, had also been exploring a cave at the end of an underwater tunnel that was 600 feet long and whose entrance was about 115 feet below sea level. After going through the sump, he discovered a cave about 170 feet in diameter and 10 to 15 feet high located slightly above sea level. Extremely beautiful wall paintings adorned this space. They were painted between 12,000 and 10,000 BCE, during the Magdalenian era, the last years of the Upper Paleolithic, a time when sea level was almost 400 feet below its current level. This remarkable site is extremely hard to get to, and it is currently not possible to admire these negative hands from 20,000 years ago. The regional management for underwater archaeological research has blocked the tunnel in order to protect this unique site that is now being studied by scientists.

The cavern of Labastide in the Upper Pyrenees could be given the title of "Horses Cave." First of all, there is the giant horse on an enormous boulder sitting on the axis of the gallery. This horse is about 9 feet long and 6 feet tall, and its head, some 10 feet above the ground, shows a truly rare artistic dexterity. A harmonious ratio connects the horse to the cave's dimensions. This is a very personal work that brings to mind the art being created today. Also in this place we can find frescoes and carvings of horses, reindeer, bison, mammoths, and bears. It seems this could be a sacred site.

The Venus of Lespugue is a masterpiece carved from a mammoth tusk 15,000 years ago. It comes from the Cave of the Curtains in Lespugue, near Saint-Gaudens in Haute-Garonne. The proportions of this mother goddess with her stylized head are clearly oriented to her maternal belly. This is undoubtedly one of the most moving pieces of our heritage.

It is also in a shelter beneath the rock, known as the Cave of the Pope in Brassempouy (Landes), that the Venus of Brassempouy was discovered. This is an admirably expressive woman's head with a stylized hood in a pure oval shape. This minuscule sculpture now figures among the riches of the National Antiquities Museum in Saint-Germain-en-Laye. I should also point out that the National Museum of Prehistory in Eyzies possesses fascinating finds illustrating the lives of our ancestors, as is also true for the Museum of Tautavel in Roussillon (Caune de l'Arago), with its remnants that testify to the lives of the people living there 455,000 years ago.

The furnishings discovered in these caves are rich and varied. In the twenty-two caves of Roc-de-Sers (Charente-Angoulême) that were used for dwellings during the Solutrean period, skeletons and a remarkable collection of Paleolithic bas-reliefs have been found. But in Aurdy (Pyrénées Atlantiques), Saint Michael's Cave possesses an amazing decoration that is similar to hopscotch.

There are many, many more caves that are much more modest in appearance, yet still pose the same questions of interpretation. These sculpted walls are not found at the entrance of the cave but at its remotest point, which is difficult to reach. It often requires squeezing through a tight tunnel where it is necessary to crawl for several dozen feet or even 500 feet. So this is no gratuitous decoration created in a spirit of art for art's sake. Some passages, maybe with a diameter between 2 and 3 feet, are also sculpted, although there is no room to step back. There is an example of this at Portel near Tarascon-sur-Ariège.

These works came to life in darkness. Undoubtedly eyesight grows habituated to the dark, and illumination that might seem quite weak to us was able to make it possible for people to work with great precision. The skillfully mastered gesture was incisive. In all parts of the world it was necessary to bring a means of lighting through one of these narrow passages. It was likely an oil lamp fueled by cabbage oil or animal fat. Torches made from resinous materials are also a possibility, branches or small logs taken from the trunk of certain trees such as Scotch pine. In East Africa it has been recorded that a branch of msasa, an oleaginous wood, can burn for fifteen minutes while casting a brilliant flame. Firewood, juniper, and charcoal were also used. But why go to such trouble to draw in such an out-of-the-way cave unless the place was sacred and reserved for initiates?

Animals are depicted in these caves most often. Is this a form of enchantment? A magical representation? But we have also seen symbolic drawings, ideograms, and geometrical designs like those on the megaliths, and I am thinking especially of the cairn of Gavrinis. In other caves there are representations of breasts, vulvas, and, in some cases, phalluses. This naturally brings fertility cults to mind, but there are also those amazing footprints, and more importantly hands, as at Gargas (Haute-Pyrénées-Aventignan). Some of these prints are described as positive because it is the hand that appears directly applied to the wall after being covered with paint. It is almost always the left hand. With negative prints the hand serves as a stencil: applied to the wall, the paint is sprayed all around it; only the outline appears, and it is most often the right hand. So what could the purpose be for making these prints in the depths of a cave that is so hard to reach? If it were simply for the sake of amusement, it would have been much easier to do this kind of thing at the cavern entrance. Five hundred handprints have been discovered at Gargas, and numerous mutilations have been noted, such as missing phalanxes. Were these the result of accidents or consensual sacrifices?

What could be the meaning of these ivory *bâtons de commandement,** which are decorated with spirals and interlacings and were found in the cave of Isturitz at Saint-Martin d'Arberoue, near Hasparren. A flute from the Aurignacian culture was also found, a 25,000-year-old pipe made from a bird bone pierced with three holes.

In Isère, near La Molière in Engins, "the pit of scriptures" offers symbols, crosses, and triangles, and anthropomorphic symbols. All these graphic signs have a solar resonance. This brings to mind the signs discovered in the Valley of the Marvels (above Nice). Could we be in the presence of a single Bronze Age civilization that has left these as

---

*[Or "command sticks," name given by archaeologists to pierced rods that may have been shaft straighteners found in the prehistoric caves. —*Trans.*]

signs of its passage? The pre-Columbian carved rocks in Guadeloupe have some strange correspondences with them.

The oldest frescoes, those of Altamira, Lascaux, Niaux, and Tassili of Sormiou, are remarkable for their concise lines and the volume given to the figurations that skillfully take advantage of the very shape of the rock to deftly stylize and render movement. But in the almost contemporary representations we no longer find this elegance and purity of drawing. The praying figure of La Roche-Clermont Château (Indre-et-Loire, Chinon) and the two lions facing forward no longer have these fresh qualities. However, this praying figure with its solar disk and hourglass—but is it an hourglass?—appears to respond to a very distinctive symbolism. Comparisons have been made to the Bogomil artistic tradition; I think we need to go back earlier in time.

After the graffiti of Provins, we should give a thought to the sculptures of Denezé, which were likely inspired by medieval art, but do not have the same grandeur.

The sculpted cave of Denezé-sous-Doué in the Maine-et-Loire department with its many figures (about four hundred) poses a problem. According to the custodians Annie and Daniel List, archaeologists and experts on the underground, three or four stone carvers produced this vast collection, whose craftsmanship is often naïve. The figures represent scenes and customs of the sixteenth century. Are these initiatory scenes, by a group of libertarian stone carvers? Or was this room with its numerous maternity scenes used to entertain the inhabitants of the region by retracing the history of this society? Only one room has been currently explored—two others need to be cleared out. The very instructive historical commentary of the custodians makes it possible to envision a more precise study of these strange and enigmatic sculptures, some of which remain unfinished. They appear to have no direct connection to each other but do show an incontestable mastery of the craft. A master stone carver, Pierre d'Angers, who had stayed at the court in Blois around 1560, allegedly indicated the motif of the sculptures to his companions.

The cave of sculptures of Royston, located twenty miles south of Cambridge, was only discovered in 1742 by going down through a vertical pit that was 15 feet long and only 2 feet in diameter. The underground chamber is carved into the chalk in the form of a pear or a cloche. Almost 25 feet high, it has a diameter of around 18 feet. Motifs are carved into the chalk at the circumference of this room. These are fairly crude figures with saints, martyrs, crucifixes, and heraldic emblems. Sylvia P. Beaumon has ventured the hypothesis that this is an underground Templar chapel in which initiatory rites took place, but nothing has emerged to support this theory.[5]

While there is a wealth of examples on French soil, I would like to point out that cave art is also quite rich in Russia, particularly in Siberia, Tajikistan, and Kazakhstan. The Tassili frescoes, with their hunting scenes, are much admired and have been studied by Henri Lhote. A similar representation can be found in the cave of Bombil Pek in Guatemala. In the southern African Kalahari Desert (Bechuanaland), the Bushmen people still live as they did during the time of the caravans. It is said that they have frescoes drawn in some of their caves, but documentation of this is quite rare. It is likely that we would find depictions there similar to those described above.

THE BURIAL CAVE

The most ancient funeral practices known to us were established by Neanderthal man and discovered in 1908 at La Chapelle-aux-Saints (Corrèze, Beaulieu). Fifty thousand years ago, man created a grave, positioned a body sprinkled with ocher in it, and left offerings of jasper tools. By honoring the dead person, thought was given to possible survival and immortality of the soul. The Neanderthal man, before the Middle Paleolithic period, some 35,000 years before our time, felt feelings quite comparable to our own when faced with death.

This is why the traces of graves appear with their rites intended to protect the deceased. In Dolni Vestonice in the Moravian region of the Czech Republic, two mammoth shoulder blades shore up the opening of a young woman's tomb and protect her. Her remains are painted with red ocher.

In the Saint-Sauveur-des-Pourcils cave (Gard), E. A. Martel discovered urns and funerary ashes from Neolithic times. Similar remnants have been found in Sauve and Trèves (Gard). In the hamlet of Raymonden in Chancelade, not far from Périgueux (Dordogne), the skeleton of a 5-foot-3-inch prehistoric man contemporary with Cro-Magnon man was exhumed.

The site of Mada'in Saleh in Saudi Arabia has revealed many tombs dug into the rock. The walls are finely decorated, and these carvings are evidence of the Nabatean civilization from 2,000 years ago.

This burial place has given rise to a variety of definitions. "The hypogeums are tombs that have been entirely excavated by hand under the ground. . . . The plan of the base of the hypogeums is formed by a generally rectangular funerary chamber preceded by a narrow entrance and connected to the ground by a more or less steep slope." This is how Gérard Bailloud expressed it, noting that the covered alley was buried in a trench, and the vertical supports and slabs were most often made of sandstone and sometimes drywall.[6]

The hypogea, graves carved in the sides of mountains, are numerous in Lower Egypt starting with the Sixth Dynasty. The Valley of the Kings contains the tombs of pharaohs and high officials, including that of Queen Hatshepsut.

There are temples and tombs in Petra such as the Khazneh Firaun, the "treasure of the pharaoh," a façade that is 130 feet high and 26 feet wide, carved into the red sandstone.

In Malta, the legendary hypogeum of Hal Saflieni extends over three levels, with numerous burial chambers to which the only access is narrow tunnels.

France has a large number of hypogea. Those of the Petit Morin valley confirm that this narrow valley has always been a privileged site. There are more than one hundred and fifty funerary monuments between Epernay and Les Marais de Saint-Gond. It should be noted that their long tunnels and narrow antechambers, then the funerary room, give an impression of a corridor of dolmens. The navetas of Minorca in the Balearics clearly give a similar impression.

The Roman catacombs are more important, but those of Paris form one of the largest necropolises in the world, as there are some six million skeletons heaped inside them.

The crypt, placed beneath the church choir, is the secret as well as the foundation and bearing frame of the construction. This mysterious choir is dark, almost totally so. Many black virgins still dwell within it, but they have also been moved quite often. The crypt of Saint Victor's in Marseille has remained almost entirely in its original state, and the Black Virgin there dwells in pretty much the same place.

The church's most prominent benefactors are buried in the crypt because this is the holiest spot, with great sacred power. In addition to the deservedly famous crypts of Chartres, Bourges, and many other churches, we should contemplate these underground sites that leave a deep impression no matter how modest the church. I have in mind the crypt of Saint Jean-Baptiste of Château-Gontier, whose two rows of speckled sandstone columns, low vaulted ceiling, and small size clearly shows the symbolic meaning of the cave where man is born and dies. I really want to stress the fact that the underground temple was originally a cave. This can still be seen at Chartres in the north gallery of the largest crypt in France: 350 feet in length with a width of 15 to 20 feet. This is where Notre-Dame-Sous-Terre (Our Lady under the Ground) is enthroned—a very different statuette from the tenth-century one that was originally an object of Druidic worship.

I also have in mind the crypt of Jouarre, one of the three oldest monuments in France.

Perhaps to better illustrate this connection between the grave and the consecrated space, the church of Saint-Michel in Bordeaux houses ninety mummies in its underground vault, which is around 30 feet in diameter. Removed from a cemetery in 1810 where the earth was quite chalky, these well-preserved cadavers gave a huge fright to some Romantics: Théophile Gautier, Taine, and Victor Hugo all visited to take a look at this sight with the help of a candle.

All of these graves placed in caves and beneath tumuli and dolmens since ancient times show that dying earns the individual a new life, whether in the form of a stay in heaven or as part of a series of reincarnations that can eventually lead to nirvana.[7]

But it should also be noted that individuals with exemplary destinies are also born and die in caves. The son of putrefaction is buried in the tomb of his past life. Jesus, Mithras, Adonis, and Attis have all been interred in caverns.

Abraham chose a cave as the burial place for Sarah and so that he too could be buried there. This cavern was called Machpelah or the "double cave," likely to clearly display the character of these two evolutionary trends. The cave of Sainte-Baume in Provence has two famous tombs that do not have a historical connection. In fact, this is the resting place of Mary Magdalene, the repentant sinner and devoted servant of Jesus, as well as that of Master Jacques, one of the three mythic patrons of the Compagnons du Tour de France.

The cavern is simultaneously a place of burial and a place of birth. This is a place plunged into darkness, and these two aspects that may appear to be opposites—life and death—are finally only "the two faces of the same change of a state of being, and this transition from one state to another has always been regarded as one that needs to take place in darkness."[8]

There is also the observation made by Maurice Broëns in *Ces Souterrains* on the desire to know how to distinguish human dwelling from human grave:

> So it seems almost incomprehensible that every artificial cavern discovered in the nineteenth century elicited the following dilemma for people: was this a residence for the living or was it a space entrusted with the keeping of their mortal remains? Much more than a body yet doomed to become a nameless nothing with the passage of time, funerary monuments of the ancients were dedicated to the disincarnate shade, an immaterial form of life for whom needs, if not outright obsessions and nostalgias, persisted. This ambivalence was rendered moot by the rite of incineration. While an urn with the few handfuls of ashes it contains can be set in any corner, the

mausoleum or the simple grave box was truly the binnacle of the deceased—even one whose remains had been scattered or had disappeared. In this case, the memorial was called a cenotaph and was given all the same considerations that in other times and places had been reserved for the sepulcher.[9]

The individual in quest for completion thereby makes a return visit to the womb of the universal mother, the earth. He goes back to the primal material from where he came, the *prima materia*. As Jung says: "The primordial idea of a regeneration through entering the maternal belly is not a sign of regression but is a successful transfer of the libido over the equivalent of the mother and, consequently, toward the spiritual."

Thanks to archaeological studies, we have realized that the cavern—whether it has cave paintings or not—is scarcely a place of habitation, though it can be sometimes turned into a refuge during harsh seasons.

The ground has given back graves and funerary objects; a ritual was perfected once man had witnessed the death of one of his fellow men. Death, one of our deepest mysteries, has left its mark on every individual that has ever imagined that the individual would go into another world. This is what Leroi-Gourhan was discussing when he spoke of the "religion of the caves."

20

The Cave on
the Divine Plane

UNDERGROUND CULTS

Without being able to define what these caves adorned with paintings or drawings represent, we have noted by the fact that they are extremely difficult to access that we should probably regard them as temples and places for initiation. I will revisit the magical power of the cavern. This can inspire thought of shamanic rites, and Mircea Eliade reports many examples in which men refuse "to wound or cut, or rend or scratch the earth with agricultural work, for this would be mutilation of our mother." The earth is therefore a human body.

Plato saw a close kinship between the earth and the woman; the female generative organ is called *delphi,* and this brings the depths of Delphi to mind. The cave is thereby the matrix in which all is born and to which everything returns: it is the immense crucible. Bernard Palissy believes that "the earth is never idle: whatever is naturally consumed inside her, she restores and reshapes anew. If it is not as one spell, she recasts it as another. Similarly the interior and the womb of the earth also labor to produce."

All life produces itself in the world below. Man descends into this primordial egg, this philosophical egg, in order to be regenerated in the site of his first birth.

The cave is mysterious not only because of the darkness that reigns there but for its limestone concretions that assume such strange shapes. Legends are born around this hole, birthplace of the human being, as well as the site of his final burial. Mythology is rich in this regard, and it is common knowledge that the conflicts between the gods are responsible for earthquakes.

The caves of Greece gave shelter to Hermes and Pan, as well as to nymphs with the Phyle Cave on Mount Parnes. In the *Odyssey* (19.188), Homer mentions that births took place in the cave of Eileithyia. Zeus was born in this cave, but he spent his childhood in another cave on Mount Dikti.

Curetes and Dactyls, the metal-smithing magicians, had caves for their homes. And the Uranian gods Zeus, Hera, Artemis, and Poseidon all have subterranean attributes.

Hermes, the son of Maia—the Earth Mother—was born in a cavern on Mount Cyllene, where he is held in high honor.

During the Nineteenth Dynasty, Ramses II had a huge temple carved into the sandstone cliff on the left bank of the Nile. This large edifice is over 100 feet high by 120 feet wide. It goes back almost 200 feet into the mountain. Four 65-foot statues of Ramses seated were placed at the entrance in his honor. Another small temple dedicated to Hathor, the goddess of love and beauty, was built in similar circumstances to honor his wife Nefertari.

I have already mentioned the very hilly region of Turkey, Cappadocia, and its mysterious underground settlements. This is the location of the cave temple of Yazilikaya; the paintings exhibited at the Ankara museum share a strange resemblance to those of Tassili. Close to the strange cone of Ürgüp there is a church that has been carved out of the rock. There are similar sites in Uçhisar and in Çavusin, with the Saint John the Baptist Chapel. There is also the huge construction of Saint Simon's Monastery in Zelve, with its chapel and hermit dwelling.

In India the creation of underground temples was primarily in the Deccan on the Kathiawar Peninsula in the state of Maharastra. In

Ajanta in the Indhyadri mountain chain, there are around thirty caves that were carved in the volcanic rock. Another thirty caves can be found in the Ellora Hills also located in the state of Maharastra, home to the famous monolithic construction that is separated from the mountain by a circular tunnel.

In Afghanistan there is the Buddhist sanctuary of Bamyan, which, in addition to its caves that are laid out in a square octagonal pattern, has two Buddhas carved in the rock that are 115 and 174 feet tall.*

Ethiopia is densely covered by rock churches carved into the red tufa. Tigray Province has ninety, but the ones on the high plateaus of Ouag and Lasta are also worthy of note. Monolithic churches can also be found in Lalibela, 20,000 feet above sea level, in the center of Ethiopia.

Persecuted Christians established places of worship in the Roman catacombs. This is an example of a banned religion that was forced to practice its rites hidden from sight. The underworld joins those who share the same faith and are persecuted for it together. Once the Christians were finally recognized, they in turn persecuted those who did not worship as they did. This explains how Christian inquisitors such as Nicolas Eymerich and Bernard Gui came to denounce heretical conventicles in turn. The Dominican Bernard Gui (1261–1331) was inquisitor of Toulouse in 1307 and bishop of Tuy in Spain and Lodève in 1324. He left to posterity a *Manual for Inquisitors*. In his uncompromising crusade against the heretics, Bernard Gui wrote that "the heretics long remain in revolt against the light sometimes staying in the mountains, and sometimes in the caves and caverns like owls and the children of darkness."

We already know that the caves are the basement windows of hell. The Greeks marked these malefic spots on their maps: in Cape Matapan near Pylos was the site of one of the gates to Hades. Other spots included Thesprotia, Heraclea Pontica, and Trémène. According to Strabo, Pluto is the master of the infernal deities. In all civilizations,

---

*[These two Buddhas were destroyed by the Taliban in 2001. —*Trans.*]

hell is located in the underworld, the lower state of mankind. The religious thought of the Hellenic poets comes close to that of Eastern Jewish traditions here, which themselves appear to have originated in Egypt or Assyria. Khmer mythology speaks of eight major hells, to each of which sixteen minor hells were attached, making for a total of one hundred and twenty-eight hells. In the Chinese concept of the afterlife, the ten hells are ruled by the ten Yama Kings of the Ten Tribunals. There are bas-reliefs in Angkor Wat depicting thirty-two hells. The Asuras, a kind of fallen demigod, can no longer leave the underground kingdom placed beneath Mount Meru and must remain, guarding the treasures buried there.

Volcanoes are also seen as the gateways to hell and the basement windows of the infernal realms. These would include Vesuvius, Etna, and Hekla.

By descending into hell and into the flames that only burn the wicked, the individual will prove his true nature. Once purified he will emerge from this ordeal bigger and better: "Visit the interior of the earth and through purification you will find the secret stone." This is the meaning behind the mysterious acronym of V.I.T.R.I.O.L.*

Rabelais also sent his hero Pantagruel into the depths of the earth (book 5, chapters 18 and 48). Dante also takes us for a walk in these regions in his *Divine Comedy,* in which hell is a funnel consisting of nine circles that grow smaller the deeper one descends. In his *Moral Works* (fragment 6) Plutarch describes several phases of initiation that unfold in the corridors of the tomb. With uncertain step, Cybele takes the underground passages of Eleusis with their many detours, and this brings to mind the journey through the labyrinth. During more recent initiations, like those in Freemasonry, the postulant is symbolically placed in darkness. A thick blindfold covers his eyes and the noise that accompanies him in his "travels" imitates those that echo through the underground tunnel.

This process of purification appears in many legends, most par-

---

*Visita Interiora Terrae Rectificando Invenies Occultem Lapidem.

ticularly those permeated by Celtic thought and the Gospel texts.

After the dramatic events at Calvary, Christ descended into hell. His experience there is described in *Saint Paul's Vision,* or *Saint Paul's Descent into Hell,* which dates from the fourth century and refers to the *Apocalypse* of Peter. This text was found in 1887 in Egypt during the excavations of the necropolis of Akhmim.[1] It is said there that the saint entered hell under the guidance of an angel. There he saw seven furnaces spitting flames and a wheel of fire that tortured a thousand souls with every turn.

The brave Saint Brendan in a flimsy craft made from reeds and oxhides painted red, caught a glimpse of Hell,[2] just as the knight Owen journeyed through it in the Purgatory of Saint Patrick. Tungdal's soul also made a three-day sojourn in this place of torment in order to bring his experience back to other men. In addition to the moralizing value of these tales we can also see that metamorphosis of the Druid hell into the Christian hell.

Medieval thought would latch onto and develop these themes in semisatiric, semidramatic treatises. Similar pictures were inscribed on the Romanesque capitals in which scenes of unbelievable torture can be seen among furnaces and the pits of hell. Caves and grottoes are truly hell's basement windows—the fiery spot at the center of the earth as imagined by Dante but also as poeticized by Jules Verne in the splendor of buried civilizations.

People can go to these natural caverns to consult the dead. Necromancy got a cool reception in Greece, where there was a greater interest in oracles. The sites of Delphi, Olympus, Calchas in Apulia, and Epidaurus are famous. Miracles are commonplace there—and even today we can see ex-votos left as thanks to the healing god. These miracles can take place both in natural caves and in the small artificial holes that have been dug out of the hillsides. Once the person coming for consultation had drunk the water of oblivion, he was inserted feet first through a narrow opening into this cavern, where he would see prophetic signs during the night. Priests would then seat him upon the "throne of memory" and interpret his dreams. Francis Vian, from whom I have borrowed this description, was describing an initiatory ceremony based on the Pythagorian and Platonic doctrines of remembering.[3] The cave of the Seven Sleepers in Ephesus is quite famous. Seven young people from the court of Emperor Decius seeking to flee their persecutors found refuge in the cave of Ephesus, whose entrance was ordered sealed up by the emperor. The seven Christian martyrs slept until the year 448, the year of the Second Council of Ephesus, where they offered evidence of resurrection while discussions were being held on just this topic. These seven sleepers had surrendered completely to the Divine Will, and the Byzantine sanctuary erected there in the fifth century became a magnet for pilgrims. The Koran also devotes a substantial place to them, and sura 18, "the Cavern," describes their slumber, which is also recounted in "Alexander's Quest."[4]

Revelations are given in caves with the Massabielle Cave of Lourdes being one of the most famous. The apparitions began appearing there on February 11, 1858. Bernadette Soubirous was then fourteen years old. This tiny cave (38 × 48 feet) with its miraculous waters draws millions of the faithful. The faith shown by the ill and crippled individuals that come here makes these pilgrimages very moving to witness. It should be noted that the site of Lourdes belongs to protohistory. Grillot de Givry has published a remarkable essay on *Lourdes, ville initiatique* (Chacornac). The Gave River that flows through Lourdes is born in Luz—meaning "light"—site of the astounding fortress that gave shelter to the Knights Templar. Is this a sign?

Without wishing to draw up an exhaustive list of underground churches, let's focus on those of Anjou. The chapel of Doué-la-Fontaine is no longer open to the public. J. and C. Fraysse have noted quite a number of other abandoned underground chapels.[5] Charles Gilbert and Jacek Rewerski mention Fontevraud, Rochemenier, Grésille, and Turquant. The troglodyte chapel of La Vignolle Manor—between Saumur and Montsoreau—has ogival arches. Other galleries have ogival shapes and are easily dubbed "cathedrals," especially as many reach heights close to 60 feet.[6]

The monolith church of Haute-Isle near La Roche-Guyon (Val d'Oise) is an extremely remarkable construction. Its barrel vault stands 25 feet high and the nave is close to 70 feet long. The church's bell tower dates back to 1700. The very odd pulpit is carved out of the rock and reached by a spiral staircase. The Louis XIII woodwork is quite well preserved. Boileau mentions this site in his "Epistle to the Advocate General François de Lamoignon":

> *It is a small village or a hamlet rather*
> *built on the slop of a long row of hills*
> *The inhabitant having neither limestone nor plaster*
> *Knows how to dig out his lodging*
> *Only the house of the Lord, a bit more ornate*
> *Appears outside the surrounding walls.*

The monolith church of Saint-Émilion (Gironde) is one of the most interesting in France. One goes down in it by means of a steep, 45-foot-long alley. The church's choir is lit by two rows of windows. It is said that this large edifice with three naves was created in the Middle Ages by disciples of Saint Émilion around 767. The church is oriented toward the four directions.

However, the most remarkable underground church remains that of Aubeterre-sur-Dronne (Charente). It possesses a reliquary carved directly out of the block. Its nave that is 57 feet by 35 feet has a vault that is 36 feet high. This monolith church is from the eleventh century. After restoration it was once again opened for worship in 1969.

There is another monolith church, an oratory of Saint Martial in Mortagne-sur-Gironde (Charente-Maritime). In the Dordogne region, 20 miles from Périgueux, the abbey of Brantôme emerges from a wall of rock. There are two captivating bas-reliefs in its cave known as the "Last Judgment."

I have already mentioned the crypt of Saint Victor's in Marseille, the cave of Sainte-Baume (Var) where the water seeping through the rock is said to be the tears of the repentant sinner, Mary Magdalene.

And these are but a few of the many places Christians have gathered. I can add to this number with the chapel of the Roche-l'Evêque, the church of Saint-Michel in Bordeaux, and that of the castle of Ferrand a few miles outside Bordeaux. I have to also mention the famous pilgrimage of Rocamadour, but I need to add that one should also go down the thirty-one steps leading to the underground church of Saint-Amadour that was built out of the rock in a natural cave in 1156. Also quite close to the Christian sanctuary is a "Cave of Wonders" that has prehistoric paintings.

There are a plethora of sacred places that have been the site of a worship that has altered over the course of the century and responds to the same human requirement: survival.

Primitive axes, whose symbolism I discussed earlier, have been found in the monolith church of the hamlet of Rémont, in the Doubs River. Pierre Minvielle[7] cites this rock chapel as the "most accomplished type of chthonic temple."

Vals in the Ariège region, not far from Premiers, also offers a good example of a Christianized cavern, as it forms the underground portion of a Romanesque church.

Maurice Broëns has cited the sculpted cave of Dénezé-sous-Doué and ventures the hypothesis of its being a cultural site by virtue of the four hundred carved figures that represent social types.[8] The curators see it as an ecumenical meeting of the Catholic, Protestant, and Jewish religions.

These underground places can bear the mark of chivalrous thought and its spiritual tradition. Of course, thoughts of the Templars immediately enflame the imagination, but we can also cite the Knights Hospitallers of Saint John and the Knights of Rhodes. As an example we can cite the "bove" of the knights, a rotunda of seven stalls in Neuville-sur-Touques, in the Orne department. The cruciform arrangement appears in Villours, close to Terminiers in Eure-et-Loir, and we have already seen that the motifs of the Royston Cave have been attributed to the Templars.

IN THE IMAGE OF THE CAVE

The individual regenerates in the womb of the earth. He is born in the cave and finishes his final slumber there. What becomes of us after death? A cult of hope is born.

We have seen that in 50,000 BCE humans conceived funeral rites, but it is primarily from the Chassey civilization, around 2500 to 1500 BCE, that we see the appearance of megalithic graves. However, dolmens, the earliest architectural monuments to have come down to the present day, date from around 5000 BCE and are likely the tombs of important leaders. France has a very large number of these relics, and the Parisian basin (Seine-Oise-Marne) has provided grounds for extensive study. The megaliths in Brittany are more recent. This mode of construction can be found on the periphery of the Mediterranean basin in North Africa, Portugal, and Corsica, but also in India.[9] The pit is more or less underground. Flat slabs of stone have been placed on the walls formed by vertically erected stone slabs to create a ceiling. In the Seine-Oise-Marne civilizations there were covered alleys buried in front of these chambers. These alleys were sometimes as long as 60 feet with slabs for sealing them equipped with a "manhole" that could be stopped up with a "cork." Earth-covered monuments like these can be found in Crécy-en-Brie and Montigny-Esbly. Their outer shape can be either rectangular or round.

Is this an improvement made to the Grimaldi grave? Cro-Magnon men in the Cavaillon cave surrounded the head of a young Italian with three blocks of stone placed vertically, with a fourth block installed horizontally.

Another prototype of the dolmen can be seen in Saint-Germain-la-Rivière in Gironde. Similar graves from the Magdalenian era have been found in Roc-de-Sers in Charente, in Chancelade, in la Madeleine à Laugerie Basse, and at Cap Blanc in the Dordogne.

Beneath these dolmens an abundant amount of animal remains and red ochre was found. The child of the Arènes Candides de Grimaldi had his skull decorated with shells and was clothed in a jacket adorned with squirrel tails. The body of a woman—primarily her head—was found in Dolni Vestonice in the Czech Republic. She had been covered in red ocher and was holding ten canine teeth of a fox in her right hand. The dead individual was the beneficiary of an important ceremony, and it is likely that the purpose of the dolmen was to shelter the deceased as a natural cavern would.

Extraordinary dolmens have been discovered, such as the one of Bagneux near Saumur. It is more than 75 feet long with a height of around 7 feet beneath the chamber. The weight of the covering stone is more than 100 tons. The stone slab covering the entrance that is oriented to the southeast is estimated to be 40 tons. This famous dolmen is more than 5,000 years old. While I have no desire to create a panoramic view of all the 6,000 dolmens in France, I cannot resist citing the remarkable mound of Tumiac in Arzon because these dolmens are covered in earth. The magnificent designs of Gavrinis with their spirals over a surface of around 175 feet, or the carved axes on the Table of the Merchants at Locmariaquer offer a moving sight that it would be remiss of me not to mention.[10]

One could never say too much about the great architectural value of the crypt of the Gavrinis cairn and the care given to building it, but I must also mention the large cairn of Barnenez (located in Plouezoc'h in the north Finistère region of Brittany near Morlaix). This is an enormous tumulus that is more than 225 feet long and is 22 to 25 feet high. Its width varies from 60 to 90 feet, and it holds eleven dolmen tunnels and nine vaulted rooms with false cupolas. Professor P-R. Giot studied and restored this monument that is a kind of terraced pyramid and dates from 5000 BCE. Another similar cairn existed nearby that was razed by a contractor. That cairn was 110 feet long, 64 feet wide, and 10 feet high. These cairns had three and four tiers.

The volume of stones used in the construction at Barnenez is around 47,000 cubic meters. As a comparison, the Great Pyramid of Cheops has a volume of 2.5 million cubic meters. But the extremely ancient Barnenez cairn should be compared to the terraced pyramid of Zoser. In Pornic, the cairn of the Mousseaux is 220 feet long by 95 feet wide. This construction with three terraces now has houses built on top of it. There are two large dolmen tunnels inside the mound.

Near Saint-Nazaire, in Dissignac, there is a small circular tiered pyramid that is 95 feet in diameter and 20 feet high. A monument in Cuicuilco, Mexico, is said to be similar to this one. All of these monuments are oriented to the sunrise of the winter solstice.[11]

With its man-made hills sheltering funeral chambers, we cannot overlook the Saint-Michel tumulus in Carnac (60,000 square meters) upon the central platform of which was constructed—as in many other places—a chapel in order to thoroughly Christianize such a place. The Doué mound between Saint-Cyr-sur-Morin and Coulommiers is also a man-made tumulus topped by a chapel. It was long regarded as an outlier left by erosion. In Saint-Salvy-de Coutens (Lisle-sur-Tarn) we find another tumulus of protohistoric origin. There are also the many poypes on the lands of Bresse, in Dombes, and on the plain of the Dauphin region. Often these earthen mounds are 45 to 65 feet high and are generally cone shaped. One of the largest is located in Villars-les-Dombes (Ain); a fortified castle was erected on top of it during the Middle Ages. These mounds are also called mottes, and they are called Hausberges in Germany. Vladimir Rosgnilk and Jacques Ravatin mentioned those boves whose purpose was the manipulation of chthonic forces, studied on the basis of waveforms detected by Enel around 1920.[12] Since that time the name EIFs have been given to these waves that appear as an indication of a harmonic field. Boves have been known under this name since the eleventh century as another word for caves.

This led Professor Ravatin to study the bove of the "Knights" in Neuville-sur-Touques in the Auge region. Maurice Broëns provides a list of the boves in his book.[13]

These mounds are also reminiscent of the *bories,* the huts built by shepherds using dry stones without any mortar. Their roofs are customarily cone shaped. They can be found in the Vaucluse area of the Ain. There are even more of them in Auvergne, near Sarlat (on the road of Saint-Amand from Coly to Montignac). They bring to mind the huts made from mammoth bones that have been discovered in Mezhyrich in the Ukraine.

A large number of tumuli have been discovered in Etruria; the Cerveteri tumulus, near the Etruscan port that neighbored Rome, possesses six tunnels that give access to rooms. One of these chambers has a diameter of 150 feet.

The pyramids appeared around 2500 BCE. We more readily talk of the great Egyptian pyramids, especially that of Cheops, but we should also consider the step pyramids in Egypt, which also appear in ancient America in greater number. For readers interested in learning more about these pyramids created by the Olmec, Chavin, Maya, and Aztec cultures, I recommend the excellent book by Fernand Schwab.[14] What we need to essentially focus on here is that these are representations of the mountain whose summit is a center that makes possible communication between earth and sky. In this re-creation of the sacred mountain, corridors were carved, along with rooms in which the remains of the important figures of the empire were laid to rest. Grandiose constructions were created in accordance with the principles of divine harmony, and Plutarch's observation of the sparkling light and clean air that reigned in the passageways of the Egyptian pyramids comes as a surprise to us. This is still the source of our anxious interrogation of these imposing masses of stone that have yet to surrender all their secrets.

I have studied the symbolism of the Tomb of the Christian Woman, which remains woefully underanalyzed. This is an immense construction in Tipaza, not far from Algiers. Nothing has been found in this tomb that was built before the Christian era. This is a strange monument that offers much food for thought. It emphasizes the dome, the re-creation of the cosmic vault. This building allows us a better understanding of the fact that the ultimate misfortune for a temple is to be turned into a sealed tomb over which guard is mounted, although it is often not guarded because there is a cadaver inside.

In the same spirit I mentioned the thirteen Jedars, pyramid-shaped tumuli that are erected over a square base. These are close to the Tomb of the Christian Woman (in Tiaret), but this one has a replica, the Madracen near Constantine.

Among others with a similar shape, I can mention the royal tomb near Monkala in the Indus Valley and the much more recent (eighth to eleventh century) but astounding Borobudur, the great Buddhist temple of Java.

THE CAVE OF THE BLACK MADONNA

I have mentioned the cave paintings and the statues of mother goddesses that appear in countless caves. They are all difficult to explain, but they do allow us to suppose that rites of initiation took place there.

The cave is a temple, and the stylized drawings that decorate it possess a magic power. These graphic works of an astounding sureness and a carefully developed sense of beauty are quite symbolic. These caves are evidence of the profound thought of an educated people who were fully aware of rites and symbols.

Man is sensitive to fertility: that of the plant, that of the animal, and that of the woman. He observes the balance between death and birth. He honors the belly of woman and its organs and worships them.

These eras that occupy a time span from roughly 50,000 to 3000 BCE are characterized by femininity. Countless tombs are in the shape of a womb, and the oracular cave of Delphi takes its name from *delphis,* which means "womb." These statuettes of women depict them with large thighs and small, round breasts. I have mentioned these marvelous figurines earlier, which because of their abstraction are frozen in a dream of eternity.

These enigmatic women, which are almost always found in tombs, have much grace and charm. Are they representations of a goddess? Ancestor worship? Are they meant to help the dead in the existence they are pursuing? All of these graves are evidence of the establishment of a form of worship and the belief in the body's resurrection.

We would like to get to know the motivations of this artist who was adept at polishing stone and creating forms with such simple tools.

Was this artistic man a wizard or priest? These statuettes represent the emotion of an era and the thought of a civilization. In places that were extremely far from each other, man has embodied his sensual and intellectual emotion regarding the appealing woman who gives birth. Within an erotic ideal he has emphasized woman's sex organs; he stressed her belly rich with a fertilized hope. Man was not afraid to assert his sexual satisfaction, but he was also a realist: it was the worship of fertility. It is necessary for nature to produce, to give birth. Because mortality is a fact of life, a high birth rate is also necessary.

These statuettes found in caves show that death could be transcended thanks to the fertility of women. This is why the woman is ritualistically naked. The veils covering her are spun from shadows. This divine Shakti that regenerates and bestows life is inviolable in her substance—which is light.

Woman is an initiated being because she gives birth. Her initiatory nudity penetrates the essence of things. She knows how to abandon the clothing that is subjective value and sensory phenomenon.

This cave shelters the ancestor of the black Cybele and Kala-Kali, who creates and destroys, but who in the final analysis is the one responsible for the springing forth of all energies. Because this Magna Mater is found under the ground, she is black in color like Demeter, Isis, Cybele, Athena, and our astounding Black Virgins. This cave, as the "universal womb, contains all the seeds of life," and it is amazing to note that while the black goddesses are many, the black gods are few in number.

In this cave comparable to the generative organ of the Great Goddess, we have found bodies honored by rites that are all so many sacrifices to the vital forces. Painted with red ocher, they may perhaps be a royal representation of blood and its regenerative properties.

I next noticed that strange statuettes were appearing in the deep crypts more recently, and even in the earth itself. They showed a mother holding on her knees or on her arm—often the left arm—a child holding the insignia of celestial royalty. This is naturally the Virgin Mary and the infant Jesus. But their hands and faces are black. Currently in sub-Saharan Africa, representations of the Virgin are based on black

women. But in France, where there are a large number of these statuettes, they should depict the woman as white, as was the standard in
the eleventh century, even though it was said that Mary had skin the
color of wheat or darker. The Song of Songs defines this quite clearly
(1:5–6; 4:3).

Often the small, wooden medieval statuette would be removed
from its underground world so that it could receive the homage of the
faithful more easily. A black virgin has been pulled from the deep quarries of Paris and placed under glass in a room at the Paris Observatory.
Statuettes have been brought up from the depths similarly in many
other places such as Saint-Roman d'Ay, Rocamadour, and Montserrat.
However, this is often a lady of the Under Earth, who reigns in a cavern, an ancient crypt over which a sanctuary has been built, quite often
on a wooded height in the vicinity of a spring.

Black virgins are located in the country that has the greatest number
of natural caves. France has more than 150 medieval statuettes, Spain
has 30, and a slightly lesser number are found in Italy. The power and
the holiness of these Virgin Mothers transformed into Black Madonnas
has inspired extremely popular pilgrimages, just as healing waters did in
Celtic tradition.

Black goddesses have been venerated throughout all antiquity and
in all civilizations. Isis, Cybele, Minerva, and Athena are black just
like Kali or the Demeter that is worshipped in Arcadia. All of these
black goddesses represent the Earth Mother, who is fecund yet remains
chaste, the womb from which all things come and to which all things
return. Demeter and Ceres stay within a cave; the Annunciation takes
place inside a cave; Gabriel's visit develops the higher faculties of Mary,
who is Eve regenerated.

Isis was highly honored in Gaul, and numerous portrayals of her
were destroyed by the Catholic clergy. One example would be Cardinal
Briçonnet, who had the statuette at Saint-Germain-des-Prés destroyed
in 1514. Initially hostile to any conversion of pagan images, the Catholic
Church later practiced a policy of tolerance. It gave its blessing and
Christianized the solstice festivals, which became Christmas and the

fires of Saint John. Crosses were carved on the menhirs. But before the black idol was converted into a Virgin Mary, how many statues were burned or buried? Just as menhirs were torn from the ground and broken, pagan statues were pelted with stones.

This eternal, supreme mother, the goddess of all eternity, appears in the Uncreated, for she is truly of all eternity. She is the crystallization of a millennial hope. Along with the worship of the woman who gives birth, and the worship of the earth, the cave, and water, Celticism has left us the image of this virgin who fertilizes the seeds within the earth, who presides over germination, and who resolves all cosmic mysteries within her bosom.

The Black Virgin is the color of the beginning of the alchemical Great Work, and Claude d'Ygé writes[15] that "all the Black Virgins analogically teach this truth: that under the earth is hidden 'the mineral light' in the deepest reaches of a despised and vile body, but it is not contemptible: *nigra sum, sed formosa*." This earth fertilized by the inner fire becomes the Immaculate Conception: unmanifested desire and universal passivity are followed by the miraculous birth. The Black Virgin, like the cavern, is the perfect mediator between heaven and earth. The color green is often connected to her worship, as can be seen in Marseille, Jumièges, and Murat. Osiris in the underworld assumed a black appearance to judge souls, but when he welcomed the adept and when he presided over births, he was green. I have referred to the importance of the color green on several occasions, as it is the color of regeneration, and of the Emerald Tablet on which the wisdom text, the credo of the alchemists, is carved. It is also that strange green ray of light, the coronal light that plunges whoever sees it into raptures.

These underground deities appear in the cave, the telluric night from which all has been issued, for we must die in one life to be reborn regenerated in another. The Virgin gives birth in the cave. She is the great creative principle and eternal feminine; she is the Mother Goddess who has taken the names of Venus and Ceres, but most especially that of the dark and maternal Isis. The latent force descends into the depths of inertia and floods the third heavenly sphere—that of regeneration—and has the color of vegetation and creation. The green ray is akin to the water of the spring that undulates like a snake. The Black Virgin centralizes these magic and telluric forces symbolized by the serpent; she rules the initiatory centers and ultrasecret temples, and her subterranean goddess power commands life.

THE CAVE AND THE LABYRINTH

The tangled passageways that lead to the caves, primarily the cavern-refuges created by man, inspire thoughts of labyrinthine paths. This is a dark tunnel with incomprehensible twists and turns, whose plan is invisible to the person who braves it for the first time. This route appears long and liberally seeded with traps, as confirmed by the lookout stations.

In another chapter I will revisit the spiritual and initiatory relationship between the cavern and the labyrinth, a theme that was the source of a magnificent study by René Guénon, But what I want to do here is evoke some of the external aspects of the labyrinth.

We naturally think of the maze of Crete. According to Pliny, a tortuous, winding underground path ended at the central chamber in which the Minotaur was imprisoned. Minos the king had ordered his architect Daedalus to construct a prison for this monster that was devouring boys and girls. Theseus was only able to slay this monster thanks to the complicity of Ariadne. I can hardly sum up here the full richness of this symbolic legend featuring a creature of fable, the half bull–half man offspring of a god and Pasiphaë, the wife of King Minos. Its blood would regenerate the one who was able to emerge victoriously from this trial. Bull fighting remains an exterior representation of an initiatory form of worship that came out from underground to be celebrated in the great sun of the arenas.

The labyrinth of Egypt, built on the island of Moeris, was attributed to Petesuchus or Tithoës. According to The Book of the Dead, the soul of the deceased, guided by Anubis, travels through the labyrinth. Thanks to a guiding thread, the soul makes its way to the tribunal where Osiris is waiting with the assistance of forty-two assessors. Herodotus, Strabo, and Diodorus Siculus state that the Egyptian labyrinth contained three thousand rooms and that the lower floor, which was underground, was the location for the tombs of the pharaohs. The maze of Heracleopolis was said to have been finished 3,600 years before Pliny speaks of it in his *Natural History* (36.19.13).

The famous labyrinths are still those of Lemnos, of the tomb of the king of Etruria, and on the island of Candia. But are these deep galleries that combine several caverns together, and are they labyrinths like those we have the possibility to see in Chartres, Amiens, Bayeux, Guingamp, and several other places? The labyrinths of the Catholic Church, widely used by the Compagnons du Tour de France, are placed on the floor. It is a mosaic whose drawing is merely symbolic, representing the winding path of the knight going to the Holy Land to defend the Holy Sepulcher. The path finally leads the faithful to the Holy Place where all those of good will shall receive their just reward.

But this "Path of Jerusalem" can only have true value in its underground aspect. The adventurous quest can only be achieved in the telluric night. The man must be alone and lost in the immense darkness in which the sound of his footsteps echoes in the silence with a monstrous intensity.

Do we have true labyrinths in the churches? As early as 1886 Adolphe Badin humorously reported on his escapades in the labyrinth of Crete in his book *Grottes et Cavernes*.[16] Paul Le Cour was fairly skeptical about the labyrinth of Knossos in Crete that Dr. Evans of Oxford discovered in 1902.[17] With the labyrinth as it appears in our imaginations, man is the prisoner of a cycle that is eternally starting over again. The man becomes lost in its knotwork and interlacings as he wanders indefinitely. Often he finds himself at the exit before he was able to discover the central chamber. Pernath, the master gem cutter in Gustav Meyrink's astounding initiatory novel, *The Golem,* must stoop low and crawl through the dark and winding tunnels that are buried beneath the old Jewish quarter of Prague to reach a room where he becomes paralyzed by the sight of a Tarot card, the Pagad.*

Yes, the "Corridor of the Black School" will cause the unwary to go astray but will nourish an enchanting power of mirage and vertigo. The man remains prisoner of a spell, that of the atmosphere of the cave.

If the man can make his way to the chamber of the carvings after having passed through the strait gate—the bottleneck—he returns to the surface with a new knowledge; a spiritual light glows in his being because he has seen. Again it is necessary to understand. He is likely not yet an initiate, but he has absorbed the words of O. V. de L. Milosz: "Its entrance is also its only exit. Birth and death are one and the same, single passage of physical movement and vice versa."

These tunnels offer access to mysterious, enchanted rooms whose magic value is detectable and in which shamanism is able to find expression. They can lead us to the revelation of the secret chamber, bathed in the greenish-white light where the incomparable Black Virgin is enthroned.

The individual, then aware, will leave this place transfigured; he will be another being, an initiate.

---

*[The Juggler, or the Magician in other Tarot decks. —*Trans.*]

21

The Cave on
the Cosmic Plane

THE CAVERN: EGG OF THE WORLD

Underground dwellings were conceived as places providing a refuge from danger. People there were "undercover," to borrow an expression from initiatory societies.

With the labyrinth, the trials of wandering underground makes a selection among individuals: some will go astray and get lost in this tangle, and others will make their way more or less quickly to the chamber "with the sculptures," illuminated by symbols. This route that was a means of protection and ritual defense against all that is outside works as well in the material world as it does in the spiritual world.

None should enter the underground room save they who are "free and of good moral character," they who have already supplied proof of their honesty, and who possess the possibility to achieve perfection.

In the cave, the image of the world, the individual regenerates. Placed beneath its protective vault, he or she is in reality beneath the mountains, between heaven and earth. There in the central chamber, with the help of priests or shamans, he or she can be transformed.

This hatching will only occur in the most secret of places, whose form will then be reproduced artificially.

According to the biblical documents, the Annunciation took place in Nazareth, a site riddled with caves. Recent excavations have revealed the existence of a pagan temple, and other caverns served as homes. It is not impossible that one of them may have been the "house of Mary."

According to tradition the birth of Jesus took place in a long cavern. It is not irrelevant to note that Jesus, Mithras, and Lao-Tzu were born in caves. It was not until a later date that their births were placed during the winter solstice, which is to say when the sun has reached the lowest point of its course and is about to be reborn and restore vigor to all living things. This is why shepherds and animals bow to those who represent the original energy. Zeus, Agni, and Dionysus were also born in caves and were hailed at that time by shepherds. For Mexicans, Chicomoztac Caverns—which can be translated as "Seven Caves"— is also the cradle of their race, just as the cave of Abu Ya'qūb is for Muslims, as can be seen in esoteric Islamic doctrine.

Miguel Angel Asturias portrayed the anxiety of the Guatemalan people in the presence of ritual magic in his admirable book, *Men of Maize*. In an interview with Francis de Miomandre, he said that the Guatemalan Maya believe that the first men were born in a cave, to which they returned when they died. The deities dwell in caves whose springs are an object of worship; women are not allowed to approach them. Tzul Taccah, god of the mountains and valleys, who made the growing of corn fruitful, dwelled there. This is why caves are sacred and were the object of pilgrimages. As examples, I can mention Pec'Moh, Santa Eulalia, and Cojaj. The symbolism of the cave appears in the Popol Vuh, the Mayan bible.

It would be tedious to list every god and demigod that was born in a cave, often perfumed caves like those of Dionysus, surrounded by immense forests with murmuring waters, and just as often in the middle of a wooded island where birds are perpetually singing: paradise.

Adam, all too likely created in a cave, found refuge in a cave beneath a mountain when he was expelled from Paradise. There he hid the gold, incense, and myrrh that he stole from the heavenly garden. The Magi kings, of which there were twelve originally but were knocked down to three by the pope, Saint Leo (440–461), offered these three items as presents to the Child King.

Caves often appear in biblical texts. When fleeing from Sodom, Lot found refuge with his two daughters in one of them (Genesis 19:30). On the death of Sarah in Hebron, Abraham—Lot's uncle—chose for her grave site the cave of Machpelah, whose name means something that is doubled. Abraham is actually at rest there, as well as two other patriarchs, Isaac and Jacob, along with their wives.

David found refuge in caves on two occasions—their names are Adullam and En-gedi. While Elijah's cave is revered on Mount Carmel, we should remember that he went into retreat on Mount Horeb for forty days and forty nights, where Moses also found shelter. According to 1 Kings 18:4, Obadiah hid one hundred prophets there, while the Song of Songs assures us that the mountaintops are riddled with caves.

It was in a rocky cave in the valley of Hebron that, after the Flood, the astonishing message of sacred science written by Hermes Trismegistus was discovered. This famous text written on an emerald or marble slab was found between two pillars. It is now known by alchemists as the Emerald Tablet.

No biblical scenes take place in caves, but artists are happy to harmoniously reflect this collective dream. Both Leonardo da Vinci and Raphael place these holy figures in caverns, but the raised finger of Saint John is pointing toward the sky.

The tomb of Jesus was dug out of the rock where the skull of Adam was allegedly housed. This place was reconstructed in the churches of the Holy Sepulcher; the one in Bruges piques our interest.

According to the Bible, births and deaths take place in caves but the radiantly beautiful Venus emerges from a shell whose whorls form a spiral. These shellfish, such as the oyster, share the image of the chalice and the cave.

The cave became a place of worship where these profound mysteries were honored. Henri Le Saux lived in the caves of Arunachala, one of the most sacred sites of India. This was the location of Ramana Maharshi's ashram in the "heart of Shiva." To reach it a person had to "crawl like a snake."[1] Gabriel de La Varende, owner of the caves in Arcy-sur-Cure, noted that the Chinese ideogram for the cave represents an inner place, a sanctuary, a pagoda which is a site of meditation and prayer.

The immense caves of Ferrand underneath Saint-Émilion are called Druid caves. The archaeologists, the Lists, have examined these caves extensively and discovered that they are oriented to be lit by the setting sun and that the number seven is preponderant there.

All of these monuments, most of which have an intentional orientation, share similar features. They are located beneath a magical mountain. The cupola and the dome are the image of the sky, just like the ceiling of the cavern. Every temple is the placement for a world axis. Inside this stunning evocation of the center of the world, with the vertical axis connecting heaven and earth, it should be noted that the top of the dome is often pierced; sometimes a pole is even used to materialize this fictitious axis. Smoke and incense, just like the soul, are able to escape through this hole; we "emerge into the cosmos," but it is also the means by which "the Eye of the World" watches us.

The cauldron, a deep chalice, with its large concave cavity is likened to the cave. In Celtic legends, in the Grail quest, the cauldron, like the Gallic cooking pot, permits all guests to sate both their appetite for food and that for spiritual sustenance. This vessel of abundance is sometimes a skull. This brings to mind the holy chalice, the cauldron of immortality, and the cauldron of resurrection. There is also the astounding Gundestrup cauldron or the *ding* vessels in China, in which offerings were boiled.

But this is also the utensil that the ogre and the witch use to cook their horrific meals: "the man, often headless, is cast into the boiling water," "the flesh came off the bones." In many Celtic tales the man emerges alive from the vat, and many times he has been rejuvenated. This is the cauldron of immortality.

According to Tertullian, John the Evangelist was cast into a cauldron like this on the order of Emperor Domitian. Thanks to the will of Jesus, John emerged from this ordeal unscathed. Albrecht Dürer made an engraving of this scene, the prologue to his *Apocalypse*.

The outer material fire has been able to unite with the spiritual fire of the tortured individual. This inspires thought of the natural heat of the belly of the earth that activates fertility, and which is also present in the chamber of reflection. The fire of the postulant joins again with the universal fire. The place of the initial initiation possesses its philosophical fire just like that of the alchemists.

Let's again note the admirable story by Gérard de Nerval, *Journey to the Orient* (the story of the Queen of the Morning and Solomon) that retraces the activity of Adoniram who had built his forges and foundries near the underground palace of Enoch. Now, according to the *Nights of Ramazan,* Adoniram, following his temporary setback, went down with Tubal-cain to this palace located in the center of the earth beneath Kaf Mountain. He returned from it charged with a new energy that allowed him to fulfill his mission.

The cave has been described as being identical with the egg. The lower part is the earth, and the upper part is the sky. This image of the world that reflects the perfect principle of organization is also contained in the secret teachings (Brahmavidya) which Sri Krishna Prem explains this way:

> The universe or Cosmic Egg is divided into two parts, higher and lower, between which the *manasic* centers—the individual egos—are located. The higher half is reflected in the lower half with each individual ego being, so to speak, the focal center where this reflection takes place. The two halves are considered as Spirit and Matter and are symbolized by the two well-known triangles intertwined around their central point. Sometimes the symbol is different and the two triangles are placed end to end giving us the *damaru* or Shiva's double drum, the *kamandalu* of Brahma, the hourglass of Saturn, and the sacred double-headed axe of the Cretan mysteries. The upper hemisphere is also designated as the Mons Philosophorum, the Mountain of the Philosophers symbolized by Mount Meru and Mount Kailash.

However, it is true that we must be careful in applying these terms of Matter and Spirit to these cosmic hemispheres, for Spirit and Matter represent the two ultimate poles of the being. In and of themselves they are beyond all strict manifestation: beyond the world of Brahma or Cosmic Egg. All the egg contains is formed by their combined play; consequently it is not in the sense of a predominant manifestation that we can speak of the Higher Hemisphere as Spirit and the Lower Hemisphere as Matter.

Each of them is divided into three (the three angles of the triangle) and the higher trinity is reflected by the lower trinity, but in reverse, just like the Kabbalah teaches that *demon est deus inversus,* the Devil is the reverse reflection of God.

The two trinities with the central part form the well-known seven worlds, the seven worlds of the manifested being that is designated in Hindu teaching by *bhūr, bhuvas, mahas, jana, tapas, satya.*[2]

We are likely here in the presence of the first manifestation of the nonmanifested couple, the whole of the world of Brahma, the archetype of the couple Adam and Eve.

Khnum, the potter of the banks of the Nile, modeled the egg of the world on his potter's wheel, perhaps the egg of Brahma whose seven shells are the seven spheres. Zeus transformed into a swan to fertilize the egg of Leda, from which the Dioscuri, Castor and Pollux, emerged. Castor and Pollux correspond to the two hemispheres of this world egg.

The swan Hamsa himself incubated the Brahmānda over the primordial waters. But when we know that Hamsa is breath, we know that we are in the presence of the divine breath, which, in the beginning, ruled over the face of the waters, and we recognize the Word.

The cosmic symbol of the stupa is also related to the cosmic egg and to the tumulus. We should note that this monument characteristic of Buddhist India is a world axis and represents a spiritual momentum that goes beyond the contingencies of manifestation.

In this astounding tangle of analogies—as I have been analyzing this cave like a world egg—shouldn't mention also be made of the fact that Kneph, the Egyptian serpent, produces an egg through its mouth? Here is another image of the Word, and it is saying the egg contains life and is the representation of the world. The same line of thought can be seen in the Celtic concept of the knot of serpents.

This is why the apse in our churches is always representative of the east when considered from the standpoint of architectural symbolism. This hemispherical concavity, this quarter-sphere vault is clearly yet another image of the cave, and of the seashell that marks the path on the pilgrimage to Santiago de Compostela.

The cave is a matrix where the seed grows. In a remarkable work, Jean Servier mentions that, in Berber culture, the cave is a sacred place: "In its form, the cave is feminine; the visitor's passing through recalls the pangs of childbirth."[3] For transmutation to take place in this egg, ceremonial acts of purification with animal sacrifices are performed.

We can imagine, from a symbolic perspective, an equivalency between the egg of the world, the chalice, and the heart. The cave represents the heart cavity considered as the center of the individual as well as the interior of the world egg.

Thoughts of the secret cavern of the heart bring to mind the color red, the color of blood and wine as well as the color of royalty. In Neolithic tombs the dead were sprinkled with red ocher. It so happens that Adam, according to Hebrew tradition, is related to *adom,* which means "red," and to *adamah,* which means "clay" or "earth." This is how by kneading the red earth the Lord formed Adam, who represents perfection.

Westphalia, where the tribunals of the Wehme were born around 1360, is called *die rote Erde,* "the red earth: it is only on this soil that raged an implacable justice that defends the interests of its inhabitants; something that implies a territorial supremacy."

René Guénon writes:

The development of the spiritual seed implies that the being leaves its individual state and the cosmic setting which is its proper domain, just as in coming out of the body of the whale, Jonah is "revived."

The belly of the whale is a maternal belly, a womb of regeneration, as Jonah had been imprisoned in it for three days, the same span of time that allowed Jesus to go down into the depths of the earth to receive the strength he needed for his ascension and full realization.

Actually, the whale, in the case of Jonah, is simultaneously destroyer (Jonah disappears) and regenerator (Jonah miraculously comes back to life), is both a tomb and a rebirth. René Guénon related this theme to that of the Hebraic Leviathan and the Hindu Makara—sea monsters connected to the sign of Capricorn—or in the Arab tradition to the "daughters of the whale" (*banāt al-Hūt*).

In his analysis of this initiatory cave, René Guénon also writes:

The new birth necessarily presupposes death to the former state, whether of an individual or of a world, death and birth or resurrection—these are two aspects that are inseparable one from another, for in reality they are nothing other than the two opposite faces of one same change of state. In the alphabet *nūn* immediately follows *mīm,* which has among its principle meanings that of death (*al-mawt*); its form represents the being completely folded in on itself, reduced as it were to pure virtuality, to which the position of prostration ritually corresponds. But by the concentration of all the essential possibilities of the being in one single and indestructible point, this virtuality, which may seem a transitory annihilation, immediately becomes the very seed from which will come all its developments in the higher states.[4]

In order for the soul to attain eternal bliss and to go beyond its own nature, it must return to its origins. It must go down into the depths of the earth. This descent allows one to seek out and bring back the stone that can only be found in the earth's womb. Initiation will not be effective until the salt and the stone have been fixed. It is necessary to descend into the pit by degrees and rediscover its successive stages because in order to reach paradise, it is obligatory to go through fire, one of the stages of initiation. With this initiatory death, realization is carried out by means of the stone, and the second initiatory death resides in sublime crystallization. From it the chosen one can draw the ascensional strength that will allow him to reach heaven.

This is how the inner man—the man of desire as Louis-Claude de Saint-Martin called him—can die to profane life in order to be reborn in spiritual light, thanks to the knowledge of the initiates.

INITIATION IN THE CAVE

We have seen that the cave paintings were created in places that were extremely hard to reach and that these caves represented the fruitful womb, the generator of new life. This part of the cavern is only accessible to a rare number of the elect. It is a strongly protected Holy of Holies.

In all traditions the place of initiation can only be reached after one has gone through a narrow gate, the image of the Maternal Matter. The dolmens with their covered alleys also have these "manholes" sealed by a stone that can only be removed by one who knows the secret.

The stone that sealed the entrance of the cave of Ali Baba would only move when someone spoke the kabbalistic phrase "Open, Sesame." It just so happens that a sesame seed is tiny, comparable to a grain of wheat. This temporal wealth inspires dreams of a more spiritual value; but Ali Baba's greedy brother, who had not evolved through the stages of wisdom, ignored the world of reflection and died in the profane world. He did not know the power of rhythm and vibration that provides harmony and makes it possible for the sensory faculties to open. He thought he was in possession of a secret whose uniquely spiritual essence cannot be passed on. The secret therefore remains in a pure state and cannot be violated. Even when it appears to have been divulged, it remains valueless in the hands of the person who has not made the necessary mental effort to incorporate it.

The desecrated parts of the caves were likely reserved for the initiation ceremonies of adolescents. Traces of footprints have been found, and the steps of the participants appear to indicate evidence of a rite.

These traces can be found in Pech Merle (Lot), Casseras (Hérault), in the cave of the Three Brothers in Niaux, and in Tuc d'Audoubert.

In addition to the footprints of children there are sometimes those of men and quite rarely those of women. Are we in the presence of an initiation rite that has a ceremonial way of walking? The marks of handprints can also give the impression of evidence of a ritual, perhaps one of a shamanic nature.

Based on the documents in our possession, it is safe to say that all initiations during antiquity took place underground, or beneath the tumuli, pyramids, and stupas that served in its place. The Eleusinian Mysteries indicate it was necessary to go down into the crypts.

Currently, the temple in the cayenne of the Compagnonnage is buried. The Freemason lodge is rarely underground, but in general this is the rule for the chamber of reflection, a trial of the earth in which the postulant remains by himself in narrow location that is painted black with alchemical and symbolic signs.[5] However the Masonic lodge traditionally has no windows. It is a closed space.

It is specified in the fourteenth degree of the Ancient and Accepted Scottish Rite—the Great Scotsman of the Sacred Vault—that the postulant has to be placed in an underground room with a vaulted ceiling, which can only be entered by a hole cut through the top of the vault.

Although our knowledge of Druid rites is imperfect at best, I should mention several forms that have been practiced by neo-Druids since 1717.[6] In one of the "groves" of the Order of Avalon, the future initiate disrobes and washes himself. Still naked and blindfolded, he is locked inside a small nook. The state of darkness caused by the blindfold and the indefinite waiting that is a stop in time brings the chamber of reflection to mind. In Celtic tradition this is how the return to the depths of the earth and the womb of the earth is evoked. Here is where the individual shall be reborn just like a seed.

But in other neo-Druidic orders, and most specifically in the Universal Druidic Order, the future initiate goes beneath a dolmen and sometimes even into a covered alley, which is dark and can appear to be a labyrinth. This groping your way through a sealed place, a kind of chthonic uterus, is also related to the symbolism of the chamber of reflection.

In a more general way, the dolmen is the recreation of the cave: it is the center, the heart, and the place of rebirth where prayer is connected to the worship of fertility.

Mircea Eliade studied the unfolding of this process. In *Myths, Dreams, and Mysteries* he writes:

> Entering the belly of the monster—or being symbolically "buried," or shut up in the initiatory hut—is equivalent to a regression to the primordial nondistinction, to cosmic night. To emerge from the belly or the dark hut or the initiatory "grave" is equivalent to a cosmogony. Initiatory death reiterates the paradigmatic return to chaos, in order to make possible a repetition of the cosmogony—that is, to prepare the new birth.

In this way, thanks to the initiatory ritual, the postulant dies to his everyday life, and he abandons his past. The rites advance him toward a fictitious death. In the darkness of the cave he is reborn to a new life, decanted from the world he has just left.

This death is given material substance by the placement of the neophyte in a coffin, a deep, dark chamber—the chamber of reflection. The nun before she takes her vows has gone to bed wearing a shroud after her hair has been cropped short. The priest and the king, at the moment of his coronation, prostrate themselves flat on the ground, with their faces on the floor. In all initiation we find an act of purification by the four elements. The awakening of the senses leads to a new perception of the organized world.

Moses was initiated in the cave of Horeb, and there he was told the unpronounceable name. But the most mysterious of the great initiation centers remains the Agartha that Ferdinand Ossendowski claims he discovered in the Gobi Desert in 1918.[7] Earlier in 1885 Saint-Yves d'Alveydre spoke of the "Master of the World" living in an initiatory center located in the heart of Asia. Despite the writings of

Jacolliot and Edward Bulwer-Lytton (*The Coming Race*), we are still hunting for this mysterious center that is supposed to have preserved the entire memory of humanity and where the spiritual riches of vanished civilizations are in the hands of the nine sages who secretly guide the world. All the knowledge of Lemuria, Mu, and Atlantis is supposed to have been consigned there. Agartha is where the "King of the World" resides. He is the powerful monarch of a center that went underground six thousand years ago. René Guénon was quite interested in this theme:

> However, the further the Kali-Yuga[8] progresses, the more difficult it becomes to attain unity with this center, which in its turn becomes more and more closed and concealed; at the same time those second-ary centers that represent it externally become rarer;[9] yet when this period finishes the tradition will of necessity be manifested again in its entirety, for the beginning of each *Manvantara*[10] coincides with the end of the preceding one, thus implying the inevitable return of the "primordial state" for humanity on earth.[11]

The cavern plunged into darkness is black like the earth. However, to turn this into a negative aspect and the symbol of impurity appears to be a very simplistic notion. Black symbolized the primordial mat-ter, and alchemy shows the ascent of matter toward the light and redemption. Black, along with the cosmogonic Trimurti, represents the original earth matter. It is the color of deliverance, the culmina-tion of a cycle that precedes regeneration. Here again we find the same notion of survival.

This place is that of the "inner desert" as Marie-Madeleine Davy might describe it.[12] Telluric forces connect the neophyte's nervous sys-tem to that of the earth. Here in this temple the individual has just won the "Great Peace." As noted by René Guénon, one must have crossed the sea of passions and united with tranquility, and possess the self in its fullness.[13] Then one can explore his inner world; one can make stable what until then had been unstable.

This creative thought acts in the darkness like Job tells us (28:3): The miner "setteth an end to darkness, and searcheth out all perfection: the stones of darkness, and the shadow of death." In a shadow-filled cell, the divine conceals itself from the gaze of the profane; in the silence of meditation the Word shall be reborn thanks to the mastery of the self. "Come ye yourselves apart into a desert place," Mark tells us (6:31). The desert: a world where landmarks no longer exist; alone, away from all distractions, but in complete humility, the intelligence awakens, thinks freely, and faithfully questions itself without shame; here transpires the salutary introspection of the responsible man, protected from all outside noises, who, in the silence, seeks to reconstruct his identity and his relationship with the absolute. Silence is his burial, strength softened by the darkness.

Thanks to this isolation, the individual focuses and meditates, his thought becomes regenerative.

In this cave where time has been banished, I think about peace and quiet, and the questioning of Rembrandt's meditating philosopher. I have thus evoked what the reflection of the postulant desiring to enter the Masonic Order should be; one that is undergoing his first test, which is likely the hardest, since to be locked up alone and without assistance causes a shock, and a rupture with the profane world. He forgets all his outside material preoccupations and meditates on the strange symbolism that is contained within this chamber of reflection.

The chamber of reflection, a place of spiritual concentration, is not always looked on favorably by Masons themselves. The man only remains inside it for several moments, and the layout of this enclosed place is not always conducive to spiritual meditation. And yet the seeker, shut away in this cave, is taking part in the ritual of death and resurrection. I have indicated that this cave was the womb in which the second birth would take place—it is the egg. The symbols themselves lead to envisioning the spiritual death of the individual who, transformed and initiated, will be revived in a higher state. The symbols through their dualism suggest the same transformation. You have only to look at the skull and the candle, death and life.

The initiatory death is a fictitious death that can only be achieved in the depths of the earth. Jung has noted that through his initiatory death, man approaches the reintegration of the cosmic night.[14]

Physical death is only the prelude to the resurrection. It cannot be nothingness, but merely a stage that corresponds to the transformation of matter. The seed buried in the ground gives birth to multiple stalks, the ash contributes all its fertilizing properties, the mystical bunch of grapes gives blood, and the wine is nothing other than the blood of the earth that conveys mystical intoxication, symbol of the regeneration of nature, as Melchizedek, king of Salem and priest of God the Highest, regarded them.

Everything is connected to everything. Man is a microcosm in which the universe is shut away. Man's durability is in his will. The man who has just undergone, through his own will, ordeals capable of changing him, who wants to associate with others to feel the same rhythms and hear the same "harmonic music of the spheres," is waking up. He engages another path that connects him to the principle and to the center: it is the "way."

And yet the individual seems to be a prisoner of his fate: birth and death are moments that are independent of his will unless he believes in the law of karma according to which the soul joins the earth at the time and to the family it chooses. Birth comes back to meet death just as the end of one cycle always coincides with the beginning of a new one. The two phenomena are connected. The hourglass opens at birth and shuts down at death, which is the opening to new births. We travel the discontinuous line of the yin-yang symbol or the Möbius strip. There is metaphysical identification. Plato summarizes this thought as follows: "Who knows if life is not actually death and death life? It is possible that we are part of the dead."

This secret temple is the balancing point, the unvarying center that houses the Principle of all cosmic activity. In this central point all opposites find reconciliation and resolution. Beneath the magic mountain the individual stands like a pillar, but he is also a ladder of light, thanks to which he can reintegrate the primal state. This is the Holy Sepulcher

of the circular form—like the imperial chapel in Aix-la-Chapelle—
inasmuch as this center of the world radiates in all directions and favors
none. It receives the radiations from all horizons that converge at its
center and find resolution.

Every sacred site is a center of the world, a place where the Great
Work can carry out spiritual transformation; but Hyperborean tradi-
tion gives us a few privileged ones to think upon: Thule, Avalon, the
Land of the Sun, Agartha.

Alchemists are often depicted as laboring over the operations of
the Great Work in underground laboratories. Alchemical books from
around 1600 were richly illustrated in the atmosphere of a "renaissance" that was seeing its final days. Emperor Rudolph II (1576–1611)
attracted artists, collected the works of Hieronymus Bosch, and
housed alchemists like Khunrath, Helvetius, Maier, and Sendivogius.
Among the fairly numerous books dedicated to the Hermetic science
it can be seen that the workshop is located under a mountain shaped
like a pyramid. "The adept should imitate the rabbit who visits the
interior of the earth. If he imitates it and does not remain blind like
his friend, he will find the 'vitriol,' the prime material of the stone,"
writes Jacques van Lennep. Here is an example in the third engraving of Stephan Michelspacher's *Cabala* (Augsbourg, 1616), but in
Atalanta Fugiens, the treatise published by Maier in 1617, we find this
image again that is also based on the symbolism of the toad. Basil
Valentine often shows that the ore must be taken out of the caves: the
Benedictine monk introduces a dragon there that goes to ground when
confronted by the lion that guards the place. This idea is repeated by
Daniel Mylius, who in 1622 published a book with Lucas Jennis in
which he says that the seven metals are housed inside a cave.

The philosophers' egg appears like a seed in the center of a globe
being hatched by a dragon. This is the cosmic vessel that has to possess
the gentle warmth of the earth. This egg remains "in the dark hollow
of the rock" as Stolcius expresses it. There are quite a few images that
reflect, in accordance with the word *vitriol,* that the prime matter has
to be found in the depths of the earth.

The spiritual center cannot be anything but hidden, as is the chaos of the flask, the dark stage of the work. Then we realize that this place of initiation possesses its own light, a bright and nondazzling clarity that cannot be seen from the outside. This middle of the world is surrounded by the profane world that has its visible lighting, but this light is nothing but darkness to the person who was able to enter the mystery and the axial chamber that is at the center of the idea. Because of its sacred quality and harmonic rhythm the supernatural light of the cavern excludes all other light, which is pale and derisory in contrast. Yet that artificial light is the one we live in.

This is why in the initiation process the cavern, after appearing dark and shadowy, becomes resplendent. This is the true light. The Three Magi were bathed in an intense glow that emanated from someone who seemed helpless and frail: the Holy Child.

The cavern then fills with light; it is the true site of initiation.

I can now bring up the admirable allegory of Plato's cave.

Men have been shackled since childhood in the cave; denied the ability to move, all they can see of the outside world are the shadows projected on the back wall of their prison. Opposite this wall is another shorter wall with a path above on which a fire is burning and along which parade men displaying objects that are silhouetted on the cavern wall. The men born as prisoners believe that these images are real and offer an exact portrayal of life, whereas the intelligible reality belongs to the individual who stays in the bright world outside of the cave.

The man who is content with his vision, without looking for its cause, remains a slave shackled in the "dark place," and his senses are deceived by a reflection. The slave must cause his chains to fall and fight against his ignorance if he wishes to attain the path, with its narrow gate, that provides access to the true light. Only a few chosen ones ever manage to contemplate the higher realities.

Much has been written about the Platonic cavern that, actually, forms part of an initiatory elevation with its line of cognition. Those born as prisoners would be the psyche fallen into the illusion of the senses, because the material world deceives the mind. We can discern here the relative nature of the true knowledge that only offers itself gradually.

This myth also shows that there is a steep ascent toward the light that only a few individuals can find footing on. The individual is blind at this time, and he will only slowly begin to perceive real forms. What he discovers most easily are shadows, then the images of men, and finally the objects themselves.

When the individual manages to understand and make himself part of the world of light, he should return to the cave in order to help his former companions who are still chained there. He has to facilitate their passage into the world of reality and into knowledge. According to Plato, this former prisoner becomes a helper and a teacher.

I have also noted the strange stage of Javanese shadow plays, the Wayang Purwa, in which the spectators form a circle around the screen, the men in such a way to see the flat leather marionettes with their movable arms while the women can only see the shadows these puppets project. Man receives the light; woman conceals herself. A number of religions have held on to similar rites.

A lot more could be said about this allegory. Plato was only describing symbolically an initiatory mystery that he shouldn't have revealed. Some of his comments refer to the symbolism of the chamber of reflection, and it would be a good idea to hunt down their constituent and most likely contradictory elements.

In the chamber of reflection, the man is plunged into darkness comparable to that of Plato's cave. The difference is that he is not chained, and he came there of his own desire. He is confronted by time and the powers of the earth, and his sojourn there is fruitful, while in Plato's cave we see a world of despair. In Masonry, the seeker knows that he is going to live again and is going to acquire new powers. In Plato's world, the individual chained to his illusion has no desire to leave his place, and if he does escape he is blinded by the rays of the sun—by the light of truth.

Plato's cave is an illustration of a dead world where it is impossible to ascend. The chamber of reflection, to the contrary, is the cave, the egg before the world, the place that opens the ways of illumination and transcendence.

In the current day where sects have become increasingly numerous and where people listen indulgently to anyone who can unveil the future by any one of multiple methods, Jules Verne has become a teacher of the esoteric sciences. Under the cover of a coded language and the inventive fable that appeals to our innate taste for adventure, Jules Verne is said to have evoked and transmitted an initiatory philosophy and even went so far as to defend the first race of our kings. It would be less risky to say that through his creative thought and poetic resources, Jules Verne simply rediscovered the great eternal myths that have haunted humanity for thousands of years. Most likely with his admirable *Journey to the Center of the Earth* (1864) we are given grounds to see a preeminent initiatory journey, since in order to reach the center of the earth, which is also the center of the idea, it is necessary to descend into the underworld by means of a labyrinth. Was Jules Verne really trying to deliver an initiatory message? Contrary to some extensive but false analyses, Jules Verne was not a Freemason. Nor was he a member of the Bavarian Illuminati, a half-Masonic, half-political group.* Like all great creators, he rediscovered the symbols that become obvious to the individual who reflects on things and grows in self-awareness. In *The Underground City* (1877) Jules Verne imagined a miner, Simon Ford, who refused to leave the depths of his coal mine. His beautiful daughter shows us the underground beauty of this place.

In *Fragments d'un journal* Mircea Eliade describes the emotion he felt upon reading Jules Verne:

I read *Journey to the Center of the Earth* by Jules Verne and I was fascinated by the boldness of the symbols, and the precision and

---

*There was a Freemason writer, J. F. Vernhes, who was a supporter of the Misraïm Rite in Montpellier in 1821. Could this be the origin of the confusion about Jules Verne the Freemason?

richness of the images. The adventure is truly initiatory and, like in all adventures of this nature, we find the wandering through the labyrinth, the descent into the underworld, the passage over waters, the test of fire, encounters with monsters, the ordeal of absolute solitude and darkness, and finally the triumphant ascension that is nothing but the apotheosis of the initiate. How perfect these images of the subterranean worlds—the other worlds—are. Equally admirable and precise is the mythology that is scarcely camouflaged by Jules Verne's scientific jargon. How have psychologists and literary critics been able to overlook up to now this exceptional document, this inexhaustible treasury of images and archetypes?[15]

Jean-Paul Loubes in *Archi troglo* mentions that Cyrano de Bergerac in *Journey to the Moon* (1650) imagined an underground habitat "as soon as the frosts begin to cool the sky." In *The Time Machine* (1895) H. G. Wells describes the world of the Morlocks, the "lower class" whose life and activity takes place underground and supports the life of the "upper class" Eloi. The underworld of this society is inhabited by slaves who have lost all notion of humanity. We can also make note of the tale in *A Thousand and One Nights* in which Aladdin, who has descended into the depths of the earth, stumbles upon a wonderful garden.

According to Goethe's story *The Green Snake*, the subterranean temple emerges "when the times have been completed." Adoniram, according to Gérard de Nerval—in *Journey to the Orient*—went down into the depths of the earth following the same journey as Tubal-cain.

We are enchanted by the cave of Ali Baba. Its fabulous wealth sparkling with all its precious stones dazzles us and brings us back to the natural riches of the cave. To enter this cave one must be initiated to know how to knock at its entrance. The stone that blocks this entrance only moves when the kabbalistic phrase: "Open, Sesame" is spoken. Is it the power of sound and the vibration of the words? We should not overlook what may seem insignificant and without value: there are forty thieves, the number of atonement. This tale contains a spiritual value that brings us beyond the glimmering of material wealth. In addition, Ali Baba's greedy brother dies as one uninitiated, as he was unable to grow in the search for wisdom. The spiritual secret cannot be communicated; it remains in a pure state and remains valueless for the person who has not made the mental effort to incorporate it.

After the treasure of Monte Cristo we think of mountains in which jewels, gold, and doubloons are piled. Pirates and freebooters hid their fortunes under the rocks. Cathars and Templars, then the Nazi regime, buried their enormous wealth, and the fortune of some people—such as Abbé Bérenger Saunière—came from the discovery of these once buried treasures.

These highly coveted material riches have always been stored in caves. In a Syrian book with the evocative title *The Cavern of the Treasures,* we learn that Adam, who was himself created at the center of the earth, stored the gold, myrrh, and incense he had stolen from paradise in a cave. As we saw earlier, these pilfered items became the gifts of the Three Magi intended for the one who had just been born in a manger carved into a rock.

Man is a dreamer. In all lands, when standing before a mound, the inhabitants of a place repeat what they were told as children: a subterranean gallery was dug beneath the hill; there at the end of the gallery a person could find a gold goat, or a golden calf, or a sack of pieces of eight, or a crown with all its gemstones. The fantastical underworld excites the human imagination.[16]

How do we discover such treasures? Deaulin and Sébillot have recorded many legends. A peasant goes down into a mine and thinks he has only stayed there for a few hours. When he returns he learns that three centuries have gone by on earth. This contraction of time is a prevalent feature in Celtic legends, particularly in the Bran cycle.[17] The person who first touches a treasure will die within the year; and if it is not him it will be one of his family. This memory is so tenacious that it gave rise to outrageous stories after the discovery of Tutankhamen's tomb and the death of several of its explorers.

The most extravagant fables concern, of course, gold mines. India and the countries of South America offer some ingenious accounts. The myth of the ant as a guardian of gold is spread across the entire world, and Herodotus provided an interpretation of it in his work (3.102). In sub-Saharan Africa gold is practically a living being that possesses feelings and can therefore easily spirit itself away.

Strange figures haunt the mines. They often appear at night in preference to day, when the moon casts a faint illumination on objects. This helps the imagination create an enchanted world. In the play of light and shadow, supernatural beings are relentlessly performing strange tasks. Next to pretty sprites, who are always mischievous but well meaning, one must know how to combat the hideous, wicked demons that live thanks to the darkness of the mine. And that is without even mentioning the will-o'-the-wisps.

These spirits break the supports of the tunnel roofs, crushing workers who they also throw stones at when they are causing their materials to rot away or cutting their ropes. They are the ones who send suffocating odors and create all the dangers that the workers have to confront. Rübezahl is a dreadful guardian in the Tyrol. Kircher has left some fine pages on these little demons, such as the easily irritated dwarfs to whom one should give presents. A bowl filled with food or an item of red clothing can usually please them.

The Little Miner, a pygmy from central France, is not always wicked. He teases and torments the miners, but in a friendly way. He blows out their lamps, hides their tools, tears their clothing, and may throw a few stones. The Little Miner continues the job when the crew has left but makes a great deal of noise while he does it. He is the one that gives them warning of danger, by imitating the snap of a wooden frame or by causing a shower of dust in a dangerous place. It has sometimes been observed that the small blows of the Little Miner's pickaxe are in reality only the sound of water drops hitting the floor of a tunnel.

The caves give shelter to an entire race of little people: the Korrigans of Brittany, the Lamiak of the Basque country, the Nichets of the Ardennes, the Jetins of the Loire, the Fadets of Poitou, the Kobolds of Germany, and so forth. The fairies of the Ariège region leave signs of their passage with goose footprints, that mysterious sign of the bustard.

In the underground galleries beneath Paris near Montsouris, there is a being with stupefying agility that jumps from one wall to the next in the complete darkness because he doesn't use any light. Woe to whoever catches sight of the Green Man; it is a sign of death. This *Diable vert* is reminiscent of the *Diable vauvert*,* who could well be the "green devil."

Pharaoh is alleged to have hidden a treasure in these Parisian quarries. Wouldn't Paris, with its symbol the ship, the "bark of Isis," have been the origin of the Parisis? The cult of Isis was celebrated in Paris, and the black virgin that remains from it is De-Dessoubs-Terre (She of Below the Ground).

When these spirits become too irritated, all work is stopped in the mine, and the galleries are filled in order to put a halt to their malevolent actions. There are a number of underground constructions that were abandoned in the sixteenth century because of the terror caused by these wicked beings. Ceremonies of atonement were performed, but the sacrifices did not manage to divert the wrath of the deities whose domain had been violated. Sometimes even the blessing and the sign of the cross performed by a priest was not enough to restore order.

It is true that some mines are discovered without the aid or authorization of the gods. Basil Valentine showed the method for using a forked stick. Illustrators and authors alike—such as Lohneis, Munster, Agricola, Lehmann, Olaus Magnus—have made some beautiful studies of the virtues of magic wands.

Like Tristan and Iseult fleeing the court of King Mark, let's go deep into the forest and find a cave to live in. The sun enters this mineral world and engenders the precious stone that becomes the culmination of a state.

---

*[*Diable vauvert* is a French expression for a place that is miles from anywhere. —*Trans.*]

Let's enter this cave of gemstones: the four gold mountains oriented in accordance with the four cardinal points surround the Himalayas.[18] Let us become that *manjusaka* tree; then, covering ourselves in the dazzling dust of the precious stones, we will once again become the stone in the illuminated cavern; we will be resplendent in our ultimate initiation.

22

Conclusion

WE HAVE MADE A LONG JOURNEY evoking the radiant luxury of our natural caves and our converted underground dwellings; we have examined the drawings and carvings of prehistoric times and looked at rites and forms of worship. The cave, like the earth, is a living being: it has a body, a soul, and a mind.

The underground havens led to amazing subterranean cities. With scant means, long underground tunnels were carved between feudal castles, connecting centers safe from prying eyes; entire cities were crafted. In our day, when we know how to condition the air, and create light and heat efficiently, we are less inventive than our ancestors. We have, though, created railroad stations, parking lots, and subway lines; we know how to dig long tunnels. We have created commercial centers with stores and shelters. The Defense Department of every nation hides workshops and reserves in caves, and they also have created bomb shelters. But with all our technology and machines, our creations remain quite weak compared to what our ancestors were able to create with unprecedented audacity. We are not as imaginative as they were.

It is therefore the lesson of the past that we must relate when describing the full scope of human spirituality that, on every continent, it has had the same concerns and essentially invented the same rites in the same eras. Contrary to what has been put forth, our ancestors were as intelligent as we are, and they knew how to resolve problems on the scale of their society and their environment.

Possessing the highest sense of the sacred, prehistoric man honored those people dear to him who died. His rites barely differ from our own, and he was able to thereby create a ceremonial structure. Archaeology is teaching us about what he thought, how he behaved, and how he created.

We can instinctively understand the initiatory ceremonies whose principal elements have scarcely varied. For we create caves by creating tumuli, dolmen chambers, and secret temples that can becomes pyramids, rotundas, and domes, all while staying in contact with the sacred mountain and the vault of heaven. Taking shape in every era is the current of an intense spirituality into which priests or shamans initiate individuals of goodwill.

But each of us needs some outside help. Even a hero like Theseus would not have been able to overcome the dark twists and turns of the labyrinth and be immersed in a baptism of blood were it not for the complicity of Ariadne, whom he rewarded quite poorly. To descend into the depths of the earth, we need a guide.

Every cave is one of the navels of the world. This center, this Principal Point is not located in just one privileged location. All these "hearts" belong to the domain of manifestation. It is within this invariable milieu that the synthesis of all opposite forces is established. It is then that the secret temple, which had remained dark until this point, lights up. It is the site of initiation. Outside of it darkness reigns, and the rest of us human beings are immersed in it.

We humbly note this enduring quality of thought: in each point of our world, tangibly in the same era, similar realizations displayed the will of man who changes his structures while remaining the same. It is an infinitely moving chain of union.

LE PUY BARBOT, MARCH 11, 1987

APPENDIX 1

Extract from the
Mytho-Hermetic Dictionary

By Dom Antoine-Joseph Pernety

(Paris: Bauche, 1758)[1]

Adiz Stone: Sal ammoniac of the Sages.

Animal, Plant, and Mineral Stone: This is the perfect elixir, composed of the quintessence of the three kingdoms. Not because it is necessary to take something from each kingdom in order to make it, but because it is their principle, and because it is the right medicine to heal their weaknesses, and to push them to the degree of perfection of which they are capable. We must not confuse the term "stone of the Philosophers" with "Philosophers' Stone." The first should be understood as the material of the work, and the second is of the work in its perfection.

Animal Stone: Human blood. This name has also been given to the different types of bezoars.

Arabic Stone: Rulland claims that this is talc, which is also called the Specular Stone, the Stone of the Moon, and Mary's Ice. See Pliny, book 36, chapter 22.

Atticos Stone: See Boric Stone.

Blessed Stone: See Perfect Stone.

Boric Stone *(Lapis borricus)*: Name that the Sages have given to their matter in the white phase. Others have called it Atticos Stone. Pandolphus (discourse 21 in *The Turba Philosophorum*) and Lucas (discourse 22) have named it Aiar.

Caduceus: The caduceus consisted of three parts: the golden rod topped by an iron knob and the two snakes that appear to be trying to devour each other. One of these serpents represents the volatile part of the philosophical matter; the other signifies the fixed part, that fight each other inside a vase. The philosophical gold symbolized by the rod puts them into accord by fixing them to one another and by combining them inseparably into a single body.

Center of the World: This is the matter of the stone of the Philosophers, and the stone itself when it is in its perfection. The Philosophers gave it this name because they say that all the qualities of the universe are as if combined therein.

Cerberus: In the meaning of the common chemists, this is niter (saltpeter), but the Philosophers understand something other than the Cerberus of fable. The Philosopher-Poets only imagined a three-headed dog with gaping jaws that guarded the gates to Hell, and who was shackled by three chains. The alchemists claim that all the fables of the ancient poets are naught but riddles, which are used to conceal the operations of the Philosophers' Stone. In consequence they say that we must understand this three-headed dog Cerberus as the matter of the Philosophers' Stone composed of salt, sulfur, and mercury, sealed within the triple vase of the Philosophers, which are the three chains that bind Cerberus, and that the matter itself is the palace of Pluto, god of Hell, and that the triple vessel is the dog with three heads that guards the palace gate and prevents entry. This last explanation appears more likely to me, for it is said that Cerberus spat out fire, which is a characteristic of furnaces. We should not understand this as meaning that the furnaces of the alchemists spit out fire, like those of ordinary chemists, for the fire of Spagyric Philosophy is not common fire but the fire of nature, a fire that causes heat without burning. And whoever knows this fire, and the way to regulate it, is well advanced in the Hermetic science.

Let him who wishes to study this science therefore have Hercules and know how to marry him at the right moment with his inseparable companion, Theseus; he will soon have the secret of the three kingdoms.

Circle: In terms of the Hermetic science, this signifies the circulation of matter in the egg of the Philosophers. It is in this sense that they call their operation the movement of the heavens, the circular revolutions of the elements, and they also call the Great Work *the squaring of the physical circle.* Michel Maier wrote a short treatise on this subject, whose title is *De Circulo quadrato Physico, sive de Auro.*

They also divide the practice of the Philosophers' Stone into seven circles or operations, yet everything consists of dissolving and coagulating. The first *circle* is the reduction of the matter in water. The second is the coagulation of this water into fixed earth. The third is the digestion of the matter, which is done very slowly; this is why the Philosophers say that the revolutions of this *circle* are done in the secret furnace. It cooks the food of the child of the Sages and converts it into homogenous parts, like the stomach prepares foods so they can be transformed into the substance of the body. D'Espagnat only accepts the existence of *three circles,* through the repetition of which one succeeds, he says, to reduce water into earth, and to conciliate the enemies, which is to say, the volatile with the fixed, the humid with the dry, the cold with the hot, and the water with the fire.

Citrine Stone: The stone pushed to the color of topaz.

Cross: Crosses in common chemistry are characters that indicate the crucible, vinegar, and distilled vinegar. But in the Hermetic science, the cross is, as it was with the Egyptians, the symbol of the four elements, and as the Philosophers' Stone is, they say, composed from the purest substance of coarse elements, which is to say, from the very substance of the element principles; and they said: *in cruce salus,* "salvation is in the cross," in similarity to the salvation of our souls redeemed by the blood of Jesus Christ attached to the tree of the cross. Several of them even pushed audacity so far and had no fear about employing the phrases of the New Testament to form their allegories and riddles. Jean de Roquetaillade, known under the name of Jean de Rupe Sciffa, and Arnold of Villanova say in their books on the composition of the Philosophers' Stone: it is necessary for the Son of Man to be raised upon the cross before being glorified, to designate the volatilization of the fixed and fiery part of the matter. John Dee* the Englishman, in his treatise on the work of the Sages, made a very extensive comparison of the Philosophers' Stone with the mystery of our Redemption. The title of his treatise is *Monas Hieroglyphica*.

Ethesian Stone: Topaz, or the matter of the work when it has reached the color of saffron.

Famous Stone: In terms of Chymistry, it is none other than the salt of urine.

First Stone: White magistery before multiplication, meaning the first sulfur of the work, the Moon of the Philosophers.

Golden Stone: Said of urine itself, in the terms of Chymistry.

Great Stone, the: This is the Philosophers' Stone.

Green Serpent: Mercury of the Sages.

Green Stone: Matter of the Philosophers in putrefaction. It is called *green* because it is still raw and has not acquired through digestion the degree of dryness and perfection it requires.

Hell: The Hermetic Philosophers use this name to describe the useless—and, so to speak, eternal—work of the false alchemists, who are continuously amid their lit furnaces and who never see God, although they desire him without cease. This means that they don't manage at all to reach the perfection of the Great Work, which would give them all the human heart needs to be satisfied in this life. Sometimes they call their matter in putrefaction "hell," because black is the image of darkness, and Hell is a place of darkness and horror.

Indian Stone: Magistery at red.

---

*[Jean de Dée in the original French. —*Trans.*]

Indrademe Stone (*Pierre lazul*): See Indian Stone.

Limestone: Also called, in Chymistry terms, copper slag.

Lunar Stone: Magistery at white.

Mineral Stone: Mercury of the Sages after the conjunction of spirit and body, meaning when the matter begins to become fixed.

Moonstone: This is talc, if we take Avicenna, who has written a long treatise on it, at his word. But the moonstone of the Philosophers is the matter of the work at the white stage.

Perfect Stone: Elixir at red.

Philosophers' Stone: The result of the Hermetic work that the Philosophers also call *projection powder*. The Philosophers' Stone is regarded as a pure pipe dream, and the people who look for it are regarded as lunatics. This scorn, say the Hermetic Philosophers, is in fact the just judgment of God, who would not allow such a precious secret be known to the wicked and the ignorant. Not only do the most famous and learned modern Chymists not consider the Philosophers' Stone to be a pipe dream, but they believe it is a real thing. Beccher, Stahl, and a number of others have defended it against the repeated assaults of ignorance and the people who ordinarily rise up against it knowing nothing about it save its name. See the preliminary discourse of the *Treatise on the Egyptian and Greek Fables Unveiled*.

Predicted Stone: Magistery at white.

Red Stone: Sulfur of the Philosophers.

Root 1: Several physician Chymists have given the name of *roots* to what others call principles and have named them differently, although they are the same things. They call roots the principles of the mixtures, the pure fixed, and the pure volatile. Moreover, all that enters into the composition of the mixture is supposedly heterogeneous, and nonroot, because it is an obstacle to the perfect union of the roots on which the duration depends, and it causes their separation, from which death ensues. It is for this reason that the union of the principles made by alchemy is permanent and incorruptible.

Root 2 (Hermetic Science): Mercury of the Sages during putrefaction.

They have said that their matter, or rather their mercury, was composed of two things from the same *root;* because in fact from one unique matter that is soft and found everywhere, as the Cosmopolite says, two things are drawn, a water and an earth, which reunited form only one thing that never separates. This joining makes but one sole *root,* which is the seed and the true root of the philosophical metals.

The root of the work is, according to Trevisan, the principal ingredient of the philosophical compound. This is why Ripley named it the base. It is the ripe sulfur of the Sun of the Sages, through whose virtue the two other mercurial substances ripen and acquire the degree of the perfection of gold. The Philosophers have also called it the *fire of nature.*

Root 3: Is also said about the principal parts of the human body, from which the others seem to take their origin. The brain is the *root* of all the ligaments, the heart is the *root* of all the limbs, and the liver that of blood. These *roots* only suffer through accident. By keeping them in good health, the entire body is kept healthy, but it is also necessary to heal the accidents to preserve the principal.

Root of the Art: The stone at white. One should not confuse the stone of the art with the stone of the work, because the beginning of the work is the manual preparation, which everyone can do crudely, instead of which the philosophical art only begins after this preparation, about which almost no Philosopher has spoken. This is why the root of the work taken in its principle is the raw matter, and the root of the art is prepared mercury and the matter at the white stage.

Root of the Colors of the Sun and the Moon: This is the mercury of the Sages united with its sulfur.

Root of the Metals: Some have given this name to antimony, and others have given it to common mercury. Both are deceiving themselves. We should understand by *Antimony* and *Mercury* those of the Hermetic Philosophers, who make the same thing, and which is itself the *root* of common antimony and mercury, meaning that in which all is dissolved.

Round Stone: Matter at the white stage.

Sanguinary Stone: The dry water of the Philosophers, which changes the bodies into spirits. It has the virtue of spiritual blood, without which nothing can be made. Flamel also speaks of it in regard to his hieroglyphic figure on which he depicts soldiers cutting the throats of children and whose blood they are putting into a small tub in which the Sun and the Moon are bathing. He says on this subject that it would be an impious and quite unconscionable thing to use human or any animal blood to do the work, and he clearly states that he is only speaking in allegory in this circumstance. The stone is vile and must be made with the seed of metals; but it is precious for its admirable effects on the infirmities of the three kingdoms of Nature.

Second Stone: Sulfur of the Sages, their mine of celestial fire.

Serpent: Nothing is more common than serpents and dragons in the symbolic figures, riddles, and fables of Hermetic Science. The two that Juno sent against Hercules, at the time when he was still in the cradle, should be understood as metallic salts called Sun and Moon, the brother and the sister. They are called *serpents* because they are born in the earth, and they live there, and they hide there in various forms, which cover them like clothing. These serpents were killed by Hercules, which means he reduced the philosophical mercury to putrefaction in the vase, which is a kind of death. The name *serpent* has also been given to mercury because it flows like water, and it moves sinuously like serpents do.

Serpent of the Caduceus of Mercury: They are the fixed and the volatile, which fight each other and are then brought into agreement by fixation.

Serpent of the Philosophers: This is also the same mercury, which, by circulating in the vase, forms small streams that undulate like a snake.

Serpent That Devours Its Tail: This was what was placed in the hand of Saturn as a symbol of the work, of which the end, so say the Philosophers, gives testimony to the beginning. It is the Mercury of the Sages according to Philalethes. Planiscampi interprets it as the spirit of vitriol distilled several times on its dead head.

Serpentine: The *Turba Philosophorum* speaks of the color serpentine, or the color green, and says that it is a sign of vegetation. Philalethes calls it the *desired greenness,* and Ramon Llull says that the matter of the work is the color of lizard green. It is likely the reason that the Philosophers called it *Saturnie végétale* ("leaden plant").

Solar Stone: Red sulfur or the magistery at red. These sulfurs are a production of the Art and not of Nature; in vain will Chymists seek them on or in the earth as a thing that it produces. It only provides the material from which they are made, just as it provides the grain from which we make bread.

Starry Stone: Sulfur of the Philosophers.

Stone 1: In the terms of Hermetic science, this word refers to all that is fixed and does not evaporate at all in fire.

Stone 2: The Sages gave this name to their material in many of the circumstances it was in, depending more or less on the state of its cooking and perfection. Philalethes says in his treatise *De vera Confectione lapidis Philosophici* that the terms *stone* and *unique stone* only mean that the material of the Sages has been pushed to the white stage by the philosophical cooking.

There are three kinds of stones. The stone of the first order is the matter of the Philosophers perfectly purified and reduced to pure mercurial substance. The stone of the second order is the same matter, cooked, digested, and fixed to incombustible sulfur. The stone lastly of the third order is that same matter fermented, multiplied, and pushed to the final perfection of the fixed, permanent, and tinctorial.

Stone and Not Stone: The Hermetic Philosophers have given this name to their perfect magistery and not to the matter they make it with, as some Chymists have wrongly thought. They have not called it stone because it bears any resemblance to stones but because like stones it resists the most violent assaults of fire. It is a very fixed impalpable powder that is heavy and has a good odor, which is why it has been called powder of projection and not stone of projection.

Stone of All Colors: Some Chymists have given this name to glass.

Stone of Bacchus or Dionysus: A hard, black stone that is often marked with red patches. Pliny, Solinus, and Albert say that crushed and infused in water, it will give the water the aroma and taste of wine, and that it will prevent drunkenness or cure it. It is from there that it takes its name.

Stone of Hephestion: Pyrites.

Stone of Medea: This is Pliny's black hematite. He talks of it in book 37, chapter 10.

Stone of Paradise: Powder of projection, the miracle of Art and Nature; some have given this name to the mercury of the Philosophers.

Stone of Silver: Mercury of the Philosophers after it has been given life, meaning it has received its soul and spirit, which is what occurs when the matter attains the white state.

Stone of the Cherubim: Sulfur of the Sages.

Stone of the Mountain: This is the Tortoise, and the Rebis of the Alchemists.

Stone of the Swallow (*Lapis chelidonis*): Small stones the size and shape of a flax seed. Dioscorides says they are found in the stomachs of small swallows, when the moon is crescent shaped. They are ordinarily in two different colors. Pliny says that they are red and mixed with black patches on one side, and the other side is completely black. The ancients attributed great properties to them, but there is a slight whiff of fable to these claims.

Stone That Is Born Wisely in the Air: This is the material of the work that Hermes said had been carried in the belly of the wind or air. It is born in sublimation, for because there is no air in the vase, volatilization cannot take place, and there is a risk the vessel would break. It is reborn there even several times because the fixed must be made volatile at each operation, which Morienus calls disposition. The wet root is the base of metals, like the most fixed; this is why it performs so many wonders, by fortifying nature and repairing its losses, which foods can only do imperfectly. When it is said that the stone contains all things, and that all things are of it and by it, this is on account of its being the radical humidity of all, the principle of all.

Stone That Saturn Swallowed and Then Threw Up: This signifies nothing but the fixed matter of the work that dissolves and becomes commingled with the volatile during the putrefaction called Saturn. He vomits it, says the fable, and it was placed on Mount Helicon, for after the putrefaction and dissolution, this volatilized matter was fixed anew and became stone again. This why the fable says that Saturn was obliged to vomit it.

Stone That Was Very Celebrated in Antiquity: According to Priscian the Grammarian, the Romans named it Abadir, and the Greeks, if we trust the word of Hesychius, Boefylos. They were believed to be alive and were consulted like the Teraphim. These stones were round and of mediocre size. Isidore, as we can see in the life written by Damascius, said that there were baetyls of various kinds, that some were sacred to Saturn and others to Jupiter or the Sun, and so on.

Touchstone: Battus was changed into a touchstone by Mercury, when he was indiscreet enough to say where Mercury had put the cattle of Admetus that he had stolen while Apollo guarded them.

Tree: This is also the name the Philosophers gave the material of the Philosophers' Stone because it is vegetative. *The Great Tree of the Philosophers* is their mercury, their tincture, their principle, and their root; sometimes it is the work of the stone. An anonymous author made this the subject of a treatise titled *De Arbore salari* (*Of the Solar Tree*). It can be found in the sixth chapter of the *Chymical Theater*. The Cosmopolite, in his "Riddle Addressed to the Children of the Truth," supposes that he was transported onto an island adorned with everything nature can produce that is most precious, including two trees, one solar and the other lunar, which means that one produces gold and the other produces silver.

Tree of Gold or Solar Tree: This is the stone at the red stage.

Tree of Life: Name that the Hermetic Philosophers gave to their mercury several times, but more commonly to their elixir because it is then the medicine of the three kingdoms, or their universal panacea because it can resuscitate the dead, meaning the imperfect metals that it raises to the perfection of silver if it is at the white stage, or to gold if it is at the red stage. For this reason they called it the *wood of life.*

Tree of Sea: This is coral and the madrepores.

Tree of Silver: Magistery at the white stage, or matter after the stage of putrefaction.

Trees: Paracelsus gave this name to the tumors and patches that darken and mar the bright natural color of the skin. He only uses this term to describe them at their onset and before they have turned into ulcers.

Unique Stone: This is the perfect elixir, which is unique because there is no mixture in the world that could be compared to it for its properties.

APPENDIX 2

Hollow Earth Mysticism

I HAVE NOT SPOKEN OF the "hollow earth" theories, a pseudo-scientific theory discussed by Louis Pauwels and Jacques Bergier in *The Morning of the Magicians* (Inner Traditions, 2008, 279, 333, 337). A secret community is supposed to inhabit caves at the center of the earth, according to the novel by Bulwer-Lytton, *The Coming Race*. This notion of beings endowed with superhuman powers alleg-edly fully influenced Hitlerian policies through the disciples of the Thule "Luminous Lodge" or "Vril Society," a secret society that was on friendly terms with the Theosophists and the Rosicrucians. This also connected it to the Order of the Golden Dawn, an initiatory movement founded by Wentworth Little in 1887. The fans of the "hollow earth" believe that "we inhabit the interior of a ball caught in a mass of rock which extends into infinity. We live pressed against the concave face: the sky is in the center of this ball." Here we have the substance of the works by the German Bender (1930), founder of the *Hohlweltlehre* movement, successor to the thought of the American Marshall B. Gardner (1913).

For Pauwels and Bergier this earth mysticism comes close to that of traditional legends (337), an opinion I don't share completely, as in the initiation concept man descends into the depths of the earth by tortuous paths and through the narrow door for the purpose of regeneration.

Superimposed upon the central fire that regenerates and purifies is the power of the Earth Mother, the living element of the cosmos to which we must return in order to be reborn. It is therefore not a place where all men live equally but a privileged place that only a select few are able to reach.

MAISONS-LAFFITTE, 1961

Notes

CHAPTER 2.
EARTH, MINERAL BLOOD

1. Mavéric, *La Réforme des bases de l'Astrologie traditionelle.*
2. Génillard, *Inconnu,* no. 13, 112–235.
3. "Si-Do-In-Dzou: Gestures Made by the Officiating Priest in the Mystic Ceremonies of the Tendai and Shingon Sects," *Annales du musée Guimet,* vol. 8.
4. Pausanias, 2.34.1. Also see Strabo and Herodotus.
5. Guénon, *L'Homme et son devenir selon le Vedanta,* 50–51.
6. Third Prapāthaka, khanda 14, shruti 3.
7. Dom Pernety, preface to *Dictionnaire mytho-hermétique.*
8. Eliade, *Mythes, rêves et mystères,* 207; see also Eliade, *Traité d'histoire des religions,* 226.
9. Davy, *Essai sur le symbolisme romane,* 107 and 127–34.
10. *Eludicarium 1,* 11, pl. 172 c. 1116 (after M.-M. Davy).
11. Mircea Eliade dealt with this subject in greater detail in his book *Forgerons et Alchimistes,* 42, 59.
12. Davy, *Essai sur le symbolisme romane,* 96.
13. Text cited by Gaston Bachelard, *La Terre et les reveries de la Volonté,* 286. See *Laura* by George Sand.
14. Palissy, *Récepte veritable,* 35.
15. Dumas, *L'Oeuf cosmique.*
16. Eliade, *Mythes, rêves et mystères.*
17. Fulcanelli, *Le Mystère des Cathédrales* [The Mystery of the Cathedrals].
18. Pernety, "Chaos," in *Mytho-Hermetic Dictionary.*

19. Charles Diot, *Les Sourciers et les monuments mégalithique,* 60.

20. Guénon, *Le Roi du monde,* 78; see also Guénon, *La Grande Triade.*

21. Schaya, *L'Homme et l'Absolu selon la Kabbale,* 81.

22. Also see Ambelain, *Au Pied des menhirs,* 80.

23. We should also note those of Paul Le Cour in *Atlantis,* nos. 10, 11, 17: *L'emolème symbolisme des Trois Enceintes*); René Guénon, "La Triple enceinte druidique," in *Le Voile d'Isis* 35, no. 114 (June 1929); L. Charbonneau-Lassay, "L'Ésotérisme de quelques symbols géometrique," in *Études traditionnelles,* no. 346 (March 1958).

24. Guénon, *Le Roi du monde,* 76; Guénon, *La Grande Triade,* 26. See also my book *La Symbolique du feu* in which I examined the symbolism of the pentagram and the G on several occasions.

CHAPTER 3.
THE TELLURIC CURRENTS

1. Guénon, *Ésotérisme de Dante,* 71.

2. In reality, traditional science tells us it is 33 meters.

3. Jacques Baurès, *L'Aventure souterraine,* 244.

4. See also Rudeaux, *La Terre et son histoire,* and Gamow, *Biographie de la terre.*

5. Vincent, "L'Univers et la Vie," in *L'Ingénieur-Constructeur E.T.P.* (March 1958). The axis, site of the greatest density, contains matter and spirituality.

6. Stanislas de Guaita, *Essais de science maudites.*

7. See the article by F. Dupry-Pacherad, "Le fabuleux Problem du mètre égyptien et les mesures de Karnak."

8. Bouchet, *Bulletin;* Bouchet, "Cours druidiques 10ème leçon."

9. Gamow, *Biographie de la terre,* 76.

CHAPTER 4. THE ROOT

1. See Marshall, *Mohenjo Daro and the Indus Civilization.*

2. Viennot, *Le Culte de l'arbre dans l'Inde ancienne.*

3. Davy, *Essai sur le symbolisme romane,* 162.

4. It would be necessary to develop all these points further. For more on the mediating tree see the magazine *Ogam,* no. 6, 16.

5. Eliade, *Mythes, rêves et mystères,* 87, 153, 260. In his *Images et Symboles* he defines the center in which the sacred is made manifest.

6. Viennot, *Le Culte de l'arbre.*

7. Du Puget, *Les Eddas,* 30.

8. The analysis of J. H. Philpot should also be noted, *The Sacred Tree,* 109–27, as well as that of A. Mac Culloch, *Eddic Mythology,* 331.

9. Guénon, *Le Roi du monde,* 56–87.

10. Viennot, *Le Culte de l'arbre.*

11. Lenormant, *Les Origines de l'Histoire.*

12. Le Cour, *La Crète et ses mystères,* 82.

13. Boucher, *La Symbolique maçonnique,* 268.

14. Tiele, *Histoire comparée des anciennes religions.*

15. It is said that the Ark and the Tabernacle are made from shittim wood (Exodus 36:20).

16. *Mahavamsa,* 144, 70.

17. Viennot, *Le Culte de l'arbre.*

18. Marques-Rivière, *Histoire des doctrines ésotériques,* 21; J.-P. Bayard, *La Symbolique du feu.*

19. For more on the subject of the construction of these two pillars and their symbolism, readers should refer to Boucher, *La Symbolique maçonnique,* 133–38, and to the entry on "La Colonne" in Lanoë-Villène's *Le Livre des symboles.*

20. Papus, *Traité élémentaire des sciences occultes,* 160.

21. Bayard, *Histoire des légendes,* 117.

22. Saintyves, *Les Contes de Perrault,* 257.

23. Doresse, *L'Empire du prêtre Jean,* 2:25.

24. Schmidt, *La Mandragore.*

25. Hildegard von Bingen, *Physicia sanctae Hildegardis Argentorati,* 1544.

26. Lévi, *Dogme et rituel de haute magie.*

27. Tercinet, *Mandragore, Qui es-tu?*

28. Lanoë-Villène, "Le Blé et l'Orge," in *Le Livre des symboles.*

29. Husson, *La Chaîne traditionelle,* 94.

30. Saintyves, *Les Vierges mères et les naissance miraculeuses,* 78. Also see *Le Goéland,* no. 78. Joan of Arc carried a mandrake with her.

31. Migne, "Fève," in *Dictionnaire des Religions.*

32. Loisy, *Essai sur les sacrifices,* 185.

33. Fulcanelli, *Le Mystère des Cathédrales,* 145.
34. Bayard, *La Symbolique du Feu,* chapter on the fires of Saint John.

CHAPTER 5.
UNDERGROUND WATER

1. Guénon, *L'Homme et son devenir,* chapter 21, footnote; Guénon, *Man and His Becoming According to the Vedanta,* 136.
2. Schuon, "La Gnose, langage du Soi," no. 333.
3. Durand, *Rationale,* book 7, chapter 14, V5:62–63.
4. See Canseliet, *Deux logis alchimistes,* 34.
5. Vincent, the review in *L'Ingénieur Constructeur E.T.P.,* 391.
6. Commentary by Horion Toki in the book *Si-Do-In-Dzou. Ban* means "the essence of water," whereas consecrated water is *alkca;* but it is also intended to quench thirst, and its offering is called *argham.*
7. Ramayana, 47.1.2–3.
8. *Bhagavata Purana,* 11.18.
9. Lanoë-Villène, "Le Bain," in *Le Livre des symboles,* 5.
10. For more on this subject, see Marrou, *Saint Augustine.*
11. Diot, *Les Sourciers et les monuments mégalithique,* 9, 20.
12. Bouchet, *Cours druidiques.*
13. Krappe, *La Genèse des mythes,* 201–6.

CHAPTER 6. THE ROCK

1. Bachelard, *La Terre et les reveries,* 188.
2. Michelet, *La Bible de l'humanité,* 162.
3. Michelet, *Le Secret de la Chevalarie,* 15.
4. Davy, *Essai sur le symbolisme romane,* 138.
5. Bayard, "Les Statues animées."
6. Genesis 28:10–32.
7. Eliade, *Forgerons et Alchimistes,* 45.
8. Davy, *Essai sur le symbolisme romane,* 138, 150.
9. Bayard, *Essai sur les representations du diable dans l'art medieval.*
10. Joshua 4:4–10.
11. Exodus 20:25; Deuteronomy 27:6.

12. Pausanias, *Description of Greece.*

13. Fernand Niel, *Dolmens et menhirs,* 31.

14. See Saintyves, *Les Vierges mères,* 28ff.

15. For more on the meaning of the opening carved into the vault, see chapter 9, "The Underground Temple."

16. These acts of vandalism—or unawareness—are still frequent today. Yvan Christ has waged a campaign in the magazine *Arts.* In the issue of June 25–July 1, 1958 (page 15), this critic mentions that dolmens and menhirs are removed to make farm buildings. To remedy a situation like this it will be necessary to educate the public, who often do not see the extent of their great sacrilege. The cinema, radio, and television should make this cause their mission.

17. Palissy, "Les Pierres" in *Discours admirables,* 263.

18. Boehme, *Concerning the Three Principles,* vol. 2.

19. Bachelard cites in his *La Terre et les reveries,* 273, the opinion of E. W. Eschmann contained in *Entretien dans un jardin.*

20. Oswald Wirth also said, in his *Notions élémentaires de maçonnerie,* 18, that the operations of the great work take place within.

21. Text published by the magazine *Atlantis,* no. 191 (April 1958).

22. D'Ygé, *Nouvelle assemblée des Philosophes chymiques.*

23. Belin, *Les Aventures du Philosophe inconnu.*

24. Bayard, *La Sacres et couronnements royaux.*

25. Bayard, "The Grail," *Histoire des légendes,* 74–85.

26. Abbé Aubert, *Histoire et théorie du symbolisme religieux,* vol. 2, 155. Also see Caillette de l'Hervilliers, *Étude sur la loi du secret dans la primitive Église.*

27. Nerval, *Voyage en Orient,* vol. 2, 432.

28. Some rapprochements can be made between some writings, actions, and ideas of Nerval and the books of Meyrink. But this parallel remains hypothetical.

29. Lanoë-Villène, "Couleurs," in *Le Livre des symboles,* 117.

30. Briant, *Le Goéland,* no. 112; also see Briant, *Le Goéland,* no. 6 from 1936.

31. Diot, *Les Sourciers et les monuments,* 30.

32. See Dubois, "Les Poypes de la Bresse et de la Dombes."

33. Lanoë-Villène, "La Couleur noire," in *Le Livre des symbols,* 222; see also Charles Le Goffric, *L'Âme bretonne,* 2nd series, 236.

CHAPTER 7.
THE GEMS FROM UNDERGROUND

1. Viennot, *Le Culte de l'arbre*, 103.

2. Crollius, *La royal chymie*, 112.

3. Barba, *Métallurgie, ou l'art de tirer et de purifier les métaux*, vol. 1, 82.

4. Eliade, *Forgerons et Alchimistes*, 17.

5. Doresse, *L'Empire du prêtre Jean*, 2:107.

6. Porta, *La Magie naturelle*, 487.

7. Bayard, *Les Talismans*.

8. Mandeville, *Le grand Lapidaire*.

9. Palissy, *Récepte veritable*, 51.

10. Exodus 28:17–20.

11. Victor-Émile Michelet, *Les Portes d'airain*, 125.

12. Cros, *Poèmes et proses*, N.R.F; Moreux, *L'Alchimie moderne*, 162.

13. Claudel, "La Mystique des pierres précieuses."

14. Victor-Émile Michelet, *Les Portes d'airain*, 62.

CHAPTER 8.
DESCENT INTO HELL

1. Maury, *La Magie et l'astrologie*, 172.

2. Strabo, *Géographie*, 13.4.14; Cicero, *De Legibus*, 2.25.

3. Couchoud, *La Mythologie asiatique*, 339.

4. Schaya, *L'Homme et l'Absolu selon la Kabbale*, 132.

5. Eliade, *Shamanism* (the descent into hell), 279, 282.

6. We find the same processes in Goethe's story, *The Green Snake and the Beautiful Lily*.

7. See the book by Francis Bar, *Les Routes de l'autre monde*, chapter 6, "Les Descents Philosophiques," and chapter 7, "L'Initiation d'Enée."

8. Persigoult, *Le Cabinet de réflexion*, 77; Bayard, *La Symbolique du cabinet de réflexion*.

9. Guénon, *Ésotérisme de Dante*, 40, 46, and 72.

10. Jacolliot, *La Femme dans l'Inde*, 184.

11. Jung, *Psychology and Alchemy*.

12. D'Ygé, *Nouvelle assemblée des Philosophes chymiques*, 76.

13. Bachelard, *La psychanalyse du Feu,* 84. With regard to Nodier, this would be Smarra's second preface.

14. In his book *Les mystères de l'art royal,* Oswald Wirth has provided an interesting alchemical interpretation, 94–95.

15. Lanoë-Villène, "Le Cygne," in *Le Livre des symboles,* 76.

16. Diricq, *Le Voile d'Isis,* no. 172 (April 1934), 172.

17. Le Cour, *Évangile ésotérique de saint Jean,* 107.

18. *The Vision of Saint Paul* goes back to the fourth century and refers to the *Apocalypse of Peter,* a book rediscovered in Egypt in 1887, during the excavation of the necropolis of Akhmim (publication by Harnack, Leipzig, 1893).

19. Guénon, *L'Ésotérisme de Dante.* Guénon noted that the architecture of Dante's hell was very close to that of the Muslim hell.

20. Richer, *Gérard de Nerval et les doctrines ésotériques.*

21. Tarbé, *Le Purgatoire de saint Patrice.*

22. Bayard, *La Légende de Saint-Brendan.*

23. See Bayard, *La pratique du Tarot* (Dangles, 1987). According to the *Gestes de l'officiant dans les ceremonies mystiques des sects Tendai et Singon—le Si-Do-In-Dzou* (Leroux, 1899), the turning wheel of the law is the preaching of Buddhist dogmas: "The force or power of the preaching breaks or destroys evil thoughts and mistaken or wicked judgments like an iron wheel crushes whatever it rolls over."

24. *Visio Tungdali* (*The Vision of Tungdal,* circa 1149).

25. Bayard, *Histoire des légendes,* 36.

26. Reinach, *Orpheus: Histoire générale des religions,* 130.

27. Stanislas de Guaita wrote in his *Au Seuil du mystère,* vol. 1, p. 158: "Evolution is the universal redemption of the Spirit. By evolving, Spirit climbs up anew. But before it climbed back up, Spirit had descended. This is what we call Involution."

CHAPTER 9.
THE UNDERGROUND TEMPLE

1. "A mentor accompanies this neophyte and guide this Telemachus of the mystery," Guaita, *La Clef de la magie noire,* vol. 2, p.191.

2. Dumas, *L'Oeuf cosmique.*

3. Eliade, *Forgerons et Alchimistes,* 42.

4. Porphyry, *On the Cave of the Nymphs.*

5. This symbolic rope in certain Anglo-Saxon rites is looped around the neck of the recipient, notes Persigoult (*Cabinet de réflexion,* 495), who also thinks of the rope of Shiva-Pashas and of certain denominations, such as the "child of the rope" used in medieval secret societies such as the Sainte Vehme, about which I have also spoken (*La Symbolique du cabinet de réflexion* and *Les Franc-Juges de la Sainte-Vehme* [Le Soleil Natal, 1991]).

6. Murt, *Recherches sur l'iconographie de l'Évangile aux XVIe et XVIIe siècles,* 71.

7. Pierre Saintyves, "Les grottes dans les cultes magico-religieux," 167.

8. "Léonard de Vinci Johanniste," *Atlantis,* no. 85 (1939) and no. 192 (August 1958).

9. Briant, in *Le Goéland,* no. 91 (May 1949). See the *Oeuvres,* Éditions Tequin.

10. Toutain, *Les Caverns sacrées dans l'antiquité grecque.*

11. Based on Pausanias, 7.31.

12. Rig Veda 1.164.9 and 144.1.

13. Siculus, *Historical Library,* vol. 4, p. 68.

14. Saintyves, "Les Grottes dans les cultes," 191, 202; Doubdan, *Le Voyage de la Terre Sainte.*

15. R. P. Boucher, *Le Bouquet sacré,* 405.

16. Carcopino, *La Basilique pythagoricienne de la porte Majeure.*

17. Guénon, "La Porte Étroite."

18. Guaita, *La Clef de la magie noire,* 668–69.

19. *Le Goéland,* nos. 75 and 99.

20. Allaix, *Introduction à l'étude de la Magie.*

21. Boucher, Jules, *La Symbolique maçonnique,* 278.

22. Bayard, *La Symbolique du Feu,* 184.

23. Marques-Rivière, *Le Yoga tantrique.* See also, David-Neel, *Parmi les mystiques et les magiciens du Tibet.*

24. Sale, *La Salade,* chapter 4, "Du Mont de la Sybille et de son lac et des choses que j'y ai vues et qui dire auz gens du pays," cited by Gaston Paris, *Légendes du Moyen Âge,* 67, 111.

25. René Guénon has made some beautiful comparisons in his "The Mountain and the Cave," in *Études traditionnelles,* no. 217 (January 1938).

26. I have provided other references in other chapters. What we have here are only underground temples.

CHAPTER 10. INITIATORY PASSAGEWAYS
AND THE TOMB OF THE CHRISTIAN WOMAN

1. Article by M. De Nériac in *Initiation et Science,* 22.
2. Bélizal and Chaumery, *Essai de radiesthésie vibratoire.*
3. M. H. Guettard's notes have not been published.
4. Stuttgart Library.
5. Philostratus, *Vita Apollonius,* chapter 15. In studying the temple of Esna, Serge Sauneron discovered the principle of blood circulation in Egyptian thinking.
6. Boucher, Jules, *La Symbolique maçonnique,* 160.
7. *Enneads* 7.7 and 7.8.
8. The bibliography will permit the reader to revisit this matter.
9. Christofle, *Le Tombeau de la Chrétienne.*
10. I have used here the dimensions communicated by M. Christofle. In his excellent account, Jean Brune took the less precise figures of Berbrugger or Caise. The blueprints were also poorly drawn.
11. Here I used the value of the circumambulation in *Le Sacre des rois,* 142–45. It seems that in this case in the corridor of this tomb we are dealing with a polar rite and no longer a solar one.
12. Éditions Émile Paul, 1929, and Éditions La Colombe. See the chapter "Le Labyrinthe souterrain."
13. Hus, *Les Étrusques* (Arthème Fayard, 1957), 86, and (Le Seuil, 1959), 24.
14. Diot, *Les Sourciers et les monuments,* 32–58.

CHAPTER 11. AN INITIATORY PASSAGEWAY:
THE UNDERGROUND LABYRINTH

1. Guénon, "La caverne et le labyrinth," 349 and 385.
2. Jules Boucher, in his book *La Symbolique maçonnique,* 168, cites several texts that show the sacred nature of the axe but draws no conclusions from them.
3. The labyrinth of Knossos in Crete was discovered in 1902 by Dr. Evans of Oxford. Paul Le Cour, in *La Crète et ses mystères,* does not think that temple palace is the famous Cretan labyrinth; see *Atlantis,* no. 180 (January 1956). Incidentally, the underground excavations of Cortyne are only ancient abandoned quarries.

4. In the book *Devises héroiques et emblems de M. Claude Paradin, revues et augmentées de moitié par Messire François d'Ambois* (Paris, 1621) there is mention of a circular labyrinth in which the Minotaur would have been enclosed.

5. It would be quite helpful to define the importance of the horned god. But this would be a departure from the subject at hand, and I refer primarily to Margaret Murray's book *The God of the Witches* and to the July 1956 issue of *Esculape*.

6. Caillois, "Les Thèmes fondamentaux de J. L. Borges," in *L'Herne: Borges.*

7. Jules Boucher, *La Symbolique maçonnique,* 94.

8. Ragon, *Rituel de l'apprenti maçon,* 66–67.

9. Plantagenet, *Causeries initiatiques,* 128.

10. Wirth, *Le Symbolisme occulte de la franc-maçonnerie,* 43.

11. Brion, "Hofmannsthal et l'expérience du labyrinthe," 177.

12. Reyor, in *Le Voile d'Isis,* 148, writes that at the time of the Crusades, the Stations of the Cross took the place of a pilgrimage to the Holy Land.

13. This is what Prévost de Cherbourg wrote about the "Reparatus" labyrinth in Orléansville, Algeria.

14. Amé, *Les Carrelages émaillés du Moyen Âge et de la Renaissance,* 31–53.

15. Schmit, *Manuel complet de l'architecte des monuments religieux.*

16. Guénon; see the chapter "Le Symbolisme du lissage" in *Le Symbolisme de la croix,* 112–13.

17. *Le Voile d'Isis,* no. 71 (November 1925).

18. One can find, however, in the book published by Jean-Pierre Laubscher called *Merveilleuse Notre-Dame de Lausanne* a very interesting chapter on the labyrinth of the Compagnonnage.

19. Waters, *Book of the Hopi.* See Louis Charpentier, *Les Jacques et le mystère de Compostelle.*

20. Marcel Brion's articles are noted in the bibliography. We should pay special attention to his book *Léonard de Vinci,* in which he devoted a chapter to the labyrinth.

21. See Lambert, *L'Architecture des Templiers.*

22. Sandoz, *Le Labyrinthe.*

23. Jean Paris, *Joyce par lui-même.*

24. James, *The Collected Ghost Stories of M. R. James,* 318–58.

25. Brion, "Hofmannsthal et l'expérience du labyrinthe," 177.

26. Hofmannsthal, *Andreas oder die Vereinigten.*

27. Given such keys, it is my wish that some publishers would translate these books with such vast perspectives.

28. Meyrink, *Le Golem.*

29. Bayard, *Le Sens caché des rites mortuaires.*

CHAPTER 12. THE VIRGIN OF THE CRYPT, FROM GREEN TO BLACK

1. Fulcanelli, *Le Mystère des Cathédrales,* 69.

2. I recommend reading the books by Marie Durand-Lefebvre, *Étude sur l'origine des Vierges Noires,* and E. Saillens, *Nos Vierges Noires,* both listed in the bibliography. See also my article in *Le Lotus Bleu: La Revue Théosophique,* November–December 1960.

3. Cabrol and Leclerq, *Dictionnaire d'archéologie chrétienne,* 10:2, columns 1892, 1991, 2395.

4. Darmeister, *Dictionnaire général de la langue française.*

5. Apuleius, *Metamorphoses* 11.47.

6. Cumont, *Religions orientales dans le paganism chrétien.*

7. Bigaine, *Considérations sur le culte d'Isis chez les Éduens;* also Saillens, *Nos Vierges Noires,* 56–184.

8. A fact noted by Dulaure in his *Histoire de Paris.*

9. Philéas Lebesque shares the same opinion in "Virgile et le culte de la Terre Mère."

10. Bayard, *Histoire des légendes,* 27, 87, 100, 116, 122.

11. Saintyves, *Les Vierges mères.*

12. Jillian, *De la Gaule à la France,* 150.

13. Ferdinand Lot, *La Gaule,* 701–02.

14. Bayard, *La Symbolique du feu,* 132ff.

15. This makes it easier to understand the role of "the Mother" in the Compagnonnage cayenne. A. Pictet, *Du Culte des Cabires chez les anciens Irlandais,* 131, studies the word "mother" in a large number of languages.

16. D'Ygé, *Nouvelle assemblée des Philosophes chymiques,* 79.

17. For more on this subject it is necessary to read Grillot de Givry, *Lourdes.*

18. Wirth, *Le Tarot des imagiers du Moyen Âge.*

19. Portal, *Des Couleurs symboliques,* 186.

20. Hugo, *Contemplations, 2,* "Ce que dit la bouche d'ombre."

21. Rig Veda, 3.1.3.

22. Lanoë-Villène, "Couleurs," in *Le Livre des symboles,* 210–31.

23. Bayard, *La Symbolique du feu,* 64.

24. Portal, "Du Noir," *Des couleurs symboliques,* 107.

25. Mazel, *Notes sur la Camargue et les Saintes-Maries-de-la-mer.*

26. Saillens pointed out this characteristic in *Nos Vierges Noires,* 128.

27. Persigoult, *Le Cabinet de réflexion,* 250, says that this temple was sacred to Diana.

28. For more on this see Jaubert, *Les anciennes Madones du diocèse de Marseille.*

29. D'Ygé, *Nouvelle assemblée des Philosophes chymiques,* 99.

30. Bayard, *La Symbolique du feu,* 120, 151.

31. This detail was noted by Saillens, *Nos Vierges Noires,* 116, and Fulcanelli, *Le Mystère des Cathédrales,* 52.

32. Portal, "On the Wind," in *Des couleurs symboliques,* 113.

33. Readers should refer to the very extensive documentation of Lanoë-Villène, *Le Livre des symboles,* in the chapter on colors, 105–45.

34. Victor-Émile Michelet, *Le Secret de la Chevalerie,* 90.

35. Duchaussoy, *Le Bestiaire divin,* 115.

36. Vincent, *L'Ingenieur-Constructeur E.T.P.* (August–September, 1957).

37. Saintyves, *Les contes de Perrault,* 273.

38. Lanoë-Villène, "Couleurs," in *Le Livre des symboles,* 132.

39. D'Ygé, *Nouvelle assemblée des Philosophes chymiques,* 95–99.

40. Fulcanelli, *Le Mystère des Cathédrales,* 137.

41. Reyor, "De la Couleur Verte," *Le Voile d'Isis,* January 1932, 44. Also see the commentary on Dante's *Divine Comedy* by Argos in *Le Voile d'Isis.*

42. I included this text in my book *La Symbolique du feu,* 107.

43. The narrative by G. Osculati appears in his *L'Illustration* (1852); in Denis's anthology, *Les vrais Robinsons*; and partially in *Atlantis,* no. 185 (January 1957).

44. Guénon, "Le sanglier et l'ours," 235.

45. Lanoë-Villène, *Le Livre des symboles,* 116.

46. Bayard, *La Symbolique du feu,* 67.

47. Vincent, in *L'Ingenieur-Constructeur E.T.P.* (May 1957), 245, and (March 1958), 107.

48. *L'Ingenieur-Constructeur E.T.P.*, no. 20 (October 1958), 435.

49. "La Nouvelle Lumière Chimique du Cosmopolite," in *Les Douze clefs* of Basil Valentine.

50. M. de Nériac, in *Initiation et Science*, no. 45 (March 1958), 22.

CHAPTER 13.
THE TELLURIC REPTILE AND THE SPIRAL

1. Oswald Wirth, *Les Mystères de l'art royal*.

2. *Études traditionnelles*, no. 346 (March 1958).

3. Duchaussoy, "La Colombe," in *Le Bestiaire divin*, 102.

4. Bayard, "Le Caducée," *Médecine de France;* Bayard, *Le Symbolisme du caducée*.

5. Doresse, *L'Empire du prêtre Jean*, 1:6.

6. *Du calice de la Sainte Cène*, chapter 63.

7. 1 Samuel 28.

8. 1 Samuel 28:7–15; Leviticus 20:27; Isaiah 8:19, 19:3; Exodus 22:18.

9. Herodotus, *Histories*, 8.41.

10. Saintyves, *Les Vierges mères*, 122.

11. Meyrink, *The Green Face*.

12. Lanoë-Villène, *Le Livre des symboles*, 1:135.

13. C. W. Leadbeater, *Les Centres de force et le serpent de feu*.

14. Marques-Rivière, *Le Yoga tantrique*, 63.

15. *Études traditionnelles*, December 1935.

16. Guénon, *Le Symbolisme de la croix*, 170; Guénon, *La Grande Triade*, chapter 5, 33–45; Guénon, *Études traditionnelles*, no. 195 (March 1936).

17. Guénon, *Le Symbolisme de la croix*, 63.

18. Yves Millet, "La gamme de Pythagore."

19. *Inconnue*, no. 13, 53.

20. Berthelot, *Les Origins de l'Alchimie*, 61.

21. Based on Vincent, in *L'Ingenieur-Constructeur E.T.P.* (August–September, 1957), 391.

22. Dumas provides many examples in his book *L'Oeuf cosmique*.

23. Dewise, *Les Zombis ou le secret des morts vivants*.

24. Bayard, *Essai sur les représentations du diable dans l'art médiéval*, sequel to *Le Diable dans la Cathédrale* by Abbé Denis Grivot.

CHAPTER 14. THE TEMPLES IN CAVES

1. Porphyry, *On the Cave of the Nymphs,* 9.

2. Utudjian, *Le Monde souterrain,* 132. Edouard Utudjian provides some useful documents on troglodytes. See also the articles by Nicholas Roerich on the underground peoples in *Ethnographie.*

3. *Revue des questions historiques,* October 1896, 365.

4. Doresse, *L'Empire du prêtre Jean,* 2:59–60. I would also like to cite the work by an anonymous author, *Relation d'un voyage du Pôle Arctique au Pôle Antarctique par le centre du monde* (1723).

5. Bayard, *Les Francs-Juges de la Sainte-Vehme* (Le Soleil Natal).

6. Reinach, *Cultes, mythes et religions,* 1:125–36.

7. Lanoë-Villène, "Couleurs," in *Le Livre des symboles,* 171–209.

8. See Cartailhac, *La France préhistorique,* and Dechelette, *Manuel d'archéologie préhistorique.*

9. Le Cour, *La Crête et ses mystères;* see also *Atlantis,* no. 180, 76.

10. On the subject of the symbolism of the "horn" it is worth referring to Lanoë-Villène, *Le Livre des symboles,* 5:79–92; Le Cour, *La Crête et ses mystères;* Bayard, "Les Dieux cornus"; Avalon, "La Corne, symbole de la autorité et de la puissance"; Murray, *The God of the Witches.*

11. Frobenius, *Destin des civilizations.*

12. See the Arthaud edition, 1958.

13. Discovered in 1957; *Le Figaro,* January 14, 1958.

14. See Bataille, *La Peinture préhistorique: Lascaux ou la naissance de l'art.*

15. Article by Ferrua in the *Osservatore Romano.*

16. These fifty extraordinary Egyptian frescoes are reproduced in *La Peinture égyptienne ancienne* by Nina Davies and H. Alan Gardner.

17. Viennot, *Le Culte,* 230.

18. Abbé Lemozi, *La Grotte, temple du Pech-Merle,* 63–64.

CHAPTER 15. BURIAL CAVES

1. Since 1961 I have attributed other values to these rites by writing *Le Sens caché des rites mortuaires.*

2. Gouwellos, *Inconnue,* no. 13, 145.

3. Bayard, *La Symbolique du cabinet de refléxion.*

4. Eliade, *Forgerons et Alchimistes,* 42; Eliade, *Traité d'histoire des religions,* 220.

5. Genesis 23 and 49.

6. Probst-Biraben, *Études traditionnelles,* 106.

7. Desnoyers, *Dictionnaire d'histoire naturelle de d'Orbigny.*

8. Bayard, *La Symbolique du temple*; Bayard, *La Tradition cachée des cathédrales.*

9. Information from G. Albert Roulhac.

CHAPTER 16.
THE UNDERGROUND FACTORIES

1. Sébillot, *Les Travaux publics et les mines dans les traditions et les superstitions de tous les pays* (1894), 460–78.

2. These divine factories appear in the epic poem in Latin verse by Jerome Fracastor, *Syphilis ou le mal vénérien* (French translation of 1796).

3. Rossignol, *Les métaux dans l'Antiquité: Origines religieux de la métallurgie,* 17; Rossignol, *Mémoire sur le metal que les anciens appelaient Orichalque,* 230.

4. Strabo, *Geographia,* vol. 2; Sébillot, *Les Travaux publics,* 398.

5. *Journal des Savants,* no. 379 (1890), 382, 392, 441, 452.

6. See Granet, *Danses et legends de la Chine ancienne,* 496.

7. Utudjian, *Architecture et l'urbanisme souterrain,* 94. See also the magazine *Le Monde souterrain.* I would like to add to these the experience of Michel Siffre, who spent two months underground during August and September, 1972.

8. Jacques Baurès, *L'Aventure souterraine,* 243.

CHAPTER 17. CONCLUSION

1. Corbin, *Creative Imagination Imagination in the Sufism of Ibn Arabi,* 96–97.

CHAPTER 18. PREAMBLE

1. Random, *L'Art visionnaire,* 158.

CHAPTER 19.
THE CAVE ON THE EARTHLY PLANE

1. Gilbert and Rewerski, *Le Monde souterrain de l'Anjou*, 13.
2. Utudjian, *Architecture et l'urbanisme souterrain.*
3. Nicolas Flamel followed the black plague of 1374 after financing the Charnel House of the Innocents. See Suttel, *Catacombes et cavités de Paris.*
4. See *L'Ingénieur-Constructeur,* no. 26 (October 1983), 20–23. A part of this reproduction is housed at the Musée Nationale des Antiquités in Saint-Germain-en-Laye.
5. For a more detailed description of the caves, readers can refer to the excellent document "Les Souterrains," *Revue Archéologia,* no. 3 (1973).
6. Bailloud, *Le Néolithique dans le basin parisien,* 146.
7. Bayard, *Le Sens caché des rites mortuaires.*
8. Guénon, "La Caverne et le labyrinthe."
9. Broëns, *Ces Souterrains,* 15.

CHAPTER 20.
THE CAVE ON THE DIVINE PLANE

1. *Saint Paul's Vision* (Hanack-Leipzig, 1893).
2. Bayard, *La Légende de Saint-Brendan.*
3. Vian, *La Grèce archaïque et classique dans histoires des religions,* 1:544.
4. Bonnet, *Artemis of Ephesus and the Legend of the Seven Sleepers.*
5. Fraysse and Fraysse, *Les Troglodytes en Anjou.*
6. A complete list can be found in Gilbert and Rewerski's book *Le Monde souterrain de l'Anjou.*
7. Pierre Minvielle, *Guide de la France souterraine,* 413.
8. Broëns, *Ces souterrains,* 110.
9. I recommend the works of Fernand Niel (his works with Robert Laffont and his book that is no. 764 in the Que-Sais-je? series published by P.U.F.), and those by Giot and R. Grosjean of the Kergal Association and of the journal *Mythologie Française.* I made two broadcasts on Radio 3 discussing this on April 19 and May 3, 1983.
10. Le Rouzic, *Corpus des signes graves des monuments megalithiques du Morbihan.*

11. Giot, L'Helgouaach, and Monnier, *Prehistoire de la Bretagne*.

12. Rosgnilk, *L'Émergence de l'Enel ou L'immergence des repères: Introduction à l'étude des forms et des champs de coherence*, vol. 1, 316.

13. Broëns, *Ces Souterrains*.

14. Schwab, *Les Traditions d'Amérique ancienne*.

15. D'Ygé, *Nouvelle assemblée des Philosophes chymiques*, 77.

16. Badin, *Grottes et cavernes*, 48.

17. Le Cour, *La Crète et ses mystères;* see also *Atlantis* no. 180 (January 1956).

CHAPTER 21.
THE CAVE ON THE COSMIC PLANE

1. Le Saux, *Souvenirs d'Arunáchala*.

2. Sri Krishna Prem, *Le Yoga de la Kathopanishad*, 133. It is also necessary to acquaint yourself with François Ribadeau Dumas's book *L'Oeuf cosmique*.

3. Servier, *Tradition et civilisation berbères*, 53.

4. Guénon, *Fundamental Symbols: The Universal Language of Sacred Science*, 153.

5. Bayard, *La Symbolique du cabinet de réflexion*, or the light in the darkness.

6. Raoult, *Les Druids*.

7. Ossendowski, Ferdinand. *Bêtes, homes et dieux*, 202.

8. "Kali-Yuga or the Black Age, the Iron Age of the Ancient West" (R. Guénon).

9. "Only a relative exteriorization is of course meant, as these secondary centers have themselves been more or less strictly closed since the beginning of the Kali-Yuga" (R. Guénon).

10. "The *Manvantara*, or era of a *Manu*, also called Mahā-Yuga, comprises four Yugas or secondary periods: Krita-Yuga (or Satya-Yuga), Tretā-Yuga, Dvāpara-Yuga, and the Kali-Yuga, which are identifiable respectively with the 'age of gold,' the 'age of silver,' the 'age of bronze,' and the 'age of iron,' of Greco-Roman antiquity. In the succession of these periods there is a kind of progressive materialization resulting from the gradual distancing from the Principle that necessarily accompanies the development of the cyclical manifestation in the corporeal world, starting from the 'primordial state' (R. Guénon).

11. "This is the manifestation of the celestial Jerusalem, which is, in connection with the cycle which is ending, the same thing as is the Terrestrial Paradise in connection with the cycle which is beginning, as explained in *L'Ésotérisme de Dante*" (R. Guénon).

12. Davy, *Le Desert intérieur*.

13. Guénon, *Le Roi du monde*, 81, 89.

14. Jung, *Psychology and Alchemy*.

15. Eliade, *Fragments d'un journal*, 232.

16. Sébillot, *La Terre et le monde souterrain;* and *Les Travaux publics et les mines*.

17. Bayard, *La Légende de Saint-Brendan*.

18. Viennot, *Le Culte de l'arbre*.

APPENDIX 1. EXTRACT FROM THE *MYTHO-HERMETIC DICTIONARY*

1. This edition of the *Dictionnaire mytho-hermétique* was republished by Éditions Denoël in 1972 through the efforts of René Alleau for the "Bibliothèque Hermetica."

Bibliography

Allaix, Henri. *Introduction à l'étude de la Magie.* Paris: Le Lien médical, 1936.

Allier, Raoul. *Magie et religion.* Paris: Berger-Levrault, 1935.

Almanach catholique français. Paris: Libraire Bloud et Gay, 1933.

Ambelain, Robert. *Au Pied des menhirs.* Paris: Éditions Niclaus, 1945.

Amé, Émile. *Les Carrelages émaillés du Moyen Âge et de la Renaissance.* Paris: Morel & Cie, 1859.

Aubert, Abbé. *Histoire de la Cathédrale de Poitiers.* Paris: Chez Derache, 1848–49.

———. *Histoire et théorie du symbolisme religieux avant et depuis le Christianisme.* 4 vols. Paris: Librairie de Féchoz et Letouzey, 1884.

———. *Histoire générale civile, religieuse et littéraire du Poitou.* 2 vols. Poitiers, France: Fontenay-le-Comte, 1885.

Avalon, Jean. "La Corne, symbole de la autorité et de la puissance," *Æsculape,* July 1958.

Bachelard, Gaston. *La psychanalyse du Feu.* Paris: Gallimard, 1992.

———. *La Terre et les reveries de la Volonté.* Paris: José Corti, 1948. Translated into English as *Earth and Reveries of Will: An Essay on the Imagination of Matter.* Dallas: Dallas Institute of Humanities & Culture, Bachelard Translations Series, 2002.

Badin, Adolphe. *Grottes et cavernes.* Paris: Hachette, 1886.

Bailloud, Gérard. *Le Néolithique dans le basin parisien.* Paris: CNRS, 1974.

Bain, George. *Celtic Art.* Glasgow: Macllelan, 1951.

Ballu, Albert. *Rapport sur les travaux du service des monuments historiques d'Algérie, 1918–1923.* Work led by Marcel Christofle.

Bar, Francis. *Les Routes de l'autre monde.* Collection Mythes et Religions. Paris: P.U.F., 1946.

Barba, Alphonse. *Métallurgie, ou l'art de tirer et de purifier les métaux,* vol. 1. Paris: Didot, 1751.

Bataille, Georges. *La Peinture préhistorique: Lascaux ou la naissance de l'art.* Geneva: Skira, 1955.

Baurès, Jacques. *L'Aventure souterraine.* Paris: Albin Michel, 1958.

Bayard, Jean-Pierre. *Essai sur les représentations du diable dans l'art medieval,* following *Le Diable dans la Cathédrale* by Abbé Grivot. Club du Livre Chrétien, 1960.

———. *Histoire des légendes.* Collection Que sais-je? Paris: P.U.F., 1955.

———. *La Légende de Saint-Brendan.* Paris: Guy Trédaniel, 1988.

———. *La Sacres et couronnements royaux.* Paris: Guy Trédaniel, 1984.

———. *La Symbolique du cabinet de réflexion.* ÉDIMAF, 1984.

———. *La Symbolique du feu.* Paris: Éditions Vega, 1986.

———. *La Symbolique du temple.* Paris: Edimaf, 1991.

———. *La Tradition cachée des cathédrales.* Paris: Dangles, 1990.

———. "Le Caducée." *Médecine de France,* no. 225 (October 1971).

———. "Le Labyrinthe." *L'Age Nouveau,* no. 104 (November–December 1958).

———. *Le Sens caché des rites mortuaires.* Paris: Dangles, 1993.

———. *Le Symbolisme du caducée.* Paris: Guy Trédaniel, 1978.

———. "Les Chemins de la tradition." Radio 3 broadcast, February 15, 1983.

———. "Les Dieux cornus," *Martini,* no. 31 (August 1958).

———. *Les Francs-Juges de la Sainte-Vehme.* Paris: Albin Michel, 1971.

———. "Les Statues animées." *Martini,* no. 32 (October 1958).

———. *Les Talismans.* Paris: Tchou, 1976.

Belin, Dom Jean-Albert. *Les Aventures du Philosophe inconnu.* Paris: Estienne Danguy, 1646.

Bélizal, André, and Léon Chaumery. *Essai de radiesthésie vibratoire.* Paris: Dangles, 1956.

Belot, Victor R. *Contes et récits des Grottes et des Cavernes.* Paris: Fernand Nathan, 1977.

———. *La France souterrain.* Paris: Marabout, 1977.

Berbrugger, Adrien. "Le Tombeau de la chrétienne d'après Shaw et Bruce." *Revue Africaine,* vols. 10 and 11, 1856.

———. *Le Tombeau de la chrétienne mausolée des rois mauritaniens de la dernière dynastie.* Blida, Algeria: Manguin, 1867.

Berthelot, Marcellin. *La Grande Encyclopedie,* vol. 21. Paris: H. Lamirault et cie, 1895.

——. *Les Origins de l'Alchimie.* Paris: Steinheil, 1885.

Bertrand, Elie. *Mémoire sur la structure intérieur de la terre.* Zurich: Heidegger, 1752.

Bigaine, Charles. *Considérations sur le culte d'Isis chez les Eduens.* Beaune, 1862.

Blanchet, Adrien. *Souterrains refuges de la France.* Paris: Contribution à l'étude de l'habitation humaine, 1923.

Boehme, Jacob (pseudonym: the Unknown Philosopher). *Concerning the Three Principles of the Divine Essence,* vol. 2. London: John M. Watkins, 1910.

Boisthibaut, Doublet de. "Notice sur le labyrinthe de Chartres." *Revue Archéologique* (October 1851), 437–47.

Bonnet, Jacques. *Artemis of Ephesus and the Legend of the Seven Sleepers.* Paris: Librarie Orientaliste, 1977.

——. *Le Livre des grottes.* Paris: Dervy, 1986.

Boucher, Jules. *La Symbolique maçonnique.* Paris: Dervy, 1953.

Boucher, R. P. *Le Bouquet sacré ou, le voyage de la Terre Sainte.* Rouen, France: Oursel, 1735.

Bouchet, Paul. *Bulletin,* no. 97 (March 1958).

——. *Cours druidiques 10ème leçon.* In *Le Temps se prépare sous terre,* no. 106 (December 10, 1958).

Bourgin, André. *Rivières de la nuit.* Paris: Artaud, 1950.

Briant, Théophile. *Le Goéland.* 1936.

Brion, Marcel. "Les Noeuds de Léonard de Vinci et leur signification." *Études d'Art,* nos. 8, 9, 10.

——. "Le Theme de l'entrelacs et du labyrinthe dans l'oeuvre de Léonard de Vinci." *Revue d'Esthétique* 5, no. 1 (January–March 1952).

——. "Hofmannsthal et l'expérience du labyrinthe." *Cahiers du Sud,* no. 333 (February 1956).

——. *Léonard de Vinci.* Paris: Albin Michel, 1952.

Broëns, Maurice. *Ces Souterrains: Refuges pour les vivants ou pour les esprits.* Paris: Picard, 1976.

Brune, Jean. "Le Secret du tombeau de la chrétienne." *Le Journal d'Alger,* February 1 to March 13, 1951.

Burrows, E. *The Labyrinth: Some Cosmological Patterns in Babylonian Religion.* London: S. H. Hooke, 1935.

Cabrol, Dom Fernand, and Dom Henri Leclerq. *Dictionnaire d'archéologie chrétienne et de liturgie.* Facsimile LXXXII–LXXXIII.

Caillette de l'Hervilliers, Edmond. *Étude sur la loi du secret dans la primitive Église.* Paris: H. Casterman, 1861.

Caillois, Roger. "Les Thèmes fondamentaux de J. L. Borges." *L'Herne: Borges.* Paris: Éditions de L'Herne, 1964.

Caisee, Albert. *Exploration archéologique du tombeau de Juba II, dit Tombeau de la chrétienne.* Blida, Algeria: Manguin, 1893.

———. *Le Tombeau de Juba II, dit Tombeau de la chrétienne.* Blida, Algeria: Manguin, 1892.

Canseliet, Eugène. *Deux logis alchimistes, en marge de la science et de l'histoire.* Paris: J. Schwmit, 1945.

Carcopino, Jérôme. *La Basilique pythagoricienne de la porte Majeure.* Paris: Artisan du livre, 1927.

Cartailhac, Emile M. *La France préhistorique.* Paris: Ancienne Librarie Germer Bailliere, 1889.

Caumont, Arcisse de. *Abécédaire ou rudiments d'archéologie.* Paris, 1860.

Charpentier, Louis. *Les Jacques et le mystère de Compostelle.* Paris: Robert Laffont, 1972.

Christofle, Marcel. *Le Tombeau de la Chrétienne.* In *Arts et Métiers graphiques.* Paris: Flammarion, 1951.

Chthonia. Publication du Centre International de Recherches Anhistoriques. Barcelona: Herder, ND.

Claudel, Paul. "La Mystique des pierres précieuses." *Fontaine,* May 1945.

"Compagnonnage." *Le Voile d'Isis,* no. 71 (November 1925) & no. 86 (February 1927).

Corbin, Henry. *Creative Imagination in the Sufism of Ibn Arabi.* Translated by Ralph Manheim. Princeton, N.J.: Princeton University Press, 1969.

Couchoud, Paul Louis. *La Mythologie asiatique.* Paris: Libraire de France, 1931.

Crollius, Oswald. *La royal chymie de Crollius.* Lyon, France: Pierre Drobet, 1624.

Crooke, William. *The Popular Religion and Folklore of Northern India.* London: Humphrey Milford, 1896.

Cros, Charles. *Poèmes et proses.* N.R.F. Moreux, *L'Alchimie moderne.* Paris: Gaston Doin, 1924.

Cross, Samuel H. *The Russian Primary Chronicle.* Cambridge, Mass.: Harvard University Press, 1930.

Cumont, Franz. *Religions orientales dans le paganism chrétien*. Paris: Guenther, 1929.

Czernicheff, Prince. *Théorie mystique des Pierres*. Paris: Bibliothèque de la revue *Psyche*, n.d.

Darmeister, Arsene. *Dictionnaire général de la langue française*. Paris: Library Ch. Delagrave, 1895–1900.

David-Neel, Alexandra. *Parmi les mystiques et les magiciens du Tibet*. Paris: Plon, 1968.

Davies, Nina, and H. Alan Gardner. *La Peinture égyptienne ancienne*. Paris: Guillot, 1953–54.

Davy, Marie-Madeleine. *Essai sur le symbolisme romane*. Collection "Homo Sapiens." Paris: Flammarion 1955.

———. *Le Desert intérieur*. Paris: Albin Michel, 1983.

Dechelette, J. *Manuel d'archéologie préhistorique*. 7 vols. Paris: Picard, 1908–14.

Demaison, Louis. *Bulletin archéologique,* 1894, 3–40.

———. *Bulletin Monumental,* 1902, 3–59.

———. *Congrès archéologique,* vol. 2. Paris, 1911.

———. *La Cathédrale de Reims*. Paris, 1910.

Deneux, Henri. *Bulletin de la société nationale des antiquaries de France,* 1920.

Denis, Ferdinand. *Les vrais Robinsons*. Paris: Librarie du Magasin Pittoresque, 1863.

Deschamps de Pas, Louis. "Essai sur le pavage des églises." *Annales archéologiques,* vol. 22.

Desnoyers, *Dictionnaire d'histoire naturelle de d'Orbigny,* vol. 6, 2nd ed. Paris: Au Bureau principal de l'editor, 1845.

Dewise, C. H. *Les Zombis ou le secret des morts vivants*. Paris: Grasset, 1957.

Diot, Charles. *Les Sourciers et les monuments mégalithique*. Bourg, France: Berthod, 1935.

Diricq, E. G. *Le Voile d'Isis,* no. 172 (April 1934), 172.

Doresse, Jean. *L'Empire du prêtre Jean,* vol. 2. Paris: Plon, 1957.

Doubdan, Jean. *Le Voyage de la Terre Sainte*. Paris: Pierre Bienfait, 1661.

Dournon, Robert, *Autour du tombeau de la Chrétienne, d'après les documents inédits de A. Berbrugger*. Algiers: Pfister, 1931; Éditions Charlot, 1946.

Drechsler, Paul. *Sitte, Brauch und Volksglaube in Schlesien,* vol. 2. Leipzig, Germany: Teubner, 1903–6.

Dubois, Saint Etienne. "Les Poypes de la Bresse et de la Dombes." In *Bulletin de la société des Naturalistes de l'Ain,* no. 46 (1932).

Duchaussoy, Jacques. *Le Bestiaire divin.* Paris: La Colombe, 1958.

Dulaure, Jacques-Antoine. *Histoire de Paris.* Paris: Baudoin Frères, 1825.

Dumas, François Ribadeau. *L'Oeuf cosmique.* Paris: Dangles, 1979.

Dupry-Pacherad, F. "Le fabuleux Problem du mètre égyptien et les mesures de Karnak." *Atlantis,* no. 203 (October 1960).

Du Puget, R. *Les Eddas.* Paris: Jouaust, 1885.

Durand, Guillaume. *Rationale divinorum officiorum,* book 7. Translated by Charles Barthélemy. Paris: N.p., 1854.

Durand-Lefebvre, Marie. *Étude sur l'origine des Vierges Noires.* Paris: Henri Laurens, 1937.

Duret, Abbé. *Notions élémentaires d'architecture religieuse.* Paris: Letouzey, 1930.

D'Ygé, Claude. *Nouvelle assemblée des Philosophes chymiques.* Paris: Dervy, 1954.

Edmond, Pierre. "Le Tombeau de la Chrétienne." *Echo d'Alger,* April 15, 1924.

Eliade, Mircea. *Le Chamanisme et les techniques archaïques de l'extase.* Paris: Payot, 1951.

———. *Le Sacré et le profane:* Paris: Gallimard, 1965. Translated as *The Sacred and the Profane.* New York: Harcourt, 1959.

———. *Forgerons et Alchimistes.* Paris: Flammarion, 1956. Translated by Stephen Corrin as *The Forge and the Crucible: The Origins and Structure of Alchemy,* 1962. 2nd ed. Chicago: University of Chicago Press, 1979.

———. *Fragments d'un journal.* Paris: Gallimard, 1973.

———. *Images et symbols.* Paris: Gallimard, 1952.

———. *Mythes, rêves et mystères.* Paris: Gallimard, 1957. Translated by Philip Mairet as *Myths, Dreams, and Mysteries.* New York: Harper, 1975.

———. *Shamanism: Archaic Techniques of Ecstasy.* Translated by Willard Trask. New York: Pantheon, 1964.

———. *Traité d'histoire des religions.* Paris: Payot, 1974.

Emmerich, Saint Anne Catherine. *Du calice de la Sainte Cène.* N.p. N.d.

Enthoven, R. D. E. *The Folklore of Bombay.* Oxford: Oxford University Press, 1924.

Ferrua, R. P. Antonio. *Osservatore Romano* (April 6, 1956).

Foucard, G. *Histoire des religions et méthode comparative.* Paris: Picard, 1912.

Fraysse, J., and C. *Les Troglodytes en Anjou à travers les ages.* Cholet, France: Farré et Fils, 1962.

Frazer, Sir James George. *The Golden Bough.* London: Macmillan, 1935.

———. *La Crainte des morts dans les religions primitives.* Paris: Nourry, 1935. Original English was *The Fear of the Dead in Primitive Religion.* London: Macmillan, 1934.

Frobenius, Leo. *Destin des civilizations: Histoire de la civilization africaine.* Paris: Gallimard, 1940.

Fulcanelli. *Le Mystère des Cathédrales.* Paris: Éditions des Champs Elysées, Omnium littéraire, 1957. Translated as *The Mystery of the Cathedrals.* Las Vegas: Brotherhood of Life, 1984.

Gamow, George. *Biographie de la terre.* Paris: Dunod, 1956.

Gauthier, E. F. *Le Passé de l'Afrique du Nord.* Paris: Payot, 1937.

Génillard, Pierre. *Inconnu,* no. 13, 112–235.

Gilbert, Charles, and Jacek Rewerski. *Le Monde souterrain de l'Anjou.* Tours, France: La Nouvelle République, 1986.

Giot, Pierre-Roland, Jean L'Helgouaach, and Jean-Laurent Monnier. *Prehistoire de la Bretagne.* Rennes, France: Ouest France et l'Université de Rennes, 1979.

Givry, Grillot de. *Lourdes, ville initiatique.* Paris: Chacornac, 1902.

Goethe, Johann Wolfgang. *The Green Snake and the Beautiful Lily.* Translated by Thomas Carlyle in 1832. Etext: John Roland Penner, 2000.

Goury, Georges. *Origine et evolution de l'homme.* Paris: Picard, 1931.

Granet, Marcel. *Danses et legends de la Chine ancienne.* Paris: PUF, 1926.

Grivot, Abbé Denis. *Le Diable dans le Cathédrale.* Paris: Club du Livre Chrétien, 1960.

Gsell, Stéphane. *Notes sur le Tombeau de la Chrétienne et guide archéologique des environs d'Alger.* Algiers: Jourdan, 1896.

Guaita, Stanislas de. *Au Seuil du mystère,* vol. 1. Paris: G. Carré, 1890.

———. *Essais de sciences maudites: Au Seuil du mystère,* vol. 1. Paris: Durville, 1915.

———. *La Clef de la magie noire,* vol. 2. Paris: Henri Durville, 1920.

Guénon, René. *L'Ésotérisme de Dante.* Paris: NRF, 1957. Translated as *The Esoterism of Dante* (Hillsdale, N.Y.: Sophia Perennis, 2004).

———. "La Caverne et le labyrinthe." *Études Traditionnelles,* nos. 214 and 215 (October and November 1937).

———. *La Grande Triade.* Paris: Gallimard, 1957. Translated as *The Great Triad.* Hillsdale, N.Y.: Sophia Perennis, 2004.

———. "La Porte Étroite." *Études traditionnelles*. December 1938.

———. *Le Roi du monde*. Paris: Gallimard, 1976.

———. "Le sanglier et l'ours," in *Études traditionnelles,* 1936,

———. *Le Symbolisme de la croix*. Paris: Vega, 1989. Translated as *The Symbolism of the Cross*. Hillsdale, N.Y.: Sophia Perennis, 2004.

———. *L'Homme et son devenir selon le Vedant.,* Paris: Éditions Traditionnelles, 1978. Translated as *Man and His Becoming According to the Vedanta*. Hillsdale, N.Y.: Sophia Perennis, 2004.

———. *Symboles fundamentaux de la science sacré*. Paris: NRF, 1962. Translated as *Fundamental Symbols: The Universal Language of Sacred Science*. Hillsdale, N.Y.: Sophia Perennis, 2004.

Guyomard, Georges. "Thèse d'Architecture sur les troglodytes en Anjou." Unpublished.

Hachesse, Abbé. "Le Symbolisme de la crèche." *Le Symbolisme*, no. 368 (Jan.–Feb. 1965): 165–68.

Hatem, Simone. *L'Empire des perles et pierres précieuses*. Paris: Plon, 1956.

Hofmannsthal, Hugo von. *Andreas oder die Vereinigten*. Munich: Corona, 1932.

Holberg, Klimius. *Voyage de Klimius sans le monde souterrain*. Copenhagen: J. Preuss, 1741.

Hooke, S. H. *The Labyrinth*. London: MacMillan, 1935.

Hugo, Victor. *Contemplations*. Paris: Gallimard, 1973.

Hus, Alan. *Les Étrusques*. Paris: Arthème Fayard, 1957, and Le Seuil, 1959.

Husson, Hyacinthe. *La Chaîne traditionelle*. Paris: Durand, 1874.

Hutin, Serge. *Des Mondes souterraines au Roi du monde*. Paris: Albin Michel, 1976.

Jacolliot, Louis (Marguerite Faye). *La Femme dans l'Inde*. Paris: Lacroix, 1877.

James, M. R. "Mr. Humphreys and His Inheritance." In *The Collected Ghost Stories of M. R. James*. London: Edward Arnold & Co., 1931.

Jaubert, Dom H. *Les anciennes Madones du diocèse de Marseille*. Marseille: Imp. Marseillaise, 1890.

Jeanmaire, H. *Dionysos*. Paris: Payot, 1970.

Jeannel, René, H. Henrot, and Claude Delmare-Deboutteville. *Notes bios-péologiques*. Paris: Éditions du Muséum, 1949.

Jillian, Camille. *De la Gaule à la France: Nos origines historiques*. Paris: Librarie Hachete, 1922.

Joyce, James. *A Portrait of the Artist as a Young Man*. London: Egoist Press, 1917. Translated into French as *Dedalus*. Paris: Editions de la Sirène, 1924.

Jung, Carl. *Psychology and Alchemy.* Princeton, N.J.: Princeton University Press, 1980.

Kircher, Athanasius. *Arithmologia.* 1665.

———. *Mundus Subterraneus.* 1645.

———. *Œdipus AEgypticus,* vol. 2, part 2, 1665.

Kohlen, Charles. *Notice sur les crypts de l'abbye de Saint-Victor-lez-Marseille.* Pamphlet, March 1864.

König, Marie. *Notre passé est encore plus ancient.* Paris: Robert Lafont, 1962.

Krappe, Alexandre H. *La Genèse des mythes.* Paris: Payot, 1938.

Lambert, Élie. *L'Architecture des Templiers.* Paris: Picard, 1955.

———. "Le Labyrinthe de la cathédrale de Reims." *Gazette des Beaux-Arts* (May–June 1958): 273–80.

Langlet, Léon. "Unpublished Studies on the Tomb of the Christian Woman."

Lanoë-Villène, Georges. *Le Livre des symboles,* 7 vols. Paris: Bossard, 1927.

Lasteyrie, R. de. *L'Architecture religieuse en France à l'époque gothique,* vol. 2. Paris, 1927.

Laubscher, Jean-Pierre. *Merveilleuse Notre-Dame de Lausanne.* Paris: Bibliothèque des Arts, Lausanne, Éditions du Grand Pont, 1975.

Laurière, J. de. "Deux mausolées africains: Le Médracen et le Tombeaux de la Chrétienne." *Bulletin Monumental,* 5th Series, 2nd year, 1874.

La Varende, Gabriel de. "Le Mythe de la grotte de l'Orient à l'Occident." *Le Monde Inconnu,* no. 49, and radio broadcast with J.-P. Bayard, February 15, 1983.

Lavedan, P. *Dictionnaire de la mythologie et des antiquités grecques et latines.* Paris: Hachette, 1931.

Leadbeater, C. W. *Les Centres de force et le serpent de feu.* Paris: Bulletin théosophique,1910.

Lebesque, Philéas. "Virgile et le culte de la Terre Mère." *Atlantis,* April–May 1930.

Leclercq, H. "Labyrinthe." *Dictionnaire d'archéologie chrétienne et de literature.*

Le Cour, Paul. *Évangile ésotérique de saint Jean.* Paris: Dervy, 1950.

———. *La Crète et ses mystères.* 1929. A portion republished by the magazine *Atlantis,* no. 180 (January–February 1956).

Le Goffric, Charles. *L'Âme bretonne,* 2nd series. Paris: H. Champion, 1909.

Le Monde Souterrain. Revue 94, Paris.

Lemozi, Abbé. *La Grotte, temple du Pech-Merle.* Paris: Picard, 1929.

Lenormant, François. *Les Origines de l'Histoire*. Paris: Maisonneuve & Cie, 1880.

"Léonard de Vinci Johanniste." *Atlantis,* no. 85 (1939) and no. 192 (August 1958).

Le Rouzic, Zacharie. *Corpus des signes graves des monuments megalithiques du Morbihan.*

Le Saux, Henri. *Souvenirs d'Arunáchala.* Paris: Picard, 1927.

Le Sacred des rois. Paris: Belles Lettres, 1985.

Lévi, Éliphas. *Dogme et rituel de haute magie.* Paris: Alcan, 1894.

Le Voile d'Isis. Special issues devoted to compagnonnage, no. 71 (November 1926), and no. 86 (February 1927).

Lévy-Bruhl, Lucien. *Le Surnaturel et la nature dans la mentalité primitive.* Paris: Alcan, 1931.

Loisy, A. *Essai sur les sacrifices.* Paris: Nourry, 1920.

Lot, Ferdinand. *La Gaule.* Paris: Fayard, 1947.

Loth, J. "L'Omphalos chez les Celtes." *Revue des Études anciennes* (July–September 1915).

Loubes, Jean-Paul. *Archi troglo.* Paris: Parenthèses, 1984.

Lübke, Anton. *L'Homme dans les profondeurs de la terre, les mystères du monde souterrain.* Paris: Plon, 1955.

Mac Cullough, A. *Eddic Mythology.* Boston: Marshall Jones, 1930.

Mahavamsa. Translated by W. Geiger. Oxford: The Pali Society, 2007.

Mainage, Abbé. *Les religions de la préhistoire.* Paris: Desclée-Picard, 1921.

Male, Émile. *L'art religieux en France,* 4 vols. Paris, 1928–32.

Mandeville, Jean de. *Le grand Lapidaire où sont declares les noms des pierres orientales avec leurs vertus et leur proprieties.* Paris: Jean Bonfons, 1561.

Marcotte, Jean-Marie. *Les Récits du Capitaine.* Montreal: Lumen, 1946.

Marques-Rivière, Jean. *Histoire des doctrines ésotériques.* Paris: Payot, 1972.

———. *Le Yoga tantrique et tibétan.* Paris: Vega, 1938.

Marrou, Henri. *Saint Augustine.* Paris: Seuil, 1958.

Marshall, Sir John Hubert. *Mohenjo Daro and the Indus Civilization.* London: Arthur Probsthain, 1931.

Martin, Dom. *Religion des Gaulois.* 1727.

Matthens, W. R. *Mazes and Labyrinths.* London, 1922.

Mauny, Raymond, and Gérard Cordier. *Souterrains-refuges, caves fortes et hypogées de Touraine,* 1927. *Bulletin de la Société des amis du Vieux Chinon* 7 no. 1. (1957).

Maury, L. F. Alfred. *La Magie et l'astrologie*. Paris: Didier, 1877.

Mavéric, Jean. *La Réforme des bases de l'Astrologie traditionelle*. Paris: Leclerc, 1912.

Mazel, Chanoine. *Notes sur la Camargue et les Saintes-Maries-de-la-mer*. Marseille: Editions Publiroc, 1935.

Meyrink, Gustav. *The Golem*. Cambridgeshire, UK: Dedalus, 2017.

———. *The Green Face*. Cambridgeshire, UK: Dedalus, 2018.

———. *Le Golem*. Translated by Dr. Émile Etthofen and Miss Perrenoud. Paris: Émile Paul, 1929.

Michelet, Jules. *La Bible de l'humanité (1865)*. Paris: Kessinger, 2010.

Michelet, Victor-Émile. *Le Secret de la Chevalerie*. Paris: Didier, 1930.

———. *Les Portes d'airain, suivies de le Coeur d'alcyone*. Paris: Éditions Véga, 1934.

Migne, Jacques-Paul. *Dictionnaire des Religions*. Paris: Nabu Press, 2011.

Migot, Robert. *Le Sang est rouge*. Paris: Éditions Alphonse Lemerre, 1933.

Millet, Yves. "La gamme de Pythagore." *Études traditionnelles,* no. 348 (June–July 1958).

Millon, Abbé A. *Le Culte d'Eau—Le culte de la Pierre*. Rennes, France: Plihon and Hommay, 1972.

Milosz, O. V. de L. *Les Arcanes*. Paris: Egloff, 1948.

Minvielle, Pierre. *Guide de la France souterraine*. Paris: Tchou, 1970.

Moreux, Théophile. *L'Alchimie moderne*. Paris: Gaston Doin, 1924.

Murray, Margaret. *The God of the Witches*. Oxford: Oxford University Press, 1931.

Murt, G. *Recherches sur l'iconographie de l'Évangile aux XVIe et XVIIe siècles*. Paris: N.p., 1916.

Mythologie Française. See in particular issues no. 4 and no. 144.

Nériac, M. de. *Initiation et Science,* no. 45 (March 1958), 22.

Nerval, Gérard de. "Le Monde souterrain." In *Voyage en Orient*, from *Oeuvres Complètes,* vol. 2. Paris: Gallimard, 1984.

Niel, Fernand. *Dolmens et menhirs*. Collection Que sais-je? Paris: P.U.F., 1958.

Noël, Pierre, *La Pierre materiau du passé et de l'avenir*. Institut technique du Bâtiment at des Travux Publics, 1943.

Osculati, Gaetano. *L'Illustration*. 1852.

Ossendowski, Ferdinand. *Bêtes, homes et dieux*. Paris: Plon, 1924.

Palissy, Bernard. "Les Pierres." In *Discours admirables*. Paris: Martin de Jeune, 1580.

———. *Recepte véritable*. Paris: Éditions Cap, 1844.

Pamart, Henry. "Études sur le Médracen et sur le Kebeur-Roumia (Tombeau de la Chrétienne)." *Revue Africaine,* 1920.

Panofsky, Erwin. *Über die Reihenfolge der vier Meister von Reims.* Leipzig: Klinkhardt & Biermann, 1927.

Papus. *Traité élémentaire des sciences occultes.* Paris: Chamuel, 1898.

Paradin, Claude. *Dévises historiques et emblèmes de Claude Paradin.* Revised and expanded edition by François d'Ambroise. Paris, 1621.

Paris, Jean. *Joyce par lui-même.* Paris: Le Seuil, 1957.

Paturot, Gérome, "Le Tombeau de la Chrétienne." *Les Nouvelles d'Alger,* March 3, 1919. Pausanias. *Description of Greece.*

Pausanias. *Description of Greece.* Cambridge, Mass.: 1933.

Pernety, Dom Antoine-Joseph, "Chaos." In *Mytho-Hermetic Dictionary.* Translated by Joseph D. Zabinski. Seattle: Ouroboros Press, 2018.

———. *Dictionnaire mytho-hermétique dans lequel on trouve les allegories fabu-leuse des poètes, les metaphors, les énigmes et les termes barbares des philos-ophes hermétiques.* Paris: Bauche, 1758. Republished with a preface by René Alleau. Paris: Denoël, 1972.

Persigoult, G. *Le Cabinet de réflexion.* Paris: Méré, 1946.

———. "La Caverne, image et porte souterraine du Monde." *Le Symbolisme,* no. 204, 1936.

Philostratus. *Vita Apollonius.* Translated by F. C. Conybeare. Loeb Classical Library, 1912.

Philpot, J. H. *The Sacred Tree.* London: Macmillan, 1897.

Pictet, Adolphe. *Du Culte des Cabires chez les anciens Irlandais.* Paris: Librarie Plon, 1924.

Plantagenet, Edourd E. *Causeries initiatiques pour le travail en loge d'apprentis.* Paris: Dervy, 2001.

Pluche, Noël-Antoine. *Histoire du Ciel.* Paris: Vve. Etienne, 1767.

Porphyry. *L'antre des nymphes.* Translation by Tabucco, followed by an essay by P. Saintyves. Paris: Nourry, 1918.

———. *On the Cave of the Nymphs.* Ann Arbor, MI: Phanes Press, 1991.

Porta, Giambattista Della. *La Magie naturelle ou les secrets et miracles de la nature.* Lyon, France: Jean Martin, 1565.

Portal, Frédéric. *Des Couleurs symboliques.* Paris: Éditions Niclaus, 1957.

Probst-Biraben, J. H. *Études traditionnelles,* no. 195 (March 1936), 106.

Ragon, Jean Marie. *Rituel de l'apprenti maçon.* Paris: C. Lacour, 1993.

Random, Michel. *L'Art visionnaire*. Paris: Fernand Nathan, 1979.

Raoult, Michel. *Les Druids*. Monaco: Le Rocher, 1983.

Regnault, Dr. "Les radiations telluriques et leur action sue les êtres vivants." *Cosmobiologie,* 4th trimester, 1934.

Régné, Jean. *Les Cavernes fortifiées de la Jobernie en Vivarais*. Privas, France: Académie du Vivarais, 1934.

Reinach, Salomon. *Cultes, mythes et religions*. Paris: E. Leroux, 1908.

———. *Orpheus: Histoire générale des religions*. Paris: Picard, 1909–24.

Relation d'un voyage du Pôle Arctique au Pôle Antarctique par le centre du monde (1723). Republished, Lausanne, Switzerland: Pierre Versins, 1976.

Rewerski, Jacek. *Troglodytes in the Samur Area*. Brinon-sur-Sauldre, France: Grandvaux, 1986.

Reyor, Jean. "De la Couleur verte." *Le voile d'Isis,* January 1932.

———. *Le voile d'Isis,* no. 172, 1934, 148.

Richer, Jean. *Gérard de Nerval et les doctrines ésotériques*. Paris: Éditions du Griffon d'Or, 1947.

Rochette, Raoul. *Sur l'Hercule assyrien ou phénicen*. Paris: Mem. Acad. Inst., 1948.

Roerich, Nicholas. *Ethnographie,* nos. 21–22 (April–December 1930).

Roscher, W. H. *L'Omphalos*. Paris: Editions Pierre Jean Oswald, 1977.

Rosgnilk, Vladimir. *L'Émergence de l'Enel ou L'immergence des repères. Introduction à l'étude des forms et des champs de coherence*. Orsay, France: Foundation Ark'Ail, 1985.

Rossignol, Jean-Pierre. *Les métaux dans l'Antiquité: Origines religieux de la métallurgie*. Paris: Auguste Durand, 1863.

———. *Mémoire sur le métal que les anciens appelaient Orichalque*. Paris: Lahure, 1852.

Ruchon, François. "Rites et Symboles de l'ancien compagnonnage." *Alpina,* December 1948.

Rudeaux, Lucien. *La Terre et son histoire*. Paris: P.U.F., Collection Que sais je?, 1947.

Russel, Robert Vane. *The Tribes and Castes of the Central Provinces of India*. London: Macmillan, 1916.

Saillens, E. *Nos Vierges Noires*. Paris: Éditions Universelles, 1945.

Saintyves, Pierre. *La Force magique*. Paris: Nourry, 1914.

———. *Les Contes de Perrault*. Paris: Nourry, 1923.

———. "Les Grottes dans les cultes magico-religieux." Afterword to Porphyry, *L'Antre des Nymphes*. Paris: Nourry, 1918.

———. *Les Vierges mères et les naissances miraculeuses*. Paris: Hachette, 1908.

Sale, Antoine de la. *La Salade* "Du Mont de la Sybille et de son lac et des choses que j'y ai vues et qui dire auz gens du pays." In Paris, Gaston. *Légendes du Moyen Âge*. Paris: Bruno Paulin, 1903.

Sand, George. *Laura: A Journey into the Crystal*. Translated by Sue Dyson. London: Pushkin Press, 2004.

Sandoz, Maurice. *Le Labyrinthe*. Paris: Plon, 1957.

Schaya, Leo. *L'Homme et l'Absolu selon la Kabbale*. Paris: Buchet/Chastel Corréa, 1958.

Schmidt, Albert-Marie. *La Mandragore*. Paris: Flammarion, 1958.

Schmit, Jean-Philippe. *Manuel complet de l'architecte des monuments religieux*. Paris: Roret, 1859.

Schuon, Frithjof. "La Gnose, langage du Soi." *Études traditionelles*, no. 333 (August 1956).

Schwab, Fernand. *Les Traditions d'Amérique ancienne*. Paris: Dangles, 1982.

Sébillot, Paul. *La Terre et le monde souterrain*. Paris: Imago, 1983.

———. *Les Travaux publics et les mines*. Paris: Guy Trédaniel, 1979.

Sénéac, Albert Burnet de [AKA "Le Liberté"], "Les Labyrinthes compagnonniques." *Bulletin du Comité des Travaux historiques et scientifiques. Section des Sciences economiques et sociales*. 1936.

Servent, Gaston. *Le Tombeau de la Chrétienne*. Paris: Erge.

Servier, Jean. *Traditions et civilisation berbères*. Monaco: Rocher, 1985.

Siculus, Diodorus. *Historical Library,* vol. 4. Cambridge, Mass.: Harvard University Press, 1933.

"Si-Do-In-Dzou: Gestes de l'offciant dans les ceremonies mystiques des sects Tendai et Singon." In *Annales du musée Guimet,* vol. 8. Paris: Leroux, 1899.

Simonin, Louis-Laurent. *Les Pierres minéralogique*. Paris: Hachette, 1869.

Soyer, Edmond. *Les Labyrinthes d'églises*. Amiens, France: Yvert et Tellier, 1896.

Sri Krishna Prem. *Le Yoga de la Kathopanishad*. Monaco: Rocher, 1982.

Suttel, René. *Catacombes et cavités de Paris*. Paris: Société d'Études Historiques des anciennes carriers et cavités souerraines, 1986.

Tarbé, Prosper. *Le Purgatoire de saint Patrice,* Reims, France: P. Dubois, 1862.

Teilhard de Chardin, Pierre. *L'Esprit de la terre*. Paris: Seuill, 1931.

Tercinet, Louis. *Mandragore, Qui es-tu?* Paris: 1950.

Tiele, Cornelis Petrus. *Histoire comparée des anciennes religions.* Paris: G. Fischbacher, 1882.

Toutain. *Les Caverns sacrées dans l'antiquité grecque.* Paris: Laurens, 1912.

Trebbi, Jean-Charles, and Nicole Charneau. *Maisons, creusées, maisons enterrées.* Paris: Éditions Alternative, 1981.

Trébuchon, J. C. *Joyaux Souterrains du Vivarais.* Largentière, France: Humbert et Fils, 1954.

Utudjian, Edouard. *Architecture et l'urbanisme souterrain.* Paris: Robert Laffont, 1960.

———. *Le Monde souterrain,* no. 96 (August 1956).

Valentine, Basil. *Les Douze clefs de la philosophie.* Paris: Éditions de Minuit, 1956.

Vian, Francis. *La Grèce archaïque et classique dans histoires des religions.* Paris: Gallimard, 1982.

Viennot, Odette. *Le Culte de l'arbre dans l'Inde ancienne.* Paris: P.U.F., 1954.

Ville, Ludovic. *Notice sur les sondages effectués dans la province d'Alger en 1864–1865–1866.* Paris: Dunod, 1867.

Vincent, Louis-Claude. In *L'Ingénieur-Constructeur E.T.P.,* no. 5 (May 1957), 245.

———. "L'Univers et la Vie." In *L'Ingénieur-Constructeur E.T.P.* (March 1958), 107.

———. The review in *L'Ingénieur Constructeur E.T.P.,* no. 8 (August–September 1957), 391.

Violet-Le-Duc. "Labyrinthe." In *Dictionnaire raisonné de l'architecture française,* vol. 6.

Visio Tungdali. Erlangen, Germany: A. Wagner, 1882.

Von Bingen, Hildegard. *Physicia sanctae Hildegardis Argentorati.* 1544.

Vulliaud, Paul. *La Pensée ésoterique de Léonard de Vinci.* Paris: Dervy, 1945.

Waters, Frank. *Book of the Hopi.* New York: Ballantine Books, 1972.

Weissen-Szumlanska, Marcelle. *L'Ame archaïque de l'Afrique du Nord.* Paris: Nouvelles Éditions Latines, 1933.

Wirth, Oswald. *Les mystères de l'art royal: rituel de l'adept.* Paris: Dervy, 2012.

———. *Le Symbolisme occulte de la franc-maçonnerie.* Paris: Ernest-Renan, 1928.

———. *Le Tarot des imagiers du Moyen Âge.* Paris: Nourry, 1927.

———. *Notions élémentaires de maçonnerie.* Paris: Le Symbolisme, 1934.

Index

Page numbers in *italics* indicate illustrations.